SPORT:

A Contemporary View

SPORT:
A Contemporary View

DONNA MAE MILLER

*Professor and Director
Department of Physical Education for Women
University of Arizona
Tucson, Arizona*

and

KATHRYN R. E. RUSSELL

*Assistant Professor
Department of Physical Education
University of Arizona
Tucson, Arizona*

LEA & FEBIGER   *Philadelphia, 1971*

Health Education,
Physical Education, and
Recreation Series

Ruth Abernathy, Ph.D., Editorial Adviser
Director, School of Physical and Health Education
University of Washington, Seattle, Washington 98105

ISBN: 0-8121-0331-9

Published in Great Britain by Henry Kimpton Publishers, London

Library of Congress Catalog Card Number 70-135688

Printed in the United States of America

Foreword

Athletes often have been chided that they are so engrossed in their own little world that they ignore the important and vital problems of the real one. I contend, however, that sport is not removed from the complexities and problems of life, that it is, in fact, a world of reality.

Those who love sport may not spend much time thinking about why it is important. They just seem to know that it is. And they make no bones about recognizing that in the sport world they face tough tests of reality. Certainly the world of sport is one of flesh and blood, of grime, aching muscles, pounding lungs and of sickening fatigue. More than this, it is a world that exposes all that a man is—in mind, body, heart and spirit. There is a definite relationship between the way a man deals with the realities and challenges of sport and the way he responds to the realities and problems of life, whether it be in terms of competition, teamwork, enthusiasm or the willingness to put forth just a little bit more.

Without a doubt, the sport world frequently provides the most genuine encounter with the problems of living. But more than presenting a world of reality, sport entreats man to stretch for something beyond mere reality. My conviction that in sport man may not only find reality but may transcend it comes not only from my experience as a pole vaulter but also from my experience as a minister. I have found that one of the great problems facing a minister is not to preach honor, courage, tolerance, patience, perseverance and the like. Such abstract attributes have little or no relevance to people. Rather, men and women seem to be moved by noble aspirations when they know how these are possible to obtain in concrete ways. In the same way, sport often reveals in concrete ways the potential in man for greatness. It dramatizes commendable acts of integrity, self-discipline and resiliency of the human spirit. In sport men and women may strive for many values, even some not always recognized in their religion. They are often stirred to thoughts

v

and deeds which are beyond the reach in less-inspiring circumstances or for less-inspired men. In short, a pole vaulter may not only grasp the skill of catapulting through the air in order to clear a high bar. He may also discover that what makes a real *champion* is the conviction that you can go as high as you dare to believe that you can.

Today, the heart of sport, of which I wrote in the 1950's, has hypertrophy. It has become enlarged in size and strength, in pulse and energy. Moreover, sport is symbolized by bold new ideas as well as the instant replay and the "image scrimmage." Scholars in varied fields are discovering that sport is a fertile field for the study of man's behavior. I am sure that it has occurred to you, as it did to me, that this is an especially appropriate time for such a book as *Sport: A Contemporary View* to appear.

There are other reasons why this book is timely. In this day of telling it like it is, a day of exhorting a man to do his own thing, the authors have presented sport in terms of the people who tell it like it is for them in the language of sport, plain-speaking and direct. The characters are credible human beings who, while knowing how to be serious, are not merely solemn. They are real men and women who may not be perfect, but whose striving for perfection is made very perceptible. And, some rather fancy literary footwork has been accomplished in combining theory with biography. The result illuminates both.

Perhaps it is not entirely a coincidence that, at the peak of a resurgence of interest in women's liberation, we find that the authors are women, although I seriously doubt that this fact is of first importance to this discussion of sport. They have played a fundamental role in the sport world for many years.

Read the book. You'll probably run into some of your old friends. You may even run into yourself. You will, above all, sense the relationship of sport to the many facets and facts of life.

Bob Richards

Preface

For several years our conviction has grown that sport stands somewhat apart in the modern world as a mysterious and compelling phenomenon. Many persons have explored and attempted to explain what is so special about sport. Indeed, the theme of sport has crept into the dialogue of many disciplines. We run across its influence in psychology with man's search for self. In philosophy we find a sport text or two attempting to clarify man's relations with reality. Step into the domain of sociology and we find sport as a locus for man's relations with other men. Observe the arts and we find sport as one of the most promising vehicles for creative expression. Enter the halls of education and we find its impact upon learning.

The dimension of sport has not only occupied the attention of widely different observers from various fields of knowledge and diverse walks of life, but also it has for all intents and purposes seized the public imagination and pocketbook. Judging from the illustrations available, it does not seem audacious to interpret sport as a pervasive and powerful plutocrat.

Pervasive? In America, sport seems to symbolize the American way almost as much as a hamburger or the Statue of Liberty. At a time that is characterized by instant change, the flurries of flights to the moon, the sounds of intercontinental aircraft rushing past with fleeting intensity, sport seems to remain a mission of permanence—inexhaustibly vital, immortally versatile. Even man's moon walk appears at times to loom but insignificantly in portent beside Saturday's game. Sport is taught in the schools and yet thousands who haven't played since their school days are daily mesmerized by sport shows on television. It appeals to adults and the children. Both sexes indulge anxiously in its mystique. The countless literary pieces devoted to the subject of sport lead one to conclude that many writers still share the feeling of a one-time editor of *Harper's Weekly* that he "had rather chronicle a great boat race at Harvard or Yale or a cricket match with the U.S. Eleven than all the prize poems or the orations on Lafayette that are produced in half a century."

Powerful? It has been said that in the arena of sport, beggars have been crowned kings and kings brought low. Sport has been likened to a social frontier, to war, love, and life itself. Some believe that sport ennobles reason, discloses mortal ingenuity and truly articulates the measure of man.

Plutocrat? Without a doubt. Technology, leisure and jingling cash in people's pockets seemingly have left no sport untouched. Some cities have even spent more for rebuilding for sport contests than for rebuilding in the aftermath of a great holocaust or a world war.

That sport should evoke such a widespread response is not surprising, embodying as it does some of the values and aspirations of man throughout the world. Yet not even the most learned interpreters have made the whole of sport into something smoothly rounded, easily understood, or well described. Nonetheless, since at the beginning of the 1970's there are all the signs that we are in the midst of an epidemic of unprecedented sport events, personalities and popularity, we were enticed to put together into some meaningful whole this "more-than" fascination encountered in the arena of sport.

But, how does one distill the essence of this experience called sport? To do so might be, as Sid James of *Sports Illustrated* said, "akin to pitching a no-hit game, or making a hole in one, or running a kickoff back for a touchdown." However, we reasoned that sport has its own means of expression. It is a dialogue of many little pieces—personal motivations, social needs, artistic expression, leisure pursuits, economic interests, language, politics, education and much more. These relationships are revealed in all kinds of literature—which, according to the literary critic and writer Joseph Wood Krutch, helps man to understand man more honestly than the quasi sciences, by showing us the world and ourselves.

If the responsibility for expressing the intangibles that defy measurement lies with the literature, then by extracting and organizing representative examples from the literature and bringing them together in one source, sport might be revealed in a way that is not expressed by its disparate parts. Certainly no century has outdone our own in presenting a literature of sport that takes the reader into uncharted realms of human experience and theoretical rationale.

Taking a clue from a Tennessee slave, who, in the book *To Be a Slave* said, "If you want Negro history you will have to get it from somebody who wore the shoe," we decided to get some of the mystique of sport from some of those who wear the shoe. At the same time, although theories in an area of study such as sport are still uncertain, the theoretical rationale available to the quasi sciences provided some possibilities for viewing the significance of sport.

This, then, was our method of exploring the dialogue and dimensions of sport. Through juxtaposition of the words of some of those who speak directly out of experience and the works of some theoreticians, we believed the whole of sport might be viewed as more than a sum of its parts. We are at pains to point out that even so modest a description may do an injustice to this one aspect of human behavior.

There is no particular principal disposition to this discussion. Nor is there intent to put theories and persons into convenient categories like players clustering around their team banners. The chapters in which all of this is developed provide several themes. Certain immutable strains emerged and produced titles and subtitles which steered the story through four channels: personal, social, cultural, and educational.

Although the discussion of sport does not necessarily fit into the framework and classifications appropriate to the quasi sciences, some theoretical formulation is presented as an introduction to each section. Thereafter, quotations are used as a kind of shorthand, with the teller's own artistry and the integrity of individual expression preserved insofar as possible. Narrative is used as sparingly as possible. In many instances embroidering on the facts and explanations would seem to demean the individual expressions.

The sports which are discussed are as subjectively and arbitrarily chosen by the authors as would be the case with any sport fan or historian. Names of worthy persons and sports that might have equal claim may be missing because of the selectivity imposed. At the same time, some sports just are not news items and material about them is scarce. Presumably some writers have found some sports either too difficult to explain or not particularly entertaining, as Jim Murray acknowledged. Paul Gallico called some sports "minor sports" or "small fry" or "more miscellany," a conviction probably shared by many other writers. Jim Murray, calling some sports "little sports," offered the dour observation that "one is not sure whether they're 'sports' or just a way out of doing the dishes." Then, too, there are disagreements about the definition of sport. Deep sea fishing, for example, may "never be a sport until you put the hook in your mouth and get into the water with the fish," Ernest Hemingway was reported to have said. Needless to say, this book makes no attempt to include deep sea fishing.

The discussion of sport which is ahead, then, is a compressed overlay of stories. Like Thomas Carlyle's idea of history, it is, in a sense, "the essence of innumerable biographies." And, in a sense it is like a story that writes itself although the authors share the sentiment of Jim Murray that the story-that-writes-itself is "like asking an overturned canoe to right itself." It is not a finished theory of sport but an exploration of the dialogue encountered in different fields—including the arts, sociology, psychology, philosophy, and physical education—synthesized and sometimes fitted to the performer's expression of his experience. It is a discussion to which any reader may wish to add a line or two, since that is the nature of the stimulating subject. It may simply provide a notion of the compelling attraction of sport to do, to watch, to read, and to write about. Or, one may wish to find his or another's story—peruse them, absorb them, admire or be provoked by them, and in so doing reap, as Wordsworth put it, "the harvest of a quiet eye."

Tucson, Arizona   DONNA MAE MILLER
                                                     KATHRYN R. E. RUSSELL

Acknowledgements

The very nature of so vast a subject as sport incurs a debt of gratitude to all those who have chronicled its genesis and who seek to account for its perennial excitement and drama. In fact, the discussion presented here derives its dialogue and dimension from the works of writers in diverse fields of intellectual pursuit who have immensely extended the concept of sport in the past few years.

Individual acknowledgments must of necessity be highly arbitrary and selective. Such a book involves the good will and cooperation of many. We wish to thank the many editors and authors who gave permission to use their published materials. We are particularly indebted to the publishers and writers of *Sports Illustrated,* on whose wide array of examples we relied so heavily. Another expression of thanks is due to Mary Pavlich Roby, whose illuminating observations prompted the idea for this book. To Bob Richards, who practices what he preaches about sport, we are grateful in many ways, but most of all because he captures the feeling of what we, as sport enthusiasts, have experienced. Special thanks also must be accorded to those individual participants and sideline observers who are quoted in these pages and without whose talents and insights this book would not have been undertaken. Finally, we are grateful to our professional colleagues and students, from whom we learn that sport is worth writing about.

Special thanks are expressed to the following authors and publishers for permission to quote from their publications.

From *Farewell to Sport* by Paul Gallico. Alfred A. Knopf, Inc., New York, 1938.

From *Instant Replay* by Jerry Kramer and Dick Schaap. Reprinted by permission of The World Publishing Company. An NAL book. Copyright © 1968 by Jerry Kramer and Dick Schaap.

From *Man, Play and Games* by Roger Caillois. Free Press of Glencoe, Inc., 1961.

From *The Story of the Olympic Games 776 B.C.—1964* by John Kieran and Arthur Daley. Revised Edition Copyright, ©, 1969 by J. B. Lippincott Company. Reprinted by permission of the publishers.

From *The Astonished Muse* (Chapter 5 and Chapter 6) by Reuel Denney. Chicago, University of Chicago Press, 1957. © 1957 by The University of Chicago.

From "A Season in the Stands" by William Phillips. *Commentary* July 1969. Reprinted from *Commentary*, by permission; Copyright (CO) 1969 by the American Jewish Committee.

From "Confessions and Vengeances" by John Ciardi. *Saturday Review* March 8, 1969. Copyright 1969. Saturday Review, Inc.

From "Dateline America—All-Pro Miniconglomerate" by David Snell. *Life Magazine* May 23, 1969. © 1969 Time Inc.

From "Does A Woman Need Sports Appeal?" by Janet Coleman. *Mademoiselle* April, 1968. Reprinted by permission of Janet Coleman c/o IFA Copyright © 1968 by The Condé Nast Publications, Inc.

From "Greed is the Name of the Game" by Stanley Frank. Reprinted from *TV Guide®*, August 9-11, 1969. Copyright © 1969 by Triangle Publications.

From "It's A Woman's Right to Play in Sports" by Robert Lipsyte. *Milwaukee Journal* (The New York Times News Service) March 23, 1969, © 1969 by The New York Times Company. Reprinted by permission.

From "Ladies in Silks." By permission from *Time, The Weekly Newsmagazine* April 4, 1969. Copyright 1969 Time Inc.

From "Let's Pull Out of the Olympics" by Roger Kahn. *Saturday Evening Post* October 10, 1964. Reprinted by permission of The Saturday Evening Post © 1964, by The Curtis Publishing Company.

From "Order in the Ball Park" by John R. McDermott. *Life Magazine* March 7, 1969. © 1969 Time Inc.

From *"Where Did You Go?" "Out." "What Did You Do?" "Nothing."* by Robert Paul Smith, with the permission of the Publisher, W. W. Norton & Company, Inc., New York. Copyright © 1957 by Robert Paul Smith.

From "Sportsmanship, As A Moral Category" by J. W. Keating. *Ethics* LXXV, No. 1, October 1964. Chicago, University of Chicago Press, 1964. © 1964 by The University of Chicago.

From "Still Rolling Up the Ratings" by Melvin Durslag. Reprinted from *TV Guide®*, April 19-25, 1969. Copyright © 1969 by Triangle Publications.

From "The Joys of Life Afloat." Copyright Newsweek, Inc., August 4, 1969.

From "The Little Team That Can." By permission from *Time, The Weekly Newsmagazine* September 5, 1969; Copyright 1969 Time Inc.

From "The Origins of Olympic Games" by Raymond Bloch. *Scientific American* August, 1968. Copyright © (1968) Scientific American, Inc. All rights reserved.

From "The Power of Picasso." *Life Magazine* December 27, 1968. © 1968 Time Inc.

From "Why Do We Love Pro Football? It's Vicious, That's Why" by Josh Greenfield. Reprinted from *TV Guide®*, October 18-24, 1969. Copyright © 1969 by Triangle Publications.

From "The Uncommon Man," (pp. 63-64). By permission from *Time, The Weekly Newsmagazine* May 23, 1969; Copyright 1969 Time Inc.

Contents

PART III. SPORT IS CULTURAL

Contents XV

PART IV. SPORT IS EDUCATIONAL

PART I

Sport is Personal

"... the infinitude of the private man."

— — —EMERSON

Henry Luce began publishing *Sports Illustrated* because "there would not be a tremendous interest and participation if sport did not correspond to some important elements . . . something deeply inherent . . . in the human spirit" (49:4). Whatever that "deeply inherent" something is, sport appears to be, first of all, highly personal. Efforts to explain it have been made by philosophers, psychologists and psychiatrists, physiologists, sociologists, anthropologists, physical educators, sports writers, and the man on the street—in short, by everybody.

The phenomenon of play, and subsequently of sport as part of play, has been noted by widely divergent observers. Among theories of play as a human phenomenon have been those of Spencer (play is needed to discharge surplus energy); Tarde (play is imitation); Lazarus (play is a recreative means of recovery from fatigue); Groos (play is preparation for adult life); Appleton (play is associated with bodily changes occurring during growth); Hall (play is recapitulation—a rehearsing of ancestral activities); Shand (play is an expression of joy); McDougall (play is motivated by instinctive rivalry); Adler (play is used to overcome inferiority complexes); Huizinga (play is a totality, an end in and of itself) (21:17). In his 1938 classic and still definitive study of the play instinct, the Dutch historian, Johan Huizinga, suggesting that *homo ludens* (man the player) holds sway over *homo sapiens* (man the thinker), asserted that "the more positive conclusion forces itself upon us that 'all is play' " (33).

Learned scholars also have explored and attempted to define, classify, and interpret reasons and values held for play, games, and sport in terms of social experiences (collective group behavior, race relations, international good will and understanding); societal groupings (socio-economic groups, subcultures); cultural institutions and forces (politics, business, religion, the arts, education, technology and leisure). Other theorists and writers have addressed themselves to the questions of how play, games, and sport contribute to: health and fitness; aesthetic and ascetic experiences; catharsis and purging of aggressive tendencies; ethical and moral growth; ego-involvement and feelings of adequacy, fear, frustration, mastery of self and environment, desire for competition, risk, imitation; ad infinitum.

Also important to understanding reasons for man's involvement in sport have been the investigations and writings relating to the structure of knowledge and the ways of knowing. Influential works in this field have included those of Piaget and Jerome S. Bruner. Their theses and those of others, such as Philip H. Phenix, grow out of a concept that human existence is directed toward the fulfillment of meanings and that education is the process of engendering essential meanings. In a similar vein, Eleanor Metheny and others have attempted to elaborate a philo-sophic theory of the kinds of meanings to be found in dance, sport and other forms of human movement and their significance in curricula planning in physical education. The terms and ideas of existential philosophy and phenomenology have become particularly relevant to current interpretations of the meanings to be found in sport. Some writers extend to the world of sport the kinds of questions about "being" and "existence" raised by Buber, Heidegger, Kierkegaard, and Sartre, to name a few existential sources. One such analytic philosophic look at the why of sport was made by Paul Weiss, professor of philosophy at Yale. In his book, *Sport: A Philosophic Inquiry* (122), Weiss attempted to classify and compare the reasons why men and women participate in or watch sports and what it is they do or see. For all of the book's "difficulties, its plodding and ponderous prose," as one reviewer stated, "it is an unprecedented effort to find abstract truth in the billion dollar business, the lonely grind, and all the other simple and complex aspects of the phenomenon of sport" (65:66).

The research done by professional scholars is beyond the purpose of this book except to provide some selected background discussion for the material presented and to provide the reader with reference sources which he may wish to pursue. At the same time it may be noted that these scholarly and authoritative works may be of little pertinence to observers and writers on the sport scene. Frank Trippett, for example, in "A Special Report on the Way You Play the Ordeal of Fun," which appeared in *Look*, stated that "fun is a vaporous notion. Everyone knows what it means, yet it eludes definition." Furthermore, as Trippett declared, scholarly studies, most of which focus exclusively on "leisure: man-at-play differentiated from man-at-work," may serve the sociological method but fall short because they conceal the size of the force at work in the fun-quest (118:24). And, Robert H. Boyle, author of the book *Sport—Mirror of American Life,* suggested that American interest in sport "is in a large measure the end product of a number of impersonal factors: industrialization, immigration, organization, increased leisure and income, commercial promotion and upper-class patronage" (6:4).

Apparently no single theory, philosophy, or observation can be credited with the creation of a coherent metaphysical or motivational scheme in which to place the significance of man's reasons for participation in sport. And sport appears to remain as varied, and therefore, as unique as each individual who participates in it. The equation for each personality may be different. When it becomes something that suits the person's life it may be the formulae for his way of life. This is the human equation.

In this section, therefore, no attempt is made to propose that a single explanation of sport is valid for all participants and spectators alike. Rather, the intent is to capture the enigma that is sport from some of those who "wear the shoe" of sport, so to speak, and from "within the sun-struck privacy of the individual heart and soul . . . the ultimate human frontier" (44:63). And, we trust that, in the words of Cervantes in *Don Quixote,* "By a small sample we may judge of the whole."

CHAPTER 1

The Participant

SPORT AND THE REALITY OF LIFE

What is Sport?

What is sport? Persons in almost all walks of life have expressed their opinion as to what, to them, the word implies. A remarkable number of these persons, from sportsmen to philosophers to political leaders, have either compared sport to life or have, in so many words, called it life. Ernst Cassirer remarked in his essay "Art" that "what we feel in art is not a simple or singular emotional quality. It is the dynamic process of life itself" (12). Like art, sport may be expected to provide a glimpse into life itself. Bernard Suits, in his essay, "What Is A Game?" also argued that games are not distinguishable from the activities that constitute life except in their rules and their goals (115b).

Edward Rutkowski pointed out that football is a microcosm of that larger reality, democracy, in which life is based on the quality of experience of all those in the society: "Football, being less than life itself, allows one to appreciate and empathize with the joy of human accomplishment, which becomes internalized and part of one's personality" (83:31).

"In reality," Howard Slusher stated, "sport, as life, is a place for happiness as well as grief. Through activity man builds anxieties, suffers pain, engages the tensions of life, and frequently challenges actual death" (88:8).

Edgar Z. Friedenberg, in his foreword to Slusher's book, suggested that the essence of sport provides a cup "into which life can be poured," and which "tells us a great deal about the people who designed and choose to drink from it" (88:ix). Further, a young man experiencing himself as an athlete "learns what it can mean to live fully in his body joyfully and exuberantly, though under self-imposed discipline" (88:xi).

Mary Pavlich, in "The Power of Sport," declared that "sport extracts

5

essence . . . the 'thingness' of things—the poise of balance, the smoothness of rhythm . . . Sport therefore is not a representation of what is real and vital but rather is reality itself." Further, she stated that it is only as a totality that one can become a sportsman: "There is no possible way to use one-third of oneself" (72b:10).

Charles de Gaulle is reported to have expressed this thought on sport: "When the Order of Merit was created in France, among the first recipients were two athletes, Michel Jazy and Christine Goitschel. That's because in sport as in life one must learn to win" (101:52).

The claims that sport is a miniature of real life are legion. Performers especially do not really disengage sport from the realities of life. Bob Richards, of Olympic pole-vaulting and "Wheaties" fame, said: "The qualities that possess the contestant are the same qualities that we need in living" (78). Roger Bannister, himself exemplifying the virtues of long and arduous efforts in running, called sport "a diversion with no purpose beyond providing a testing ground larger than a chess board but smaller than life itself" (2). Thus, the expressions of those who "wear the shoe" of sport tend to validate the theories that sport intensifies the dynamic process of life itself.

Who Am I?

One of the metaphysical questions that philosophers wonder about is a person's sense of identity. Many persons spend much of their lives trying to discover the answer to this question. Odd though it may be, sport is full of searches and provides even unsuspected opportunities for self-discovery.

Sport may spotlight in its comedies and tragedies one's vanities, one's insecurities, and even one's deep-seated frustrations. For example, when the Green Bay Packers played against the Minnesota Vikings, Jerry Kramer sprained an ankle and spent the entire second half of the game on the sidelines feeling frustrated in a way probably typical of most sideliners:

> I kept bouncing around the bench trying to look spry . . . I got a little paranoic. . . . Maybe they didn't need me . . . all of a sudden I felt like an outsider . . . I was jealous (41:138).

Ty Cobb, one of the greatest and most criticized baseball players, in his book *My Life in Baseball—The True Record,* shed light on some factors that made him "an aggressive, imaginative, daring performer." It wasn't that he considered baseball as a career but that his overwhelming need was to "prove himself a real man." Furthermore,

> once an athlete feels the peculiar thrill that goes with victory and public praise, he's bewitched. He can never get away from it (14).

Or, sport may help a person contemplate "The Shears of Fate, The Loom of Life," as Bob Crozier, a Jesuit priest and teacher of English, put it. To the question of how a priest can involve himself in racing, Crozier explained the feeling he had about the Indianapolis 500:

> I think that Lorca's successful defense of the bullfight applies with equal force to motor sports: "Where else in the world amid such dazzling splendor and beauty can man contemplate death?" (19:81).

The participant's impressions and understanding may even help him face the fact that life is sometimes merely contentious and prickly. Such may be the case with Arnold Palmer, for example, for whom

> golf is deceptively simple and endlessly complicated. A child can play it well, and a grown man can never master it. Any single round of it is full of unexpected triumphs and seemingly perfect shots that end in disaster (71:28).

Perhaps one may discover that the most important thing in life is not the triumph but the challenge. Again, for Arnold Palmer golf meant

> facing up to a challenge—or even relishing a challenge—is what sport is all about. . . . The real pleasure is in pulling off the impossible (72:34).

Or, to Jean-Claude Killy:

> Skiing is not a beauty contest; it is a battle against yourself always to the frontiers of the impossible (39:57).

On some occasions a player may find that his real self is obscured by every kind of camouflage that his imagination has been able to invent. But veiled behind the lies one tells about himself, the real self may be trying to communicate. A practicing psychiatrist, Beisser, in his book *The Madness In Sport,* presented the case studies of several athletes who sought psychiatric treatment. Their stories provide considerable evidence that, as intimately as the mirror on the wall, sport has an uncompromising way of revealing that real self which is expressive, if not verbal, and which is sometimes neurotic. Take the case, for example, of the basketball player "who played the game too well." To him it was not just a game but all there was, and, as Beisser noted: "Wherein lay the flaw in his character." What he could not tolerate was

> the transition into manhood which meant he would have to be responsible for himself, for his pleasure, for his aggression, and could no longer be diffused within the team. He had to stand alone (4:27).

Or take another instance from a player who was not a psychiatric patient, yet who seemed to express perhaps what others have felt about the problem of deriving complete self-satisfaction from sport. Tommy Novis, of the Atlanta Falcons, reported to spend hours watching films, studying his play books, even recording his defensive assignments and playing the tape before he goes to sleep, said:

Seeing good teammates thrown aside, traded and cut, it makes you start
thinkin' too much about playing for yourself (121:89-90).

And, while sport may drive home the besetting agony of defeat
sometimes it honors Leo Durocher's statement that "nice guys finish last,"
or points up the words of Jim Tatum, who said that "winning is not
the most important thing. It's the only thing." For such a reason as
winning, sport may provide man a chance to prove himself as best.

Who's Best?

From the time of Homer's "Come on, no hanging back, no more
delay . . . who's the winner?" (*The Odyssey*, Book 21), sport as a
respected arena of man's competitiveness has been a way of discovering one's superiority. Roger Caillois, in his book *Man, Play and Games*,
suggested that games are created for a number of reasons, among them:
"The need to prove one's superiority . . . The desire to challenge, make
a record, or merely overcome an obstacle" (11:65).

Investigations by Francis J. Ryan pointed out that the good competitor uses his opponent as a temporary enemy and develops rivalries
with that opponent (84). This kind of behavior, however, is not necessarily bad. Ernest Dichter, President of the Institute for Motivational
Research, indicated that one human need is for competition: "Most of
us need enemies because they offer a way to establish our own superiority" (25).

The notion that sportsmen do possess a kind of superiority is attested
to in some interesting psychological studies which have been made on
the personality structure of exceptional athletes. Examination of the
personality profiles of athletes by psychologist Bruce C. Ogilvie indicated
that this "special breed" could be described, among other words, as
emotionally stable, self-assertive, self-assured, self-disciplined, self-reliant,
venturesome, and able to handle emotional stress. Racing car drivers,
ranging all the way from novices to Grand Prix stars, tended to be "the
most tough-minded" sample of all the groups tested (68).

Some sport performers who attest to the desire to be the best include
the following:

Ted Williams, who derisively called himself Teddy Ballgame, is considered one of the game's greatest and the last of the .400 hitters. In his
autobiography *My Turn At Bat,* as reported in *Look,* he stated:

What nobody understood is that I wanted to be the best . . . The percentage
that you can get out of yourself is what you strive for (46:88).

Bill Russell, the all-time, all-pro center of the Boston Celtics and
considered by many to be the greatest defensive basketball player of all

time, in announcing his retirement from basketball, explained why he played the game:

> I played because I enjoyed it . . . but there's more to it than that. I played because I was dedicated to being the best. I was part of a team, and I dedicated myself to making that team the best (82:18).

Joyce Hoffman, named by *Surfer* magazine as Woman Surfer of 1964, declaring she definitely needed an outlet for competition, stated:

> I have to be the best. It's really a big deal with me. I don't know why . . . I guess it's inborn in me . . . If I didn't think I was considered the best I'd quit (80:98).

Graham Hill, one of the world's fastest car racers, put it this way:

> That's the whole point of racing, really, to prove you're best. If you don't believe it, then you're prepared for defeat, aren't you? (20:26).

Part of the discovery of one's superiority or proving oneself as best may come in defying and overcoming the laws of nature. Or, the contestant may pit his judgment, not only against nature and the whims of chance, but against another worthy opponent. The Russian poet and sportsman Yevtushenko put it this way:

> True sport is always a duel: a duel with nature, with one's own fear, with one's own fatigue, a duel in which body and mind are strengthened (124:112).

When Ted Williams was inducted into the Baseball Hall of Fame, his acceptance speech contained this sentiment:

> Baseball gives every American boy a chance to excel, not just to be as good as someone else but to be better than someone else. This is the nature of man and the nature of the game (108:9).

The ski jumper, Bjorn Wirkola of Norway, said "that big jump . . . does not scare me . . . It makes me want to jump the more . . . On a perfect jump you are master of all the elements" (69:45).

And Joyce Hoffman, who was just mentioned, explained her ideas about surfing in the following way:

> It's really a neat feeling, this big thing between you and nature. You have to outthink the wave, you're mastering nature, you're making the wave give you something (80:110).

One writer, noting that surfing has boomed because it is the "quickest-stoking sport ever," stated:

> Slicing along the front of a wave evokes a feeling of rising from the sea to conquer the world. The water is alive with sparkle, and the surfboard makes a hissing sound like a thousand yards of tearing silk (70:32).

Matador Carlos Arruza, who during his career earned an estimated 4 million dollars bullfighting, declared of this sport:

What a sense of beauty and power . . . to control this deadly animal and do it gracefully . . . I . . . heard the crowd cheering for the first time and that was very sweet too, though nothing compared to the exciting secrets the bull and I had . . . shared . . . (16:47).

George Young, third-place finisher in the steeplechase at the 1968 Olympics and named the World's Indoor Track Athlete that year, spent 18 years making himself one of the greatest distance runners in the world. Commenting on his intended retirement, he stated:

I can't see running without something like the Olympics to look forward to. If there was someone to run against, it might make a difference (119).

Floyd Patterson, one of the world's great boxers, fought even in his graying years because it was "a way of life." What motivated Patterson in a solitary journey that "has cost him his wife and more than once has driven him into monastic seclusion?" One reporter quoted Patterson as saying:

But the real thing, the thing that sends it right through you, is the moment two strange men seek each other out. They come together and find out who will succeed and who will fail. There is no competition like it in the whole world (40:23).

Sometimes the contestant seems to know he is best. Muhammad Ali, formerly known as Cassius Clay, one of the most controversial personalities in sports, was stripped of his title and threatened by a jail sentence following his refusal to be inducted into the army. Of the boxing world he dominated he had this to say in an interview with *Newsweek* (prior to the Ali-Frazier fight early in 1971):

I don't have to prove I'm better than Joe Frazier or anyone else. You're the champion until someone beats you, and nobody had beaten me. All those people who like boxing are missing me more than I miss the sport (67:52).

Perhaps the idea of proving one's superiority is best summed up in the words of Vince Lombardi, as told by Jerry Kramer:

There is no room for second place here. There's a second place bowl game . . . held in a hinky-dinky town, played by hinky-dinky football players. That's all second place is: Hinky-dinky (41:65).

And, one of the paradoxes of sport seems to be that while the desire to compete, to be best, may be tantamount to destroying one's opponent, also present is the feeling of togetherness, comradeship, even love.

Togetherness and Love

The story of sport gives one an appreciation of not only the complexity of man's struggles with himself and his opponents, but also of the vastness of his feeling of togetherness and love for others. The statement, "may the best man win," seems to express at once both the

hrowing-down of the gauntlet of challenge to an opponent and a
declaration of good will toward the opponent. The strong kinship
with one's own teammates is an object of numerous personal testimonials
and pep talks. Probably representative of locker room aphorisms
throughout the country is this one: "The main ingredient to stardom is
the rest of the team." But, something beyond teamwork seems to char-
acterize what happens in sport, and perhaps more than any other sport,
football has brought forth expressions of an individual's involvement
so deep that it extends beyond the rasp and the roar of the combat on
the playing field.

Jerry Kramer reflected upon what he felt about the Green Bay
Packers by comparing his feelings to those expressed by Kahil Gibran
in the passage "My Friend" in *The Prophet.* In the words of Kramer:

> We're all different . . . and yet we all go down the same road, hand in hand
> . . . no individual on this club will go directly against another's feelings, no
> matter what his own opinion is . . . I guess it all comes down to consideration,
> or maybe it's what Coach Lombardi . . . called love (41:82-83).

Often called "Mr." and "The Man," as well as dictator, tyrant, martinet,
and more, Coach Vince Lombardi seems to have personified the idea
of love for his players. Speaking about his decision to return to coaching,
Lombardi declared that what he missed most was not the tension, the
crowds, the game on Sunday, the winning, the spotlight, the fame and
all that.

> There's a great—a great closeness on a football team, you know, a rapport
> between the men and the coach that's not like any other sport. It's a binding
> together, a knitting together . . . That's what I missed most (35:33).

Fran Tarkenton, commenting about his happy association with the
Minnesota Vikings and what they had gone through together on the
field, said:

> I've never seen any place in the world, any human activity, where love is
> more exemplified than on the pro football field. You go through so much to-
> gether (116:42).

Similarly, Bill Russell described the game he had played formally or
informally for twenty-six years in this way:

> To me, one of the most beautiful things to see is a group of men coordinating
> their efforts toward a common goal—alternately subordinating and asserting
> themselves to achieve real teamwork in action . . . Often, in my mind's eye, I
> stood off and watched that effort. I found it beautiful to watch (82:18).

And, in the event that one may conclude that closeness is a characteristic exclusive to the team sports, here are some examples provided
by other sportive events. Marty Liquori, when he appeared to be heir
apparent to the throne of Jim Ryun, America's premier miler, while

acknowledging that he and Ryun only meet under adverse conditions of racing, stated:

> It's not like I have a great rivalry with Ryun, or that I hate him . . . I really respect him . . . It's a friendship, something special we have between us . . . we've been through the school of hard knocks (62:21).

Stephen Van Dyke, the youngest skipper in the 1969 transatlantic sailboat race (a grueling 2,750-mile voyage from Newport, Rhode Island, to Cork, Ireland) described the rewards that transcended silver trophies in this way:

> I'm not hell-bent on winning. I want . . . a feeling of having met a singular challenge with my crew . . . That was the greatest sense of comradeship I've ever experienced (66:63).

An NBC special television show called "The Daring Old Men," which was narrated by Kyle Rote, himself a former daring old man with the New York Giants, perhaps captured the essence of togetherness in sport with the comparison that "nothing except war brings men closer together than professional sports."

Not for the love of it alone, however, but for other reasons as well, sport may be seen to reflect a person's nobility, even under intolerable conditions, and to be a means of expression of his concept of a higher **self.**

It's Uplifting

The ancient Greeks believed as Aristotle stated: "There is a life which is higher than the measure of man." Because of their philosophy and ideal of life—love of perfection and beauty of body, mind and spirit—this concept of areté, a unity of the virtues of body, mind, and spirit in the pursuit of excellence, had its place in every sport of the Greek people. Describing some of the sporting contests of the early Greeks, as glorified in Homer's *Iliad*, Raymond Bloch wrote:

> Contests of physical strength and skill were believed to invigorate and renew the youth of the participants, to activate the powers of the gods and, by inspiration, to restore to the dead . . . some of their lost powers (5:79).

In modern times, many persons sense in the fragmentation of life and the dehumanization of man the destruction of body-mind-spirit. Earl V. Pullias, a professor of higher education, hypothesized that there is a principle in sport that involves the essence of experiencing the unified self, the opportunity to taste, as it were, the best that is in man (76). Insofar as sport may be considered to be play, the words of sociologist David Riesman reinforce the promise of sport for the development of competence in the art of living.

Play may prove to be the sphere in which there is still room left for the would-be autonomous man to reclaim his individual character from the pervasive demands of his social character (78b:276).

Former President John F. Kennedy, a football player and avid fan, may be considered one of those who counted the arena of sport among those experiences which add a dimension to man's living, to enhancing his concept of value and worth, and to providing an expression of the self in pursuit of an ideal. Addressing the Football Hall of Fame with a speech called "The Importance of Participation," Kennedy quoted Theodore Roosevelt, who had said:

> The credit belongs to the man who is actually in the arena—whose face is marred by dust, sweat, and blood; who knows the great enthusiasms, the great devotion, and spends himself in a worthy cause; who at best if he wins knows the thrills of high achievement and if he fails at least fails while daring greatly so that his place shall never be with those cold and timid souls who know neither victory or defeat (38:705).

And, there are those present day philosophers who see the meaning of sport achievement as a reaching for excellence in and through the body. In his book, *Sport: A Philosophic Inquiry*, philosopher Paul Weiss provided definitions of the various prerequisites for athletic dedication, such as "desire" and "commitment," and showed that in philosophic terms at least, they need not be considered vague "intangibles." They can be treated as "real," that is, as much a part of an athlete's identity as his strength or his speed (122). In his book *Man, Sport and Existence*, Howard Slusher described sport as a sphere of involvement with religious implications. In sport man can transcend himself, both emotionally and intellectually, as much as in reasoning or prayer (88).

In his book *The Heart of A Champion* (78), the Reverend Bob Richards, twice Olympic pole-vault champion, described the diligence, dedication and downright goodness of sport champions. As one writer put it, many readily acknowledged that the message of sport is in Richards' dictum, "stretch for something beyond." One may more fully appreciate Richards' belief in his own prescription as one observed him, in his forties, engaged in daily workouts that would not only discourage backsliders but would exhaust men twenty years younger; and, at the time of this writing, as if to prove that the stout heart triumphs over the faint spirit, he was preparing to undertake a cross-country run.

The following further illustrations serve to validate the theory that sport truly articulates the measure of man, causing him to go beyond self, to learn that ancient lesson articulated by Aristotle, "not to listen to those who exhort a man to keep a man's thoughts, but to live according to the highest thing."

John Cruickshank, writer and literary critic, declared that sport, which was the main occupation of his student days, was the place where he had his only lessons in ethics. Writing about the period when he played games and acted in plays, which he loved with unequaled intensity, he said:

> Even today, the stadium . . . and the theater . . . are the only places in the world where I feel innocent (19b).

In an essay written for *Sports Illustrated*, Yevgeny Yevtushenko, who nearly became a soccer player instead of a poet, acknowledged the importance of sport in the embodiment of the concept of striving toward harmony of the physical and mental:

> Only a harmony of the two elements leads to kindness, and kindness is the fullest expression of one's humanity (124).

He discussed the embodiment of such harmony in the Russian poet Pushkin, who "stood on a granite pedestal of fame created by his own efforts," yet who was able to get off that pedestal to be a boxer, fencer, marksman, swimmer, horseman, and hunter.

Stanford University gymnastic coach Don Millman, referring to gymnastics as a way of life, explained that "by that I mean it's the primary way a person develops himself as a human being" (116b:8). Mrs. Doris Brown ("Brownie"), part-time teacher, part-time student and at age 27 considered to be the pioneer U.S. woman distance runner, described running partly as a means of fulfilling a need to give back to others what they have given to her and a way of making herself better.

> Even the books I read that inspire me in my running are those that talk about human character (62b:70).

Similarly, Andrea Mead Lawrence, well-known skier, examining the role of the sport to the total person, said as follows:

> I feel that all the past experiences have their own intrinsic value, that their significance is not contingent on their leading to victory . . . Those experiences have not only made the skier a winner, they have been woven into the very fabric of his consciousness, making him what he is—and will become—not only as a performer but as a person (42:20).

Senior editor of *Sports Illustrated* Roger S. Hewlett expressed his passion for the sport of boating in these words:

> To me a boat is something that matches your soul's yearnings. The joy of boating is compounded of promises, and it excites with uncertainty. It speaks to man's longings as well as to his vanity, and to his pride as well as his humility (92:4).

Bob Crozier too saw harmony of man in the triumphs and troubles of car racing:

The letters of Paul to the churches are written against a background of racing. Their grasp of life, molded in part by the foot racing, horse racing and chariot racing of his time will be further illuminated by the machine racing of our time for those who can see the machine not as a cold impersonal menace, but as a supple extension of man. Motor racing has, in fact, become the symbolic and ritual enactment of the harmony of man and machine in an industrial civilization (19:81).

Not unmindful of the fact that some of the best baseball players have been something less than staunch citizens, Jay Wright, poet and playwright and one time catcher in professional baseball, declared that baseball affords the opportunity "to play beyond the crassness, the artificiality and the grubbiness that are part of this 'American' game . . . or a good many, the game looks like life, where a man goes into it challenged, exhilarated, proud and all alone" (123:39).

According to Jerry Kramer, Vince Lombardi constantly impressed upon his football players the importance of striving for perfection with such words as:

when we don't use our ability to the fullest, we're not only cheating ourselves and the Green Bay Packers, we're cheating the Lord; He gave us our ability to use it to the fullest (41:31).

And, as if to prove Lombardi was right, Kramer himself said that "unless I play a perfect game, without a single fault, I'm disappointed in myself" (41:90).

Lacrosse coach Donald Kelly of Washington College in Maryland, who annually fielded "the best small college team in the country," had less tough but equally singular philosophy:

You can't be tough. These boys are not paid for this. You have to make them accept the challenge of playing above themselves (58:35).

Perhaps the belief that sport caters to the higher and harmonious self was best summed up by one reader who pointed out that Columbia's collection of studious athletes have succeeded through determination and faith and concluded:

As Swinburne wrote, "Body and spirit are twins: God only knows which is which" (99:78).

Whether or not body and mind are twins is considered in the next section.

A Way of Thinking

The Sound Body in the Sound Mind. Throughout history the study of the nature of reality has been concerned with the nature and relationship of body and mind. The historic tradition of the "body's place" and the philosophic "betrayal of the body" is cited in numerous references

(28, 52). The Greek concept of areté, the Roman ideal of *mens sano in corpore sano*, the British concept of the playing fields of Eton as the seed-ground of military victory, Rousseau's call for "retour à la nature," and the words of numerous philosophers since that time have repeatedly underscored the need for physical fitness. In early America the persistent theme of Higginson's provocative articles, particularly in the *Atlantic Monthly* (31), was, as John Lucas pointed out, that "'physical health is a necessary condition of all permanent success.'" Lucas declared that Higginson's series of articles, titled "Saints and Their Bodies," "was an amazingly comprehensive argument for a renaissance of the Greek conception of life, the return of mankind to spiritual sanctity, fear of God, and the ability to 'walk a thousand miles in a thousand hours'" (48:55). The contemporary American expression of alarm at the "Soft American" once again called attention to what the Greeks avowed, that the rational pursuit of knowledge demanded the rational discipline of the body.

The Thinking Body. Although the study of the relationship of mind and body historically may have presumed that mind and body exist independently, so too has such study revealed that, as Joseph Wood Krutch put it, "Body and mind are connected in some way for which simple rationality has no name and which it is difficult for it to conceive." Philosophers and scientists of today, no less than throughout history, have attempted to explain that connection.

The theory that kinesthetic or motor intelligence is one of the significant forms of human intelligence is not new. It has been the purpose of numerous books, articles, monographs, and research studies to show that activities of the mind do not take place only in the "head" or if they do, they have no special priority over those which take place in the neuromuscular system. Starling, a British physiologist, introduced in the 1920's the idea of a "wisdom of the body," which, as reported by Ernst Jokl, M.D., had "suggested itself to him while reading, in the *Book of Job*, the phrase 'who hath put wisdom in the inward parts'" (36).

In another article, this one appearing in *The American Scholar*, Stanley Burnshaw, drawing from numerous early writings including Walter B. Cannon's *The Wisdom of the Body*, reasoned that, as the title, borrowed from John Donne's *Paradoxes and Problems, XI*, stated, "The Body Makes the Minde." As noted in this article: "For swift and exact knowledge of when to begin, what to do, and when to stop, the cleverest brain would be hard put to match this lower body's wisdom" (10:27). And Alfred A. Messer, M. D., in an article entitled "Creative Thinking Made Easy," set forth the theory (also proposed by other scholars) that physical activity actually may be an important ingredient in creative problem solving (58b). Similarly, the central idea in contemporary education emerges from a philosophy of man's multisensory ways of knowing. From the study of what Jean Piaget called sensory-motor intelligence, educators have come to share the conviction that there is no mind except in the reaction of the body. As Harold Rugg put it, we not only move with the body, we think with it and imagine with it.

Other scholars, these more specifically within the domain of sport and dance, have written eloquently of the union between sport (or other forms of movement experiences) and thinking itself. Margaret H'Doubler, noted dance educator, wrote in the early 1930's and reiterated in a dance lesson in her eighties, that "movement sensations are as real as any other sensations and the brain handles them in the same manner . . . it is the same principle of sensorial, perceptual and conceptual cortical activity." Eleanor Metheny, noted physical educator, drawing upon the works of neurophysiologists, psychologists, and philosophers, asserted that "movement is too much like thought to be less than thinking" (59). And in *Sport: A Philosophic Inquiry*, Paul Weiss treated the "bodily relevant mind" as a vector—the mind providing the body with a controlling future. Body and mind are not closed off from one another. Rather, they are linked by emotions and they offer excellent agencies for unifying men (122:39).

Sport Intelligence. In a similar vein the high place accorded the role of the so-called intellect in sport is illustrated throughout the recorded history of sport. In Homer's *Iliad*, Nestor's lecture to his son Antilochus, as pointed out by Bloch, revealed that "the race would not go necessarily to the swiftest horses but to the driver who exercised the most careful thought and surest wisdom" (5:79). Today, most sports are considered to have more interest than just as a contest between skilled athletes.

Miller, for example, following the lead of J. P. Guilford, who contended that there were many "faces of intellect," studied, as one facet of skill intelligence, the visual-perceptual abilities of champion athletes. Champion athletes (both men and women) in basketball, fencing, gymnastics, swimming, and volleyball were found to be superior to low-skilled performers on some selected measures of the ability to perceive, to analyze, to interpret, and to react instantaneously to visual cues in space (59b). Even the sport of spectatorship, as Charles H. Page pointed out, involves more than merely watching. It involves a great deal of cognitive activity and an increasing knowledge or expertise (38b:21).

It is beyond the scope of this book to cite the thoughts and words and laboratory evidence of all those who have been concerned with the power of sport in terms of getting the body "into shape," or in expanding the intellect, or in being a form of thinking. Rather the

2

purpose here is to cite examples appearing in popular literature which may be considered as bearing out theoretical insights. A few such examples may be representative of the many.

Typical of the writings of those who believe that sport and intellect go together, even in such obvious activities as running, is this brief summation by Tex Maule, who, calling relay racing "the thinking man's race," simply stated that "the winner may well prove the race goes not to the swift but to the smart" (53:74).

The "brainy" part of the game also comes in for its share of copy. For example, "baseball strategy is a brain battle" full of countless and suspenseful maneuvers designed to outsmart the opponent. Some well-known pieces of stratagem include the "suicide squeeze," the "hit-and-run," the "intentional pass," and by means of these "mindful" decisions a lot of ball games are won or lost (125).

Although one may suspect that the football line is the one sport in the sport world which is characterized more by brawn than by brain, Jerry Kramer, former all-pro right offensive guard of the Green Bay Packers, portrayed the truth of the matter as he variously described his preseason preparations:

> Playing against Karras is like playing a chess game . . . you've got to be thinking all the time . . . Logically, you don't want to do the same thing every time . . . great tackles beat you with their quickness and intelligence . . . To an extent quickness comes with experience and understanding (41:78, 104, 105, 106).

Others may write colorfully of the power of sport to extend prowess, memory, reason, imagination, judgment, and creativity. Calling good golf a "state of mind," Arnold Palmer wrote:

> concentration means a total and forward-looking relationship between the mind and the challenge—and the essence of that relationship is . . . not destructive but creative, not the throttling of instincts but the release. . . . I am trying to rediscover my personal resources, re-group them and match them to the challenge (71:41).

While some may simply state that they think better in sport than in words, writers such as Jay Wright supply the words as well. Asking himself what baseball, as a profession, as a game, as a way of life meant to him, he reflected upon his former days as a catcher and stated

> the game and its environment shaped all my perceptions that followed . . . the intrepid, ingenious "intellectual" . . . makes his way by a highly developed sense of baseball perception. Judgment . . . can be taught. As he thinks through game situations that recur like profane mythological events, the ball-player sees what maneuver most profits him and his club (123:33, 37).

Citing examples of how sport helped people survive in dire situations—for example, a Soviet pole-vaulter, who used a Nazi flag pole to leap over a lethal wire to escape from a prisoner of war camp, or the goalkeeper Zhmelkov, who would catch enemy sentries by making his famous leaps—Yevtushenko, the Russian poet, declared that "in the 20th century the mind has a hard time, and in difficult moments the body can help the mind—and the other way around" (124).

And, for those who disavow the thesis of "faculty psychology," or that mind at times enters into particular activities in distinct ways, this tale offers at least a humorous counterpoint. It seems that at a certain elementary school the teacher held up one finger of her left hand, saying, "That's one," then holding up one finger of her right hand, she queried: "Can anyone tell me what this adds up to?" Peter, age three, answered: "A ball and a strike."

Despite the criticism that man neglects the means for getting "in shape," laboratory findings reported support the contention that some sportsmen and joggers "run for their lives" and to "grow young." On the basis of health benefits produced in one such project at Leisure World, a retirement community in Laguna Hills, California under the direction of Dr. Herbert deVries of the University of Southern California Gerontology Center, a conclusion was drawn that sport and exercise may prolong human life by slowing down the aging process. Parallel reports by scientific authorities reported that the most efficient hearts were to be found in (in descending order): professional cyclists, long-distance runners, amateur cyclists, cross-country skiers, boxers, handball players, gymnasts, wrestlers, and weight lifters (30:12-27).

Other literature shows that most persons, not just the skilled athlete, accept the invitation to get the body on the move, and in rather dramatic ways. For example: In March of 1968, a field of 1,698 people participated in the English Cross-Country Championships. Only 104 participants failed to complete the run across plowed fields, over fences, and through streams. During the same month in Salen, Sweden, 7,887 skiers participated in the world's longest ski race—a distance of 50 miles. Of the 7,887 starters, 7,705 of them completed the course and in so doing, more than half of the finishers had skied for more than 11 hours (112: 14-19).

Another article offered the possibility for the less than muscular giant to participate in "true football," if he had the physical-mental wherewithal to do so. In a study of soccer, undertaken for the United States Olympic Committee after the 1964 Olympics by Arthur D. Little, Inc., the Cambridge, Massachusetts, research organization, it was pointed out that many persons participate in soccer because:

> Soccer opens up the opportunity for others to participate in the athletic program who would otherwise be eliminated because of small size or weight . . . Soccer has action . . . roughness . . . beauty . . . everything . . . and, conditionwise, a football or baseball player could not last 10 minutes on a soccer field (37:28).

Many persons speak of a psychophysical alchemy which transforms the body and mind. We may best understand this concept in the words of Roger Bannister, who stated:

> I sometimes think that running has given me a glimpse of the greatest freedom that a man can ever know, because it results in the simultaneous liberation of both body and mind (2:229).

The evidence, however, for this psychophysical alchemy is not merely the subjective testimony of sportsmen. It is described in many case histories of neurologists and orthopedic surgeons. For example, Erns Jokl, M.D., asserting that a skilled movement is characterized by "accom paniment of mind," cited cases which exemplified the wisdom of mai imposing his will upon nature. Among such examples were those Olympic athletes who had become involved in accidents which had caused major damage to the body. The significance of these case histories according to Jokl, lay in the fact that they "changed their destiny by making defiant and heroic decisions of their own," and that

> performance techniques did not rest upon reflex-controlled inborn patterns . . . Rather, they had to be synthesized from mental images of their own (36:15).

The body-mind relationship is evident also in the laboratory-tested concept. For example, Francis Hellebrandt, M.D., conducted an experi mental project designed to study the crossover effect (from the highest reasoning apparatus to the primitive brain centers) in muscle control The consequences of pushing human beings to the point of exhaustion seemed to have application to sport. One person was reported as saying

> You feel some pain, but after a while . . . You forget the pain. You forget everything but achieving the objective (103:6).

One of the dedicated sportsmen who may support the contention tha it is necessary to overcome a natural human reluctance to push to the pain threshold, reacted with this comment:

> By driving the service muscles beyond the control of our cerebral cortex and allowing the primitive brain centers to take over, the competitive swimmer will receive the superhuman strength necessary to dominate and win all com petition (103:6).

The reporter of this study added the dour observation that the joyfu sportsman "does not indicate who would win if one agonized swimme met another in the same event" (103:6).

Blowing Off Steam

Closely connected with the concept of the mind-body relationshi found in sport is the idea that sport may act to rid man of detrimenta

motions. Long before William James urged man to find a moral equiva-
ent to war, the cathartic character of sport had been the topic of much
iterature. More recently, probably the most controversial studies of
nan and animal have to do with the biology of aggression. Notable
among such studies has been that of Dr. Konrad Lorenz, Director of
he Max-Planck-Institute for Physiology of Behavior in Bavaria. Lorenz
proposed that sport is "a specifically human form of non-hostile combat,"
and that the value of sport today is the "cathartic discharge" of the
aggressive urge. Sport, he stated, "educates man to a conscious and
esponsible control of his own fighting behavior" (47:281). Even
porting contests between nations might be regarded as a safety valve.
f sporting contests channel aggressions, nations could indeed make
port, not war.

Walter E. Schafer, citing his own research findings and the works of
ames Coleman, David Matza, Willard Waller, and others, pointed to
ome ways in which competitive sports in the schools serve a "social
control function"—inhibiting abnormal interests, harnessing adolescent
nergies, encouraging yet controlling physical force, providing oppor-
unities to struggle against an enemy, and exerting a deterring influence
on delinquency (84b:29-44).

Doctor Robert A. Moore, a psychiatrist at the University of Michigan,
old a sport panel at a meeting of the American Medical Association
hat "sports provide an exceptional opportunity for expression in a
imited way of aggressive and sadistic impulses." Sport helps the
mentally ill recover and helps the mentally healthy stay healthy, he
asserted, and also provides "an escape outlet for frightening and con-
using sexual urges."

Perhaps like laughter, sport may represent an effective antidote for
ear. Or it may simply provide simple pristine joys not readily available
elsewhere, yet so necessary to man's psychic equilibrium. To the ques-
ion of what motivates the "little sportsman," those people who "cheer-
ully gather, at their own expense, for an evening of karate, or volleyball,
or horseshoe-pitching, or fly-casting, or surf-casting, or billiards," Jim
Murray simply opined, "I sense the joy, and I envy" (60:54).

From the conjecture that sport provides a safety valve and that it
makes winners and losers all rather smug together in sharing a secret
oy flow fascinating illustrations in the literature. Some of these are
cited elsewhere throughout various sections of this chapter and the next.
A few are added here which seem to focus primarily on the cathartic and
he for-the-fun-of-it motive.

The element of ritual found in sport may meet a profound need in
he human psyche, even when such a need is unrecognized. One means
or expression of hope is the sport *festival* of the Indians for whom the

Sierra del Tarahumare, a stretch of high mountain range in Mexico's remote barranca country, is named. As Lamberto Alvarez Gayou, an authority on Mexican sport, is quoted as saying, "There is no doubt they are the best runners in the world, not for speed but for distance." These Indians refer to themselves as "Raramure," which means "foot runner." They brighten their lives by turning to festivals, and at each festival except the one celebrating death there is a game. A kickball race called "rarajipare" is the most important and festive game—the length of the laps being anywhere from three to 12 miles. Before the men race there is a dance. When the chief was asked what the dance signified, "as if he considered the question absurd," he replied, "We've always danced this way—what difference does it make?" (87:67)

Others may satisfy their needs for release by daring and daffy stunts which may be classified by strict taxonomists as more sporting than sport; nonetheless, among such men is Mira Slovak, who in 1964 became the champion of "cavorting in small planes." His "delight in the never done," as reported in *Time,*

> helps me unwind and stop being a part of the computer . . . If you think you are so great . . . then you won't feel that way too long . . . out there (117:64).

The lure of the sea turns some men and women into modern adventurers. Hugh Whall, a veteran of numerous boat races, stated the following:

> For all sports, this is the most habit-forming, the most expensive, the most exasperating, the most exciting, the most soothing, the most strenuous, the most uncomfortable and the most fun . . . always, though you thank God a race is over, you jump at the chance to sign for the next one (100:33).

Said another sailor, Hank Wulff:

> If I don't do something that scares the . . . out of me, I'd turn to Jell-O in a matter of minutes (66:63).

Although some may speak of the body's rebellion against agonizing usage, still they describe hard physical work as being satisfying. Before the 1968 Olympics, Buddy Edelen worked out by running 130 miles a week along the streets of Sioux Falls. As he put it:

> You get so tired you're preoccupied with pain . . . If I don't run for a day or two I get irritable and nervous as if something's been stolen from me (45:40).

J. Kenneth Doherty stated that for some people running is a "challenge even when it is a hardship; play even when they hate it" (26:64). Runners who bear out such a statement include Ron Clarke, world famous distance runner, who insisted that he runs for fun.

> I eat and live like ordinary people. I make no sacrifices. For me, training and competition are recreation (9:24-25).

n 1966, when Jim Ryun, who at the age of 17 became the first high
chool boy to break the four-minute mile, was selected as *Sports Illus-
rated's* Sportsman of the Year, he said:

> I've tried to explain to people that there is more satisfaction than pain in hard
> workout . . . work can be satisfying. If running hurt as much as people seem
> to think it does, I wouldn't go out on the track in the first place (114:47).

Golf fans, who, unlike football or baseball fans, *play* their favorite
port, speak almost seductively of their hopeless addiction and inevitable
eturn to the game following a single well-played shot. Alistair Cooke,
he host of Omnibus TV show of the 1950's and chief American cor-
espondent of the *Manchester Guardian* for 20 some years, wrote in a
jvial vein about this marvelous mania, in which his "lifelong purity"
vas, as he described:

> defiled in a single afternoon . . . I was taken out with a bag of oddly-shaped
> sticks to fumble around . . . My only qualification for writing about this
> marvelous mania is that I have been majoring in golf for over three years and
> may be in time to deter some other intended addict (17:33).

Still others write derisively about the spoilers of that fun element in
port. Robert Paul Smith's delightful little book for everybody who was
nce a kid, *"Where Did You Go?" "Out." "What Did You Do?" "Nothing."*
iumorously yet seriously reprimanded the "covey of overseeing grownups"
anging around today's Little League baseball players and "making it
o bloody important." What he remembered joyfully was:

> the sound of a ball in a glove, and the feeling in my fingers when the bat
> threatened to split (you vibrated clear up to your ears, and somebody hollered
> at you to hold the label up) . . . And then there was the little kid who had
> been given a glove that we thought was much too good for him . . . we
> advised him that the only way to really truly properly break it in was to rub
> it in with horse dung and leave it in the sun . . . Oh, all the wisdom. A kid
> hit a bunch of fouls. We know what to say. "He's gonna have chicken for
> supper" (89:13-14).

Fair Game

Part of the fun and cathartic character of sport seems to come from
he fact that sport sponsors approved controls—a chance to let off steam
n an approved way. As Caillois suggested, games provide "the desire
o invent rules, and to abide by them whatever the cost" (11:28).
Certainly sport motivates people to live by the rules concerning safety
if limb and property, deportment and manners, and rules concerning
ionesty and honor. The rules are generally understood and accepted by
everyone, and when the umpire calls the play he applies the same rules
o everyone. This same code of fair play, General Douglas MacArthur
jointed out in a report to President Coolidge on American participation

in the Ninth Olympic Games held in Amsterdam in 1928, "embraces th highest moral laws and will stand the test of any ethics or philosophie ever promulgated for the uplift of man . . . it instinctively follows religion that has no hypocrisy . . . and binds man to man in links as tru as steel" (51:348). In fact, as Lorenz more recently suggested, "even i the face of the strongest-aggression-eliciting stimuli" the demands fo fairness and chivalry must be respected (47:281).

Rita Wetzel, a Kansas City psychologist, studied the personalities o more than 100 race drivers who competed at Sebring and conclude that "we have learned that he [the race driver] is more apt to be rather dapper person who respects the rules of society and channels h aggressive tendencies into competition" (113:14).

Edward Rutkowski likened football to a living model of Plato concept of the republic. He conceived an artificial prototype based upo notions of practical justice and drew an analogy between the coac and the philosopher king who must deal with justice. Like Plato concept of the republic, the football game contains elements of orde discipline, and communal dedication (83:31).

Günther Lüschen explained why, on the basis of the structural rela tionship of sport and culture, "in the culture of sport we find not onl the values of achievement but also of fair play and other affiliativ orientations" (50).

Known as "friend of sport," Pius XII, an enthusiastic swimmer an horseman in his youth, was the first pope to install a gymnasium in th Vatican. At the time of his death, *Sports Illustrated* shared with reade Pope Pius XII's reflections on sport, which indicated that he saw i sport something that corresponds to man's desire and need for restrain Here, in Pius' own words, are standards to strive for:

> Loyalty that excludes taking refuge in subterfuges, docility and obedience to the director charged with training of the team, the spirit of self-renunciation when one has to fade into the background to further the interests of the team, fidelty to obligations undertaken, modesty in victory, serenity in adverse fortune, patience toward spectators who are not always moderate . . . and in general that chastity and temperance recommended by the ancients themselves (102:27).

Rex Stout, a prolific writer and typically ardent fan, stated simpl that "baseball is a test of whether or not there is justice in the world" (7 And Yevtushenko even called sport "a cleaner business than literature (*A Precocious Autobiography*).

What, then, are some illustrations of the kind of discipline and cor formity desired by man and insisted upon in the rules and standard of sport? An incident at a university in Oregon in which the footba coach told one black athlete to shave his beard touched off a walkout c 47 black students on the campus. Following this, a writer, expressing h sympathy with the coaches, made the observation that champions should "go first class." He cited the instance of Madeline Manning, winner of the 800 meter run in the 1968 Olympics. In one of her visits to high schools a small group shouted for her to raise a clenched fist as they were doing. Instead she "tilted her chin high and stood with dignity." The "good kids drowned out the shouters with applause." The writer added this point:

> We don't expect the bank teller to come to the window dressed in overalls, we don't expect the waitress to slide up to our table with a mop in one hand and her flower beads dangling in the soup bowl . . . if a football coach feels it's in the best interest of his team and his school to insist on clean-shaven players in the huddle, then I hope he has the guts to carry out his rules (55).

Although bonuses and payments to "amateurs" under the table may be, as stated in one article, "as common as barked shins" around the soccer league, the bugaboo, "professionalism" in sport has always found its opponents. In the 1912 Olympics at Stockholm, prodigious Jim Thorpe won gold medals in the decathlon and pentathlon but was forced to return them when he was accused of professionalism. More recently, according to Ress and Brown, "two of the best-made images in the pantheon of sports," Jean-Claude Killy of international skiing fame, and Sir Stanley Matthews, retired British professional soccer wizard, wound up as somewhat tarnished idols in print because of alleged professionalism. Although, according to one writer, Killy's image was far from destroyed, and although he asserted that his conscience was clear, scandal, prospects of investigations, and pressures of controversy were put upon him. As for Matthews, the British Football Association found the soccer club of which he was manager guilty of both illegal payments to and recruiting of schoolboys and amateurs. The club was summarily expelled from the league. The writers of one article concluded that people do not like to have their gods suddenly turn into ordinary corrupted mortals—however uncertain or hypocritical the cause for emotion may be" (79:22-25).

Probably symbolizing the joy of youth and life and girls even more than Killy, Joe Namath, the dazzling New York Jet quarterback, made integrity in sport an even bigger issue by his financial interest in a night spot which gamblers allegedly frequented. Reminding themselves of the infamous pro baseball's Black Sox scandal of 1919 and the college basketball scandals of 1951 and the following years, protective sport "bosses" ordered Namath to divest himself of his interest in the night club. Pete Rozelle, commissioner of professional football, emphasized that while there was no evidence that Namath was "personally involved in any illegal activities," his associations might give "the appearance of

evil . . . and thereby affect . . . the integrity of his sport." The writer of
this newspaper article added:

> That is the nature of the glass house in which live the sports world, and
> therefore the players, the owners and all other personnel (77:65-66).

In 1970, the downfall of another hero, Denny McClain, star pitcher
of the Detroit Tigers, made numerous headlines and magazine reports
(85b). Although the disclosure of McClain's involvement in a book-
making operation dominated by mobsters led to his temporary suspension,
some persons thought the suspension was too lenient. One report, de-
crying the fact that sport itself had been besmirched, wrote:

> Despite prevalent cynicism, people generally have a respect for the honesty
> and integrity of sport that they do not have for other aspects of contemporary
> society (113b:9).

Some writers decry the "cult of victory" in sport over the "code of
honor," tabbing the "will to win" as "kill to win." Examples such as
boxing are cited "where the savagery is built-in and unavoidable";
basketball, which "has to have doctors standing by with needle and
thread and bone-splints"; football, which is a form of "trench warfare"
in which many a player leaves the field "with his teeth in his hand";
horse racing, in which there is "more rough riding and horse pileups than
in Ben Hur." Jim Murray's conclusion again implied a wanted ethic.

> Athletics today don't need a sportwriter, they need a combat correspondent
> . . . the games become not skill, but chance—not marksmanship but Russian
> Roulette (61:32).

A similar example is provided by the brush-back pitch, legitimate in
baseball, the purpose of which is to keep the batter restless enough
that he is unable to dig in. Although its intent is not to knock down or
maim the batter, writers have raised the question, "why should the
batter be penalized for his skill or luck by having to test his reflexes
against a speeding baseball?" Rick Reichardt, for example, who at the
time of this reporting had hit 12 home runs, also had been hit nine times.
Despite avowals that pitchers don't throw to hit batters, some confessed,
"It's all part of the game," while another person, declaring that baseball
is not a contact sport, implied the purpose of controls in these words:

> It's beauty and drama are not enhanced by the sight of a man writhing on the
> ground (106:19).

Whether spectators are proper fans or hoodlums has been of concern
to some writers. One of the few sports where "proper fandom" and
good manners still predominate may be tennis; however, one U.S. Davis
Cup captain at one time,

as part of the effort to keep tennis abreast of the times, urged tennis fans to forget their country club manners and to start yelling at tournaments like the fans at baseball, football, hockey and basketball games (91:17).

At least one writer felt a warning was in order and emphasized restraint. Lest the thing get out of hand he recalled for readers:

the time when the mob seethed over the field to ruin a Giants-Browns football game in New York . . . and the time when youngsters invaded the outfield at Yankee Stadium . . . to commit mild mayhem on Mickey Mantle (91:17).

Another report cited the example of Bulgaria, which found an effective method of dealing with unruly soccer fans and players. At a traditional grudge match, a judge and a number of clerks presided; those present were informed that anyone causing a disturbance would be tried at once, and a list of offenders and their punishment on a previous occasion was read. The result of this method was that "the match was played peaceably, and when players accidentally fouled they apologized profusely to their opponents" (110:14).

Of the factors tending to destroy the rules of the game, and thus, sport itself, none has received more attention within recent years than the use of drugs by the athlete participating in organized games. The arguments for writing antidrug regulations and enforcing them are convincing evidence that, without the discipline of rules which equalize competition, there is no sport. More than the fact that drugs seem to constitute a health problem is the pervasive feeling of guilt, cheating, and the intangible matter of what sport is all about. Bill Gilbert, in one article of a three-part series called "Drugs in Sport" which appeared in *Sports Illustrated,* stated that the time has come to make some rules. The rules, he declared, retain the mystery and drama of sport because:

they are designed to focus on the men themselves: to measure their weaknesses, virtues, speed, strength, agility, stamina, intelligence, instincts, resistance to pain and pressure and their control . . . Short of slipping robots into the lineup, the use of drugs . . . is the most dehumanizing practice of the lot (29:32, 35).

What will be the end of the wide use of drugs by athletes remains to be seen. At this moment in history, this vastly complicated problem serves to remind the reader that man finds in sport, now as in the beginning, the simple distinction that sport motivates men to want to live by the rules.

Despite these serious problems, however, it is worth noting, and perhaps a fitting summary to this section, that even the controls in sport have their aspects of fun and levity. Some writers humorously point to, as well as rationalize, the subtle infringements on the rules by perceiving the basic principles of the art of winning games without really cheating. Classic among such writings are those of Stephen Potter, who gave the world such household words as "gamesmanship," "ploy," "gambit," and "one-upsmanship." In one of his several books, *The Theory and Practice of Gamesmanship,* he put forth the specifics of good gamesmanship and such refinements as the following:

> Do not attempt to irritate your partner by spending too long looking for your lost ball. This is unsporting. But good gamesmanship . . . can be practiced if the gamesman makes a great and irritatingly prolonged parade . . . looking for his opponent's ball . . . approved ways of saying "bad luck" for the opponent while still operating within the rules of the game (75).

Midway in the 1969 baseball season, legal grapplings over the language of the standard player's contract and its so-called reserve clause led John R. McDermott to give this extralegal view:

> If it pleases the court, I would like to finish out the season and get out . . . I'd be willing to study baseball law at my fishing camp. In time I could be a coach. Then I could instruct young pitchers on the rules and evidence regarding spitters, shiners and brush backs, and all those IRS regulations pertaining to major league players with bowling alleys and fried chicken drive-ins (56:83-84).

While sport may be among one of the comforting facts of life in that it provides a glimpse of the reality of life—discovering oneself and others, being pulled toward the higher self, experiencing the unified self, releasing pent-up emotions in an acceptable and accepted way—it may also be comforting because it provides a way of escaping the reality of life. Such is the topic of concern in the ensuing section.

ESCAPING REALITY

In this "disordered epoch" when man appears to live on quicksand with outer space as his only terrestrial frontier, one reason for the popular appeal of sport may be that, for some persons, it is a way to deal with the absurdity of a world they no longer seemingly control, a world they can no longer describe easily in rational terms.

An article on life and leisure appearing in *Newsweek* stated, in reference to people's yen to battle the sea in boats: "There aren't many places left for a man to find such elemental challenge—or such heady authority. The American male, pinned in the conflicting demands of his complex world, no longer rules anything" (66:58).

Beisser, who had opportunities to study athletes who became psychiatric patients, found that for some, sport was a means to "act out certain desires that were unacceptable elsewhere"; for some, sport provided a way of "relating to people in what was otherwise a forbidding world"; for some, sport was "a way of pleasing or identifying with or of rebelling against parents." Beisser, in short, found in the case histories that a sport may represent "a place of anachronistic refuge" (4).

As Caillois suggested, a socially acceptable way of escaping the confusion of contemporary life is derived from games, which make possible "pleasure in secrecy, make believe, or disguise" (11:65). Frank Trippett, defining illusion as meaning literally "in-play," stated that "fun takes such myriad forms it smacks of illusion." The origin of fun is not concealed, he asserted, despite the vast literature that makes a mystery of this love. The nub of fun's mystique may be found in the infant, and it is here that we recognize ourselves in "disequilibrium—and that ineluctable tandem sensation, the sense of other worlds—this is the essence of fun, this is the quarry of the human fun quest . . . Man loves the sea for the same reason an infant loves being rocked. Life is disequilibrium. Stillness is death" (118:33).

Also among the attitudes and impulses provided by games, as identified by Caillois, is "fear or inspiring of fear," and, "the intoxication, longing for ecstasy, and desire for voluptuous panic" (11:65).

Some writers have described "eustress," or pleasant stress, as fun, proposing eustress-seeking as a possible component of a common motivation to participate in sport (30b, 39b). Harris, describing the joy of being "on the 'brink of catastrophe,'" cited several works as being supportive of this theory and suggested that "the process of transferring anxiety or fear into pleasure composes the very essence of participation" (30b:36).

Here, then, are a few illustrations of the myriad forms sportive events take and some ways in which man expresses his feelings as he seeks an escape from reality.

Out of This World

Florence Chadwick, considered the best long-distance swimmer the world has known, at the age of 41 tried to swim across the treacherous North Channel of the Irish Sea, a distance of 21 miles. About swimming she commented:

> Life seems so much simpler swimming. The experience must be similar to that of a flyer above the clouds by himself—I am also in my own little world out there (13:52).

As described by Gilbert Rogin, according to Harvey Powelson, a psychiatrist at the University of California at Berkeley, a subculture of surfers arose after the war which had its own myths, mores, and folk heroes: "They said the hell with the ordinary ways of making it, but they were left nothing. Surfing seemed to be a bodily statement of what they felt" (80:106). One such person cited was Fred Van Dyke, a celebrated big-wave rider who spent four years in psychoanalysis. As a result of his "hang-up on big-wave riding," Van Dyke reportedly told

his analyst, "I want to be helped but please don't take my board away."
Of surfing he stated:

> Guys ride big waves for ego support, to compensate for something that's
> lacking in their lives . . . They have an underlying feeling that they're not
> doing anything with meaning . . . Surfing gives you that feeling of accomplish-
> ment (80:104).

Phil Edwards, one of the world's best on a board and said to be "the
Manolete of the sport" who was responsible for "giving the sport its
Jack Armstrong look," said people surf for two reasons. When it started,
he reflected, it was a form of rebellion against an organized spoon-fed
society. The other reason was as follows:

> when that big, hollow, motherless wave comes crashing down behind you, and
> it vibrates the whole ocean . . . and you come out of it alive, and you're so
> stoked you can't stand it . . . It is being unplugged from life for just a second.
> God, it's the neatest thing (70:35).

Admitting there is a lot of escapism in boating and likening boating
to taking a mistress, Roger S. Hewlett, a senior editor of *Sports Illustrated*, said the desire to own a boat

> is prompted by a need . . . to make a solid and tangible commitment to a
> dream . . . you will lavish foolish attention on her and make harsh and exacting
> demands and in return she will share with you a moment near perfection
> (92:4).

In considering the idea that sport provides pleasure through make
believe by transporting the individual from one role to another, one might
believe, as Arnold Palmer, who stated:

> I want to march right up over the next hill and on and on . . . Physically I
> am on the golf course, but spiritually I am just floating around it in a happy
> daze. I have to make a deliberate effort to reach out, pull myself back to
> reality and get down to the business at hand (71:28).

Or, one might concur finally with the feelings of a gymnast describing
his experience:

> The ceiling trades places with the floor; then the floor with the ceiling. And
> then very abruptly and seemingly miraculously, you find yourself standing on
> your own feet. You feel like you have transgressed into one exciting world
> and then back again. You feel wonderful. You cannot name what that feeling
> is, but it does not matter. As long as it is there, you will keep returning to that
> world (57:6).

Immortal Thrills—Way Out

What motivates the professional sportsman, Jim Murray divined,
"has to be panic." The home-run hero "just might hit the home run
despite the small knot of fear in his stomach" (60:53). But, what about
the precarious adventures of the nonprofessional sportsman? Contrary

to Euripedes' warning in *Bacchae* that "if man, in his brief moment goes after things too great for him, he may lose the joys within his reach," some of man's achievements, involvements and commitments, kept or unkept, say not only that he is mortal but that he, like Prometheus, is capable of reaching into the highest heavens to snatch fire from the hand of God. Although such adventures may be as Euripedes declared, 'a way of madness and perversity," apparently they become for some a way of escaping madness and perversity.

Among those nonprofessionals who actively and consciously flirt with danger are a wild and winning breed of men who venture across oceans in small boats. The first transatlantic yacht race was sailed over 100 years ago by professional crews. Since that time ocean yachtsmen by the score work their own boats. The modest prizes for the first 5,600-mile Pacific Ocean marathon through unpredictable weather and water were a trophy and one half the return expenses from Tokyo to San Francisco (64). What motives carry sailors into the solitary blue? Obviously they are not racing for money. *Sports Illustrated* staff writer Hugh Whall, a veteran of numerous distance boat races, stated:

> The things that drive men to race on the ocean must be pretty much the same as those that drive him to drink (100:33).

The book, *Why Man Takes Chances,* draws together psychologic, sociologic, anthropologic and literary materials from a conference in which nine persons were invited to explore "stress-seeking" behavior and such related phenomena as seeking danger, fear, and anxiety. Samuel Z. Klausner, editor, reminded the reader that "only in play and sports can an individual who creates artificial obstacles, pursues contests, and tempts fear achieve full toleration" (39b:iii).

Charles S. Houston, describing the motivations of mountain climbers who could choose an easier route yet cling to sheer cliffs in ascents, even deliberately made at night or in bad weather, reiterated his convictions of the call of controlled risk:

> climbing is one of the few activities where the stress is clear, apparent, and freely sought . . . a quest for self-fulfillment (39b:57).

Faced with what Pogo called an "insurmountable opportunity," some men delight in doing what has never been done. Such "uncommon men," as they were labeled in *Time,* include: Bruce Tulloh, the former British Olympic distance runner who at the time of this writing was attempting to run from Los Angeles to New York in a record 66 days; four other British men who made a 16-month, 2,000-mile dog-sled trek across the Arctic; stunt man Evel Knievel, who raced a jet-powered motorcycle down a ramp at 280 miles per hour with the idea of jumping across the Grand Canyon; Henry Carr, a professional football back and a former Olympic 200-meter dash champion, who raced a pacer (horse) over a 110-yard course and won by 10 yards ("I never beat the horses at the betting window so I wanted to see if I could beat them on the track").

But, "honors for freakish firsts," *Time* granted to Aleksander Wozniak, a Polish exile who walked 33 miles down the Thames River on 3-foot long canoe-shaped wood shoes. "Daring or daffy as these ventures may be," the report continued, "none has attracted a more mixed assortment of self-styled adventurers" than a transatlantic air race stunt sponsored by the *London Daily Mail*. At least one "among the dozens of publicity seekers and assorted kooks in the race" of 390 contestants, Mira Slovak found the challenge "in the flying, not in the frills." His aircraft was the smallest to ever cross the Atlantic. Although Slovak's cavorting in small planes has cost him a broken back, a broken leg, 28 teeth and badly damaged kidneys, he said:

> I love the challenge . . . In this country, you can try for anything you want and what I want is to be an uncommon man (117:63-64).

And, while Sharon Sites Adams, a 39-year-old housewife, completed a perilous solo voyage across the Pacific Ocean in a 31-foot boat, another voyage of courage was being enacted somewhere in the mid-Atlantic. English adventurer John Fairfax was in the midst of a journey that would make him the first man to row the ocean single-handed. Despite the outcome of his trip, one is reminded of that ancient bit of wisdom, "it is not necessary to live, it is necessary only to sail the seas."

To portray adequately either the greatness or the madness in sport would be a task worthy of the pen and brilliance of Homer himself. Within the context of this book only an overview is possible. Even so, the foregoing glimpse of the participant in sport permits the possibility of probing into some of the subtleties of man's personality, of telling some of the dilemmas of his travail and of recording portions of his delirious joy.

The attraction of sport for the spectator also is fascinating. A glimpse at this aspect of sport follows in Chapter 2.

CHAPTER 2

The Spectator

Although one may not agree with Reuel Denney that "it is important to detect in sports-mindedness a desire to feed the sources of 100 percent Americanism, spectator benches, and the star system of the Big Game" (24:124-125), one can hardly deny that many sport consumers can be classified as spectators. And, whether or not the spectator, as Denney described him in 1957, "still serves to mask the deficiency of the participant system" (24:128-129), watching, discussing and reading about sport is the pastime of millions of Americans, who, as Beisser noted, have an insatiable appetite for sports and "will take them anyway they can get them." Beisser described an instance in World War II in which the attacking Japanese troops used not only weapons but shouted invectives intended to demoralize as indicative of the overwhelming enthusiasm for sports in the United States. One such invective was, "To hell with Babe Ruth." Beisser commented, "So far as I know they did not defame the religions of America, vilify our economic system, or condemn motherhood. Instead they selected a sports hero as representative of what Americans loved most" (4:1). Despite the lack of readily documented and consistent evidence for the meanings and motivations found by spectators of sport, there is no lack of evidence that the viewing audience is vast and exuberant.

THE RUSH TO VIEWING PLEASURE

A glimpse at some highlighted statistics provides some evidence of the resistless attraction of sport to the spectator.

Football fever has resulted in a season which now encompasses the regular season schedule, preseason games, conference championships, divisional championships, postseason games, bowl games, super bowls, all-star games—a season that now covers about six months. In fact, across the land on New Year's Day watching bowl games is as much a custom as is making resolutions. If the viewer is a skillful channel switcher, he can pick up the excitement from three if not all four of the New Year's Day bowl games (Sugar, Cotton, Rose and Orange) and warm up a few days in advance with the Gator, Liberty, Citrus, Blue Bonnet, Tangerine and Sun Bowls.

In 1968, when the New York Jets played the Baltimore Colts in the third Super Bowl game, it was "Super Sunday for Super Spectator," as one writer called it.

> the sixty million (which is equal to 800 sold-out Orange Bowls, or 400 times the population of Plato's Athens) were bathed as one in the . . . cathode tubes (35b:87).

The NCAA Television Committee reported that in 1969 an average of twenty-five million persons viewed each football game telecast. According to the National Collegiate Sports Service in 1969 there were 27,626,160 spectators attending college football games, an increase of 600,314 over the all-time high set in 1968 (62c:2).

Statistics of local exuberance included: The New Orleans Saints fans bought 75,000 pennants in 1967 (the club finished its home season with an average attendance of 75,463) (111:8). In 1968, when the Dallas Cowboys were to play a preseason, or what some called an exhibition, game on a humid, hot August evening, some 72,000 Dallas fans "left their air-conditioned homes to watch" (54:10-13). *Sports Illustrated* in the 1967-1968 season had 13 outside covers, 60 pages of inside color photographs, 57 stories or, a total of about 150,000 words—all on football (93:6).

The game of professional *basketball* now encompasses the United States. Perhaps typical of basketball's significant advancement are these telling statistics: In November, 1946, a crowd of 17,205 fans watched the New York Knickerbockers play their first basketball game in Madison Square Garden. Some 21 years later, 1967, 430,448 fans watched the Knicks play in the Garden. In those 21 years the Knickerbockers have been losers (0 for 21), but they have continued to bring the fans because "New York is a pro town and a basketball town." When the new Garden on top of Penn Station was completed it held 19,500 seats and, as one writer declared, "win or lose, the Knicks will be even more of a bonanza" (23:28). After years of frustration, the loyal Knickerbocker fans were properly rewarded as the 1970 Knick team won the N.B.A. championship. A crowd of 52,693, the largest ever to see a basketball game in the United States, saw Houston defeat UCLA in the Astrodome, January 1968, and 150 television stations in 49 states provided viewing for the largest television audience in the history of basketball (34:16-19).

In *baseball*, despite the fact that the Houston Astros, for example, in 1965 established that a winning club is not necessary to attract fans (they passed the one-million mark for attendance that season), and despite the fact that a large share of the population attends games (105:10), the game of professional baseball, 100 years old in 1969, was considered to be in trouble by some writers because attendance was sagging. Red Barber, one of the nation's best known sports announcers and syndicated sports columnists, as well as numerous other opinion-making fans, sounded alarms and offered many proposals for change. For what purpose were changes suggested? None other than to make baseball relevant to the spectator, and to help "regain excitement and motion, action and pace," and to bring the fans back to the ball park (3:155). The various "media and moguls," according to Jim Brosnan, responded with the following: "Move in the fences. Move back the mound. Lower the mound. Juice up the ball. Shrink the strike zone. Outlaw the slider. Bring back the swingers of '29" (8:84). Some long-range changes anticipated included subsidizing college and high school teams.

Although William Johnson pointed out that the advent of television destroyed baseball's minor leagues (minor league clubs dropped in number from 488 in 1949 to 155 in 1969), he emphasized the vast influence that television has had in making baseball a new sport passion of the country (35b:102). Through the magic wonders of television, for example, in 1969 10 million Americans viewed NBC's baseball Game of the Week, the Los Angeles Dodgers versus the St. Louis Cardinals— more people than watched the Cardinals play from 1926 to 1946.

Another report pointed out that a compelling reason for consideration of a change in playing time of the World Series games was possible audience attraction. An estimated 55 million people watched the 1967 All-Star Game, which ended at 11 p.m. Eastern Daylight Time, as compared to 12 million viewers for the 1966 game played in the afternoon (109:9). But, whether or not the promoters think baseball can be saved, and whether or not it has "changed its position in the pecking order of sport," apparently it still remains somewhat of a compelling national pastime. In fact, Ellis E. (Woody) Erdman, play-by-play voice of the Giants, indicated that he would like to plug in on the voltage:

> If 60,000 people will shiver and freeze and get soaked . . . isn't there some
> way we could harness all that electricity? (90:85)

Although fans spend countless hours in front of their television sets watching baseball and football games, the boom in other sports is now bigger than bingo. Attendance at official Professional *Golfers'* Association tournaments in 1967 was 1,768,205—nearly double the gate of 10 years earlier (85:17).

Some 12,000 fans paid the price of admission to watch the $100,000

Firestone Tournament of Champions in *bowling* in 1966 and an estimated 8,000 fans were turned away because the building could not accommodate more (96:80). Crowds averaging 14,000 a game—a figure virtually undreamed of when the National *Hockey* League expanded into six new cities in 1967—jammed into the St. Louis arena (63:58).

Typifying the *surfing* craze are such facts as: Station WKFD in Narragansett, Rhode Island called itself "the summertime surfing station"; a surfing meet at Nantunuch Beach, New England drew 20,000 spectators while another 15,000 came on a cold, drizzling June to watch the second annual New England championships (70:30-37).

In the first issue of *Sports Illustrated* (August 16, 1954), the popularity of various sports according to number of participants and spectators was rated. *Softball* was rated as the champion of spectator sports. In the years 1955-1960 during which the International Softball Congress World Tournament was held in Rock Island, Illinois, it drew 187,760 spectators (95:71). By 1960, some said the game had died, and that fast-pitch softball was hardly more than a memory (97:78). Another reader in *Sports Illustrated* answered the above by pointing out that softball hardly seems like a dying sport. If so, how does one explain the 1964-1965 home-attendance figure of 211,000 of the Pekin Lettes, an Illinois women's team which is not even a national champion (98:79)? Softball has been accepted on a demonstration basis for the Pan American Games, the Asian Games, the Central American Games and there is talk of introducing softball competition in the Olympics in 1972.

The game of *soccer* has been a passionate sporting pastime of such disparate countries around the world as Spain, Mexico, Great Britain, Latvia, Brazil, Germany, and South Africa. In 1960, the World Series of English soccer—the Football Association Cup final—held at London's Wembley Stadium attracted 100,000 spectators. In 1967 the World Series of soccer was televised via satellite and attracted an audience of 10 million in the United States, and 400 million around the world. In January, 1967, 29,205 spectators watched the Brazil-Argentina game in Los Angeles; in September, 1966, 41,598 spectators viewed the Santos-Milan game at Yankee Stadium; in the summer of 1967 a capacity crowd of 28,000 fans saw the Benfica of Lisbon versus Santos of Brazil game at Downing Stadium in New York City. Starting in April, 1967, the American sports audience was treated with its first look at soccer seriously. Although it remains to be seen whether, in the words of W. B. Cutler, Board Chairman of the NPSL's Chicago Spurs, "the public's going to have to be educated to it," the entrepreneurs speculated that the game would burgeon in the United States (37:22-28). One observer who felt that "within its limitations soccer is far more demanding and precise a drama than football or basketball" stated that soccer may have killed itself in America because of mismanagement and because the players were mostly foreign. Nonetheless, he concluded optimistically that "in a way, soccer is like flag waving—it's not dead, but it is sleeping" (81:21).

Pro *tennis*, too, has been seeking a new face in order to gain the glamour and television exposure that other sports have. Throughout the Forest Hills Tournament the spectators were sparse, "totaling 21,000 by charitable count," compared with the 36,000 who in March, 1966, paid to see the same group play at Madison Square Garden under the new promotion tactics (22:58-62).

Among the vast multitude of sport spectators also are those from the upper echelon. One survey taken by *Esquire* submitted six questions to all members of the 1968 Congress (27:149-154). One question was as follows: "Would you prefer an evening at the theatre, the ballet, the opera, or a sports event?" The results showed that 34 percent of those responding answered "sports event" or specified a particular event such as baseball. In total, 54 percent indicated a preference for sports events alone, or in addition to the other options offered.

The magnitude of the miracle of televised sport and the revolutionary impact of television upon the geography, economics, schedules, esthetics, and the very ethos of sport are superbly dissected by William Johnson in a series of five articles, "Television and Sport," appearing in *Sports Illustrated* (December 22, 1969 to January 26, 1970). One can hardly deny from this reading that televised sport has indeed changed the country's way of life. Whether or not the commercial basis for televised sport will dwindle and sap the prosperity of sport, a possibility which Johnson discerns, it may be incidental to the fact that there are millions—*millions* of "super spectators" waiting out there for the televised transmission to begin.

And, spectatorship is not limited to America. On an international scale, the "World of Sports" made its first appearance on television (by the American Broadcasting Company) in May, 1961. This production of the Penn and Drake Relays, which was live and on tape from both Philadelphia and Des Moines, marked the beginning of 19 telecasts which were shown over 140 stations. Designed to put international flavor into Saturday's routine sports television viewing, these telecasts showed important sports events from foreign countries including soccer, and track and field, baseball, professional tennis, open golf, and other assorted events originating in the United States. In addition, commentators considered experts in their field provided the narrative (104:14).

In 1969, more than 200 spectator boats crowded the San Francisco Bay to watch the start of the first solo boat race across the Pacific Ocean, a 5,600-mile marathon with five contestants from different countries (64:86).

Although *automobile racing* is an integral part of the automobile industry's development program (i.e., improving the safety and performance of passenger cars), participation in sports, stock and drag car racing involves a multitude of spectators and sports fans. Europe's foremost automobile race, the 24-hour Le Mans Race was attended by 200,000 spectators in 1966 (its thirty-fourth running).

In Montreal, Canada's fabulous Expo '67 offered plenty to the sport fan. A dramatic transcontinental canoe race was held. A fleet of 15 yachts raced across the Atlantic for Montreal. Canadian and United States Indian teams presented the first North American Indian Lacrosse Tournament (the first of its kind in the continent's oldest sport). An international track and field meet pitted performers from the Americas against those from Europe. Elsewhere in Canada in this centennial year more than 70 international championships took place, including a $200,000 Canadian Open at Montreal's Municipal Golf Club.

The *greatest show on earth*, the Olympic Games, since they were revived in 1896, testify to the impressive spectator appeal of athletic festivals. Stadio Olympico, begun by Mussolini for the 1944 Olympics, which were cancelled because of the war, was rebuilt for the seventeenth Olympiad held in Rome, 1960, to seat 100,000 people. Asia's first Olympics, the 1964 eighteenth Olympiad, changed the face of Tokyo, Japan. Tokyo's 10½ million population mushroomed by an estimated 30,000 foreigners (15). In 1969, some 80,000 persons jammed into the University of Mexico's transformed Olympic Stadium to witness the opening ceremonies of the nineteenth Olympiad of the modern era.

WHY THIS MARVELOUS MANIA?

The best key to the "why" of spectator sport may simply be the right which Jefferson proclaimed in the Declaration of Independence, the right to pursue happiness. Or, the collective enterprise behind the mass appeal of sport may be the more tangible catalysts—more leisure time, greater earning power of more people, the impact of television. Such explanations, however, soon dissolve into metaphysics at the touch of the philosopher, sociologist, psychologist, and journalist. Some of the explanations of the motivation behind the phenomena of sport offered by widely divergent thinkers and observers are chronicled throughout this book. In the following section some literature is presented that gives a perspective of spectator addiction as well as the group meanings to be found in spectator sport. Some of these will be found to parallel those suggested by the performer in the previous section.

Identification—Wish Fulfillment

George Plimpton, ever since his involvement as a quarterback with the Detroit Lions from which developed his book *The Paper Lion*, has studied the superfans. In an article entitled "The Celestial Hell of the Superfan" he stated:

> The superfan has a primary need for identification with the football team: sitting on the bench, hanging around the locker room, calling the football stars by their first names—these are all wish-fulfillments (74:109).

Plimpton concluded with his own superfan addiction:

> While there might be a brief respite from time to time . . . the disease had me thoroughly in its throes . . . absolutely hooked (74:120).

John Underwood similarly suggested that people identify with a football team, and he is of the persuasion that college football is something the pros cannot duplicate. The college game, he proffered, is better esthetically, technically, imaginatively, and it is more entertaining. One big difference, he indicated, between college and pro football, and the reason the pro fan is not seeing football is that pro football is exactly what it is presented to be:

> a highly entertaining creature of television . . . perpetuated by the piquancy of the forward pass and the adman of Madison Avenue . . . the thrill factory of the quick touchdown (120:96).

The college game on the other hand is:

> more diversified or less one-sided . . . not stereotyped . . . engenders more spirit and emotion . . . an intimacy . . . operates on a more exalted plane, because of its traditions (120:96).

Other writers have also attested to the importance of identification with a team, yet they may not agree with Underwood, who sensed a lack of tradition or ancient rivalries in the pro game. One writer, as cited by Reuel Denney, suggested that one of the reasons for bad sportsmanship was that people seemed more interested in identifying with a winner than in the spectacle of the game (24:130). The late Bob Murphy of *The Minneapolis Star* once asked about the Minnesota Twins' fans: "Have you ever noticed how they refer to the Twins as 'we' when they win and 'they' when they lose." In 1965, when the Twins won the American League pennant, they were certainly, as William Leggett put it, "the first-place darlings of the upper-Midwest" and that was a real "we" year in Minnesota (43:16).

Perhaps the identity motive was best summed up in this statement by David H. McConnell, New York millionaire, who, when asked why he "bankrolled" a National Football League franchise in New Orleans, responded by saying that "I could go out and buy 200,000 acres of timberland, but then what would I do? Cheer for the trees?" (115:9).

Of Play and Work—A Reversal of Relationship

In *The Madness of Sport,* psychiatrist Arnold R. Beisser made the observation that the remarkable state of American dedication to sport has come about in part as the result of an inability to find meaning in the traditional value and purpose of work. Entertainment alone, he suggested, does not account for the fans' loyalty and commitment and their willingness to pay handsomely, to endure inclement weather and personal sacrifice for their sport events. Clearly one must look more deeply. One explanation may be in the complete reversal of the relationship of work and play. According to him, one of the paradoxes of sport is that the anachronistic definitions of work as serious and important and play as not no longer hold. Much contemporary behavior makes it appear that the opposite is the case because as the preoccupation with sport grows, the preoccupation with work diminishes. Some sports which began as play no longer have a playful and light-hearted characteristic, but, instead have assumed all the qualities of hard work.

> As traditional work becomes less familiar and serious, sports assume the characteristics formerly associated with work. Player and worker become paradoxical terms (4:14).

Frank Trippett, on the other hand, suggesting that "Americans are on a fun-jag of almost incalculable dimensions," asserted that "most scholarly studies of the subject fall short precisely because they focus exclusively on *leisure*: man-at-play differentiated from man-at-work." Agreeing with other observers that "most of the time the fun quest has worn us out as though it were an ordeal," Trippett declined the faddish moral diagnoses which imply the American to be in some way incapable of fun. To explore only man-at-leisure, therefore, is to conceal the force at work in man's fun quest—the force of the play instinct (118:24-34).

It's A Young Feeling

In a way, Trippett may have been saying that the motivation behind the fun of sport, as with any other quest for fun, is a young feeling. Fun "comes at birth. We must look at the infant and recognize ourselves." And, further, "disequilibrium is the very stuff of infantile joy" (118:33).

Gary Valk, present publisher of *Sports Illustrated,* in a salute to sportswriter Ezra Bowen, sounded the universal note that you may be a feeble old man of 20 or a kid of 50, but "watching and discussing and reading about sport is in part a means of keeping fresh the remembrance of great things past" (94:4). And it does not matter, according to Valk, what the precise definition of "great" is or how far past the past is.

As a result of involvement with Little League baseball, parents have been known to pummel one another, lifelong friendships have been shattered, and even Carl Stotz, who founded Little League baseball, will no longer have anything to do with the "Frankenstein" it has become. Yet, adults can no more keep their long noses out of Lilliputian baseball than they can keep from playing with their children's toys. As Lloyd Shearer noted:

> Little League has become a near-basic ingredient of American life . . . bringing youngsters and families closer together (86:6-7).

Vladimir Nabokov stated in his novel *Ada* that "independent and original minds must cling to things or pull things apart in order to ward off madness or death." Perhaps one of the things human beings cling to most is youth and sport may provide the wherewithal to do so.

The Need To Let Go

As noted by Nabokov a person appears to need to pull things apart. Denney in 1957 found in the "inveterate and compulsive" American spectator an anxiety strangely connected with his role as a spectator as evidence of the fact that "the mass media have generally been occupied with an extensive attempt to teach people how to behave" (24: 137). Whether or not the spectator of today is anxious about his sportsmanlike behavior, apparently he is anxious to let off steam. According to Murray Korngold, a Beverly Hills psychiatrist who declared that people were suffering from what he called "The Bah, Humbug! Syndrome," people need a new kind of holiday which, he declared "should be completely cathartic, an experience of pure pleasure . . . where you can get your true emotions out in the open and forget taboos" (1:53).

Psychiatrists may have no sure cure for the "blahs" or for the hollow, commercial ring implicit in such traditional celebrations as Christmas; but, apparently spectator sport offers an acceptable means of purging some aggressions, impulsions, frustrations, and rowdiness. One example of fans being acceptably boisterous comes by way of the *London Daily Mail,* which rated the soccer spectators for sportsmanship and good behavior. In 1966, when the Liverpool spectators led the field with a rating of 79.52 points out of a possible 100, team secretary Peter Robinson was reported as saying:

> We are fond of our crowd. They are noisy, vociferous, well-behaved and very sporting (107:19).

Ernest Dichter, who declared that spectator participation, with its "rhythmic interplay between tension and relaxation," provides a controlled form of "letting go," pointed out that baseball, "a sublimated and refined form of war . . . could theoretically come to satisfy our warring instincts without killing anybody . . . not even the umpire" (25:160).

Josh Greenfield claimed that Americans loved pro football because it is vicious—because of its "nitty-gritty violence." In the "protective removes" of our living rooms, behind a James Bond cover, we can observe with delight an "otherwise naked and repellent violence."

> Rendered bland by . . . television . . . our nerve endings are untouched by the violence. Psychically numbed, we watch the entertainment provided by huge padded surrogates brutally assaulting one another . . . we can thus have our cherry pie and eat it too (29b:48).

The magazine *Commentary* presented some thoughts by William Phillips, cofounder and chairman of the editorial board of *Partisan Review*. Among his comments was this statement:

> All sports serve as some kind of release, but the rhythm of football is geared particularly to the violence and peculiar combination of order and disorder of modern life. Baseball is too slow, too dependable, too much like a regional drawl. Basketball is too nervous and too tight; hockey too frenzied; boxing too chaotic, too folksy. Only football provides a genuine catharsis (73:66).

The Authentic Life—Order, Beauty, Excellence

The violence of football may be an example of a form of order-disorder, as noted by Phillips, which people can accept more readily than violence in other aspects of living. Ernest Dichter also pointed out that games such as baseball satisfy a basic need of people to bring order into chaos:

> it introduces a neat, clear framework where things add up in logical and understandable fashion (25:158-160).

In still another dimension, Norman Cousins remarked that "the sense of beauty, the capacity to be awakened and enlarged by a tender experience, the possibilities for compassionate thought—all these are being crowded and pressured by the language of force" (18:24). Applying this concept to sport one might conclude that, in one sense, the spectator pits sport against the language of force and other contemporary experiences such as nudity, pot, street riots, disorders, violence, and the trappings of life in general.

Some persons see the arena of sport as being one of the remaining places where the beauty of simple excellence is celebrated. Woody Erdman sees big time sports as a place where excellence is mandatory. According to David Snell, a senior editor of *Life*, Erdman thinks as follows:

America hungers for the real thing, and the reason the very heavens reach out to men like Joe Namath and Jim Brown has little to do with their anti-heroic private lives; it is because they brought authentic excellence to the playing field (90:85).

For Intellectuals

Part of excellence historically has been the intellectual life. This aspect of sport motivations has been illustrated previously in Chapter 1 with regard to the participant's desire to be best. One further comment is added here in reference to the spectator. This comment once again comes from Phillip's article in *Commentary* (a magazine for intellectuals which, *Sports Illustrated* suggested, has paid but little attention to sport over the years). As William Phillips opined:

> Football is not only the most popular sport, it is the most intellectual one. It is, in fact, the intellectuals' secret vice. Not politics, not sex, not pornography, but football, and not college football but the real thing, pro ball, is the opium of the intellectuals (73:65-66).

Collectors' Item

Part of the intellectuals' thirst may be slaked in gathering the facts and figures of the sport world. According to Gerald Holland, there is a strange breed of sport fanatics "whose fun is playing old records." They dote on statistics and fine examples of technique and demonstrate their prowess at bull sessions. The difference between "fan" and "nut" is that

> a fan can take a track and field meet and leave it, but a nut is never done with it. He must study it and analyze it and fit it into his encyclopedic knowledge of other meets (32:46).

Holland cited such examples of "track nuts" as Art Hoffman of Los Angeles who prides himself on having seen 64 under four minute miles run on the North American continent, and Jim Dunaway, a contributing editor of *Track and Field News*, who helped defray his expenses at the Olympics in Melbourne by setting up a one-man news bureau and covering athletes who were not otherwise closely observed by representatives of their home town papers (32:46-47).

Sociability

A thousand explanations of the why of spectator motivations might all add up to a quantitative one—sport represents a social group that is easily identified and commonly understood. Each person may need to feel that his interests are validated by a relationship to those generally shared by some larger group of individuals. To describe the social inducements and power of sport is the task of the next few chapters.

REFERENCES

1. *Arizona Republic (The)*, "The Bah, Humbug! Syndrome," December 26, 1965, p. 53.
2. Bannister, Roger. *The Four Minute Mile*. New York: Dodd, Mead and Company, 1955.
3. Barber, Red. "Can Baseball Be Saved?" *Reader's Digest*, April, 1969, pp. 155-160.
4. Beisser, Arnold R. *The Madness in Sports*. New York: Appleton-Century-Crofts, 1967.
5. Bloch, Raymond. "The Origins of the Olympic Games," *Scientific American*, August, 1968, pp. 79-85.
6. Boyle, Robert H. *Sport—Mirror of American Life*. Boston: Little, Brown and Company, 1963.
7. Brosnan, Jim. "Little Leaguers Have Big Problems—Their Parents," *The Atlantic*, March 1963, pp. 117-120.
8. Brosnan, Jim. "Where Have All the Hitters Gone?" *Look*, May 13, 1969, pp. 84-93.
9. Brown, Gwilym S. "Ron Runs the World Ragged," *Sports Illustrated*, July 26, 1965, pp. 24-25.
10. Burnshaw, Stanley. "The Body Makes the Minde," *The American Scholar*, Winter, 1968-1969, pp. 25-39.
11. Caillois, Roger. *Man, Play and Games*. Translated by Meyer Barash, New York: Free Press of Glencoe, Inc., 1961.
12. Cassirer, Ernst. "Art," *An Essay On Man*. New Haven: Yale University Press, 1944.
13. Chadwick, Florence. "Triumph For A Cold Cruel Sea," *Sports Illustrated*, November 7, 1960, pp. 49-52.
14. Cobb, Ty, and Stump, A. *My Life In Baseball, The True Record*. New York: Doubleday and Company, 1961. Also see "Last Inning of an Angry Man," *Sports Illustrated*, August 21, 1961, pp. 50-56.
15. Connery, Donald S. "Tokyo Changes Face For Asia's First Olympics," *Sports Illustrated*, May 8, 1961, pp. 38-41.
16. Conrad, Barnaby. "Homage to a Peerless Matador," *Sports Illustrated*, August 1, 1966, pp. 44-52.
17. Cooke, Alistair. "Goodby, Mr. President—Hi There, Arnie," *Golf* (Incorporating *Golfing Magazine*), March 1968, pp. 32-34.
18. Cousins, Norman. "Toward a New Language," *Saturday Review*, May 24, 1969, p. 24.
19. Crozier, Bob. "The Shears of Fate, The Loom of Life," *Sports Illustrated*, May 29, 1967, pp. 79-84.
19b. Cruickshank, John. *Albert Camus and the Literature of Revolt*. New York: A Galaxy Book, 1960.
20. Daley, Robert. "When You're No. 2 You Drive Harder," *Sports Illustrated*, August 15, 1966, pp. 24-30.
21. Daniels, A. S. "The Study of Sport As An Element of the Culture," pp. 13-22, in Loy, John W., Jr., and Kenyon, Gerald S. (editors). *Sport, Culture and Society*. Toronto: The Macmillan Company, 1969.
22. Deford, Frank. "A Man To Lead the Pros Out of Darkness," *Sports Illustrated*, June 20, 1966, pp. 58-62.
23. Deford, Frank. "New York Gets A Top Team at Last," *Sports Illustrated*, October 23, 1967, pp. 28-38.

24. Denney, Reuel. *The Astonished Muse.* Chapter 6, pp. 121-137. Chicago: University of Chicago Press, 1957.
25. Dichter, Ernest. "Should You Be A Fan?" A Uniroyal Advertisement, *Reader's Digest,* May, 1968, pp. 158-160.
26. Doherty, J. Kenneth. "Why Men Run," *Quest,* Monograph II, Spring 1964, pp. 61-66.
27. *Esquire,* "Salvaging the 20th Century," (35th Anniversary Issue), October 1968, pp. 149-154.
28. Fairs, John R. "The Influence of Plato and Platonism on the Development of Physical Education in Western Culture," *Quest,* Monograph XI: Our Heritage, December 1968, pp. 14-23.
29. Gilbert, Bil. "Drugs In Sport: Part III, High Time To Make Some Rules," *Sports Illustrated,* July 7, 1969, pp. 30-35.
29b. Greenfield, Josh. "Why Do We Love Pro Football? It's Vicious, That's Why," *TV Guide,* October 18-24, 1969, pp. 45-48.
30. Hamilton, Andrew. "How to Grow Young," *Parade,* April 27, 1969, pp. 12-27.
30b. Harris, Dorothy V. "On the Brink of Catastrophe," *Quest,* Monograph XIII, January, 1970, pp. 33-40.
31. Higginson, Thomas Wentworth. "Saints and Their Bodies," *Atlantic Monthly,* I, March, 1958.
32. Holland, Gerald. "Some Fanatics Whose Fun Is Playing Old Records," *Sports Illustrated,* August 2, 1965, pp. 46-47.
33. Huizinga, Johan. *Homo Ludens: A Study of The Play-Element In Culture.* Boston: The Beacon Press, 1950.
34. Jares, Joe. "A Dandy In The Dome," *Sports Illustrated,* January 29, 1968, pp. 16-19.
35. Johnson, William. "Arararararargh!" *Sports Illustrated,* March 3, 1969, pp. 28-30 ff.
35b. Johnson, William. "TV Made It All A New Game," *Sports Illustrated,* December 22, 1969, pp. 86-101.
36. Jokl, Ernst. "The Acquisition of Skill," *Quest,* Monograph VI, Symposium on Motor Learning, May, 1966, pp. 11-26.
37. Kane, Martin. "The True Football Gets Its Big Chance," *Sports Illustrated,* March 27, 1967, pp. 22-28.
38. Kennedy, John F. "The Importance of Participation," in Herbert Warren Wind (editor), *The Realm of Sport.* New York: Simon and Schuster, 1966, pp. 703-705.
38b. Kenyon, Gerald S. (editor). *Aspects of Contemporary Sport Sociology,* Proceedings of C. I. C. Symposium on the Sociology of Sport, University of Wisconsin, November 18-20, 1968. Chicago: The Athletic Institute, 1969.
39. Killy, Jean-Claude. "Skiing Is Not A Beauty Contest," *Sports Illustrated,* November 18, 1968, pp. 50-57.
39b. Klausner, Samuel Z. (editor). *Why Man Takes Chances.* Garden City, New Jersey: Anchor Books, Doubleday and Company, Inc., 1968.
40. Kram, Mark. "They're Still Waiting for Jerry," *Sports Illustrated,* November 6, 1967, pp. 19-23.
41. Kramer, Jerry. *Instant Replay.* Dick Schaap (editor), New York: The New American Library, 1968.
42. Lawrence, Andrea Mead. "Let's Not Spoil Their Sport," *Sports Illustrated,* February 3, 1964, pp. 18-21.
43. Leggett, William. "Everybody Pick Up A Drum," *Sports Illustrated,* August 23, 1965, pp. 16, 71.
44. *Life,* "Leisure Could Mean a Better Civilization," Editorial, December 28, 1959, p. 63.
45. *Look,* "The Splendid Splinter Swings Again," April 29, 1969, pp. 88-92.
46. Lorenz, Konrad. *On Aggression.* Translated by Marjorie Kerr Wilson. New York: Harcourt, Brace & World, Inc., 1966.

47. Lovesey, John. "Straight Man In a Twisty Race," *Sports Illustrated*, June 1 1964, pp. 40-42, 45.
48. Lucas, John A. "A Prelude to the Rise of Sport: Ante-bellum America, 1850-1860," *Quest*, Monograph XI: Our Heritage, December, 1968, pp. 50-57.
49. Luce, Henry. *Sports Illustrated*, Editorial, March 13, 1967, p. 4.
50. Lüschen, Günther. "The Interdependence of Sport and Culture," Paper presented at the Annual AAHPER Meeting, 1967.
51. MacArthur, Douglas. "Athletic America," Excerpts from a *Report to President Coolidge on American Participation in the Ninth Olympic Games*, Amsterdam August 22, 1928.
52. Maheu, Rene. "Sport and Culture," *International Journal of Adult and Youth Education*, (UNESCO), XIV, 1962, pp. 175-176.
53. Maule, Tex. "The Battle to Win the Thinking Man's Race," *Sports Illustrated*, May 14, 1962, pp. 74-75.
54. Maule, Tex. "By Any Other Name," *Sports Illustrated*, September 2, 1968, pp. 10-13.
55. McAuley, Regis. "Child Home Fetes Mrs. Manning," *The Tucson Citizen*, Tucson, Arizona, March 15, 1969.
56. McDermott, John R. "Order in the Ball Park," Life, March 7, 1969, pp. 83-84.
57. McDonnell, Patrick. "The Bar and The Body," *Modern Gymnast*, IX, March 1967.
58. Mechem, Rose Mary. "The Game on the Eastern Shore," *Sports Illustrated*, March 27, 1967, pp. 30-35.
58b. Messer, Alfred A. "Creative Thinking Made Easy," *Fitness for Living*, 33 E Minor Street, Emmaus, Pennsylvania.
59. Metheny, Eleanor. *Connotations of Movement In Sport and Dance*. Dubuque, Iowa: W. C. Brown Company, 1965.
59b. Miller, Donna Mae. *The Relationship Between Some Visual-Perceptual Factors and the Degree of Success Realized By Sports Performers*. Unpublished Doctoral Dissertation, University of Southern California, June, 1960.
60. Murray, James. *The Best of Jim Murray*. New York: Doubleday and Company, Inc., 1965.
61. Murray, James. "Athletes' Will To Win Tabbed 'Kill To Win,'" *The Arizona Republic (Los Angeles Times Service)*, March 6, 1963, p. 32.
62. Myslenski, Skip. "The Pressure Cooker," *Sports Illustrated*, July 7, 1969, pp. 18-21.
62b. Myslenski, Skip. "A PTA Meeting Is Tougher," *Sports Illustrated*, December 8, 1969, pp. 69-70.
62c. *Newsletter*, President's Council on Physical Fitness and Sports, Washington, D.C., March, 1970, p. 2.
63. *Newsweek*, "No Blues for St. Louis," December 23, 1968, p. 58, 61.
64. *Newsweek* "The Solo Breed," March 31, 1969, p. 86.
65. *Newsweek*, "The Metaphysical Game," June 2, 1969, pp. 66-67.
66. *Newsweek*, "The Joys of Life Afloat," August 4, 1969, pp. 58-63.
67. *Newsweek*, "Will Ali Fight Again?" April 7, 1969, pp. 52, 54.
68. Ogilvie, Bruce C. "The Personality of the Male Athlete," *The Academy Papers*, (published by The American Academy of Physical Education), March, 1968, pp. 45-52.
69. Ottum, Bob. "Norway Will Run And Jump Away With The Nordic Events," *Sports Illustrated*, February 5, 1968, pp. 43-47.
70. Ottum, Bob. "Riding the Wave of the East Coast's Surfing Boom," *Sports Illustrated*, July 18, 1966, pp. 30-37.
71. Palmer, Arnold. "My Game and Yours," *Sports Illustrated*, July 15, 1963, pp. 28-42.
72. Palmer, Arnold. "Joys of Trouble," *Sports Illustrated*, July 26, 1965, pp. 34-38.
72b. Pavlich, Mary. "The Power of Sport," *Journal of the Arizona Association for Health, Physical Education, and Recreation*, Vol. 10, No. 1, Fall, 1966, pp. 9-10.

73. Phillips, William. "A Season In The Stands," *Commentary*, July 1969, pp. 65-69.
74. Plimpton, George. "The Celestial Hell of the Superfan," *Sports Illustrated*, September 13, 1965, pp. 104-120.
75. Potter, Stephen. *Golfmanship*. New York: McGraw-Hill Book Company, 1968.
76. Pullias, Earl V. "The Role of Sport in Higher Education," D.G.W.S. National Conference on Sports Programs for College Women, Estes Park, Colorado, June, 1969.
77. Rathet, Mike. "Protective Sports Bosses Fear Soiling by Gambling Dirt," *The Denver Post*, (New York—AP), June 22, 1969, pp. 65-66.
78. Richards, Bob. *The Heart of A Champion*. Westwood, New Jersey: Fleming H. Revell Company, 1959.
78b. Riesman, David, Glazer, Nathan, and Denney, Reuel. *The Lonely Crowd*. New Haven: Yale University Press, 1961.
79. Ress, Paul, and Brown, Gwilym S. "A Tale of Two Idols," *Sports Illustrated*, March 18, 1968, pp. 22-25.
80. Rogin, Gilbert. "An Odd Sport. . . And An Unusual Champion," *Sports Illustrated*, October 18, 1965, pp. 94-104.
81. Rudman, Steve. "Soccer's Sleeping, Not Dead," *The Salt Lake Tribune*, August 5, 1969, p. 21.
82. Russell, William F. "I'm Not Involved Anymore," *Sports Illustrated*, August 4, 1969, pp. 18-19.
83. Rutkowski, Edward. "What is Football?" *Journal of Health, Physical Education, and Recreation*, September, 1967, pp. 30-31.
84. Ryan, Francis J. "An Investigation of Personality Differences Associated With Competitive Ability," and "Further Observations on Competitive Ability in Athletics," *Psychosocial Problems of College Men*. Bryant M. Wedge (editor), New Haven: Yale University Press, 1958, pp. 113-139.
84b. Schafer, Walter E. "Some Social Sources and Consequences of Interscholastic Athletics: The Case of Participation and Delinquency," *Aspects of Contemporary Sport Sociology*, Gerald S. Kenyon (editor), Proceedings of C.I.C. Symposium on the Sociology of Sport, University of Wisconsin, 1968, pp. 29-44.
85. Seitz, Nick. "Golf: Big Business, Big Pleasure," *The Book of Golf* (produced for PGA with the cooperation of *Golf Digest*), 1968, pp. 17-19.
85b. Sharnik, Morton. "Downfall of A Hero," *Sports Illustrated*, February 23, 1970, pp. 16-21.
86. Shearer, Lloyd. "Little League Baseball," *Parade*, May 28, 1961, pp. 6-7.
87. Shrake, Edwin. "A Lonely Tribe of Long-Distance Runners," *Sports Illustrated*, January 9, 1967, pp. 56-67.
88. Slusher, Howard S. *Man, Sport and Existence*. Philadelphia: Lea & Febiger, 1967.
89. Smith, Robert Paul. *"Where Did You Go?" "Out." "What Did You Do?" "Nothing."* New York: Pocket Books, Inc., Cardinal Edition, 1957.
90. Snell, David. "Dateline America—All-Pro Miniconglomerate," *Life*, May 23, 1969, pp. 85-86.
91. *Sports Illustrated*, Editorial, June 13, 1960, p. 17.
92. *Sports Illustrated*, Letter From the Publisher, July 10, 1967, p. 4.
93. *Sports Illustrated*, Letter From the Publisher, January 22, 1968, p. 6.
94. *Sports Illustrated*, Letter From the Publisher, March 4, 1968, p. 4.
95. *Sports Illustrated*, "19th Hole," August 8, 1960, p. 71.
96. *Sports Illustrated*, "19th Hole," June 20, 1966, p. 80.
97. *Sports Illustrated*, "19th Hole," July 4, 1966, p. 78.
98. *Sports Illustrated*, "19th Hole," July 18, 1966, p. 79.
99. *Sports Illustrated*, "19th Hole," February 12, 1968, p. 78.
100. *Sports Illustrated*. "On The High Seas—A Wet Wondrous Way To Joy," July 4, 1966, pp. 32-34.
101. *Sports Illustrated*, "People," July 18, 1966, p. 52.

102. *Sports Illustrated,* "Requiem For A Friend," October 20, 1958, p. 27.
103. *Sports Illustrated,* "Scorecard," November 7, 1960, p. 6.
104. *Sports Illustrated,* "Scorecard," May 8, 1961, p. 14.
105. *Sports Illustrated,* "Scorecard," June 12, 1965, p. 10.
106. *Sports Illustrated,* "Scorecard," June 13, 1966, p. 19.
107. *Sports Illustrated,* "Scorecard," June 13, 1966, p. 19.
108. *Sports Illustrated,* "Scorecard," August 8, 1966, p. 9.
109. *Sports Illustrated,* "Scorecard," August 21, 1967, p. 9.
110. *Sports Illustrated,* "Scorecard," December 11, 1967, p. 14.
111. *Sports Illustrated,* "Scorecard," December 25, 1967, p. 8.
112. *Sports Illustrated,* "Scorecard," March 18, 1968, p. 14.
113. *Sports Illustrated,* "Scorecard," May 20, 1968, pp. 13-14.
113b. *Sports Illustrated,* "Scorecard," March 2, 1970, p. 9.
114. *Sports Illustrated,* "Sportman of the Year, Jim Ryun," December 19, 1966. p. 47
115. *Sports Illustrated,* "They Said It," July 26, 1965, p. 9.
115b. Suits, Bernard. "What Is A Game?" *Philosophy of Science,* January, 1967, pp 48-56.
116. Tarkenton, Fran, with Jack Olsen. "Dear Norm: I Cannot Return," (Part 3 "Quarterback On The Run"), *Sports Illustrated,* July 31, 1967, pp. 36-42
116b. *The Stanford Observer,* "The Beauty and Esthetics of Gymnastics," March 1970, p. 8.
117. *Time,* "The Uncommon Man," May 23, 1969, pp. 63-64.
118. Trippett, Frank. "A Special Report On The Way You Play The Ordeal o Fun," *Look,* July 29, 1969, pp. 24-34.
119. *Tucson Daily Citizen,* "Young Has 2 Races Left," February 19, 1969, p. 29
120. Underwood, John. "The College Game Is Best," *Sports Illustrated,* September 20, 1965, pp. 94-103.
121. Walf, David. "The Best Man Loses—and It Hurts," *Life,* November 29, 1968 pp. 89-90.
122. Weiss, Paul. *Sport: A Philosophic Inquiry.* Carbondale, Illinois: Southern Illinois University Press, 1969.
123. Wright, Jay. "A Diamond-Bright Art Form," *Sports Illustrated,* June 23, 1969 pp. 32-39.
124. Yevtushenko, Yevgeny. "A Poet Against the Destroyers," *Sports Illustrated* December 19, 1966, pp. 105-128.
125. Young, Dick. "The 'Hit-and-Run' Is On!" A Uniroyal Advertisement, *Reader* *Digest,* May, 1968, pp. 180-182.

PART II

Sport is Social

*"Today, religion apart, world sport represents the most
comprehensive organization in social spheres."*

— — —Carl Diem

If sport is personal, so too must it be social in the sense that, as
Cooley stated, "Self and society go together as phases of a common
whole" (19:8).   Sport is said not only to represent microcosms of
society—divisions of labor, codes of ethics, government, ideologies, myths,
religious practices, and so forth—but also, to help determine the structure
of society. Within "the social matrix," to use Celeste Ulrich's term (101),
sport may be recognized as a locus for man's group feelings, identity,
mobility, integration, assimilation, and diffusion.

Sport as one aspect of man's social nature is the concern of the ensuing
section. As such, it is not intended as a theoretic treatise in sport
sociology. Considerable literature and some empirical studies are available to the reader concerned with the sociology of sport. Ruth Abernathy,
although she has repeatedly suggested the need for sophisticated studies
in sociology related to physical education, pointed out that "sensitivity
to the impact of social influences is not new to physical education."
Rosalind Cassidy has written extensively in the area and for years has
called attention to the imperative need for study of the impact of the
society on the planning of physical education programs (1:33).

John W. Loy and Gerald S. Kenyon, in their book *Sport, Culture, and
Society* (48), brought together a wide array of research studies from
physical education and the social sciences in presenting a part of the
body of knowledge of the sociology of sport. A basic assumption underlying their selection of articles to be reprinted was that sport can be
considered as both a dependent variable (sport can be explained in

49

terms of other social systems), and an independent variable (sport as a factor in explaining the nature of other social systems). A number of essays and research studies stemming from European interest is also provided within that text. Earlier Kenyon and Loy themselves made a plea for the study of physical activity as a sociologic and sociopsychologic phenomenon and offered a valuable discussion of techniques of scientific inquiry of sport (41:68-69).

In reviewing the theoretic efforts in sport sociology, certain of the following works must be acknowledged as fundamental. Among these one of the earlier and most notable works linking sport (in the sense of its being a form of play) to culture is that of the Dutch historian, Johan Huizinga. In his book *Homo Ludens* (31), he described how play pervades all social institutions and phenomena and theorized that it should be considered as an end itself rather than a means to some other end. Another whose work is of considerable interest to the social scientist is that of sociologist Roger Caillois, who, suggesting several reasons for games, attempted to show that the type of games a society encourages reflects its health (12). David Riesman and Reuel Denney (66), in describing how American football changed from Rugby to a different game, attempted to show the basic cultural traits (ethnic differentiation and social mobility) of the American society. P. C. McIntosh, in *Sport and Society* (54) described sport as a social institution on an international scale. Some relationships shown between sport and politics indicated how sport can be used as a powerful tool of nations.

Roberts, Sutton-Smith, and coworkers, as cited by Loy and Kenyon (48:40), hypothesizing that games model the maintenance problems of a given society, use the illustration of the United State wherein, through sport and games, youth may rehearse competitive roles without the anxiety experienced by adults striving for success. Gregory Stone proposed hypotheses concerning the relationship between sport and socioeconomic status (96) and sport as "Play and Dis-Play" (95).

The interest which is manifested in sport throughout various societies of the world has been elucidated in scholarly works too numerous to mention in detail. The reader may be most interested in early American sport. According to John Richards Betts (7), among the most useful works to be consulted are these: John A. Krout, *Annals of American Sport* (New Haven, 1929); Jennis Holliman, *American Sports, 1785-1835* (Durham, 1931); Foster R. Dulles, *America Learns to Play: A History of Popular Recreation, 1607-1940* (New York, 1940); Robert B. Weaver, *Amusements and Sports in American Life* (Chicago, 1939); and Herbert Manchester, *Four Centuries of Sport in America, 1490-1890* (New York, 1931); and, for certain aspects of antebellum sport Arthur M. Schlesinger and Dixon R. Fox (eds.), *A History of American ife,* 13 vols., (New York, 1927-1948). Another recent book of selected eadings, *Sport and American Society,* edited by George H. Sage, brings ogether a widely diverse literature on the subject (67b).

On a world-wide scale, the International Committee for the Sociology f Sport, which began in 1964, and is affiliated with the International Council of Sport and Physical Education and the International Sociological Association, has become a center of recent developments in the eld. This committee has conducted numerous workshops, conferences, eminars, and research projects devoted to selected aspects of sport.

Other recent developments in the sociology of sport include a series f symposia sponsored by the Committee on Institutional Cooperation Conference Group on Physical Education. The C.I.C. is made up of one nember each of the Big Ten universities and the University of Chicago. he results of the first of such symposia, held at the University of Visconsin, comprise the contents of the report *Aspects of Contemporary port Sociology* (40). As Günther Lüschen, General Secretary of the nternational Committee on Sport Sociology, pointed out in this report, bout 3000 publications may be classified as being related to the field of he sociology of sport although a number of problem areas of study have ot as yet received much attention (40:3).

The First International Congress of Sport Psychology, held in Rome n 1965, and the publication of its proceedings, *Psicologia Dello Sport,* vas an important landmark in the development of sport. Proceedings of he Second International Congress of Sport Psychology, held in Washington, D.C. in 1968, comprised 101 addresses and reports, representing the vork of authors from 23 countries. Numerous articles in the volume are evoted to the social aspects of sport and play (40b). The Third International Congress, scheduled for Madrid in 1972, will no doubt add continued progress in understanding the psychologic-sociologic dimensions f sport phenomena.

All this literature, in addition to those other works too numerous to ite, obviously attests to the fact that, as a social being, man produces multiplicity of activities, which in turn, express, reflect, and determine is behavior. One such activity is sport. In the ensuing section the ocial side of sport, as it is revealed in contemporary popular literature, presented. Some social theory is interwoven in the introductory comnents as well as some of the literature which confronts the reader with lan's perennial social problems. For the most part, however, this section, ke that which has preceded it, is composed of extracted bits from those vho "wear the shoe" of sport and who in some way confirm a belief nat sport touches a common nerve evoking group feelings that words lone cannot describe, and that it taps the mainstream of humanity, nowing us that people everywhere are much the same.

CHAPTER 3

Sport and Collective Enthusiasm

THE FAN AND HIS FLAME

Mere contact with sporting events has a contagious fascination even among the most improbable participants and spectators. A richly diverse group of spectators—doctors, lawyers, merchants, and women—become an ardently devoted gathering with nothing whatever in common except sport. At the same time, as pointed out by Huizinga, "a play-community generally tends to become permanent even after the game is over." It's a feeling of being "apart together" (31:12). Or, as Cozens and Stumpf expressed it: "Common interests, common loyalties, common enthusiasms, those are the great integrating factors in any culture . . . sports have provided this common denominator in as great a degree as any other factor" (20:56).

Arnold Beisser, from insights gained in case studies of athletes who had become psychiatric patients, offered an explanation of the behavior of the masses of Americans who participate directly or vicariously in sport. He concluded that those people who watch in the grandstand or play in the field "are performing rituals which in every respect constitute an integral part of American life and are in no way deviant." Sport in general may represent "the remaining stronghold of the archaic family structure . . . a locus for the expression of the competition, physical strength, and social rituals of a bygone era" (6:148-150).

Similarly, Howard Slusher made the existential observation that sport, like religion, "offers its 'followers' a grouping of myths, symbols, and rituals that facilitate the total experience" (73:127). In his foreword to Slusher's book, Edgar Z. Friedenberg, touching upon some implications of "the erotic functions of athletes," stated that "athletic events occur, and have always occurred, in an atmosphere of erotic tension and excitement that enriches their contribution either to sacred or secular occasions" (73:x, xi).

53

Gregory Stone's inquiry into sport and status in the mid-fifties, as reported by Boyle, showed that the spectatorship of sport is a "necessary food for conversation and provides mutual accessibility to anonymous members of the mass society" (10:95). And Ernest Dichter, noted authority on human behavior, said that "a fan belongs." Explaining what all the shouting in baseball is about, Dichter noted that "the enthusiasm itself fulfills basic human needs." He likened the twentieth century American fan, who has his own team fighting with honor to fulfill his aspiration, to the Roman Caesar, whose gladiators defended his name, or the British queen, who has her own supporting corps. By associating oneself with thousands of other people, a reassuring feeling of warmth and unity is produced. "The yelling of the crowd is like an enormous emotional steam bath" (23:158).

The theories and observations provided in Part I and in Chapter 5 may be added to the foregoing theories regarding man's social behavior. The following examples serve to illustrate any of the theories which state that sport-crowd behavior is a fundamental form of human behavior.

Baseball crowds perhaps best illustrate the contagious and collective enthusiasm of spectators. The first professional baseball league was formed in 1871, and since that time, baseball, the native American sport, has commanded the attention of Americans for the better part of six months of each year. As Jacques Barzun warned:

> Whoever wants to know the heart and minds of America had better learn baseball (5).

Perhaps at no time was Barzun's statement a more evident truth than when the astronauts had just returned from their historic walk on the moon and were greeted in their isolation trailer by President Nixon, who asked: "Did you get the results of the All-Star game?"

Still other evaluators of the American character consider carefully what pleases the American about baseball. Peter Von Zahn, German-born historian, news correspondent, and author, asserted that citizens of America seem to have "the urge to measure, calculate and compare," perhaps partly because of the early days of capitalism. Baseball's "strict formality," wrote Von Zahn, "allows the performance of each player to be measured absolutely in a plethora of statistics and percentages." Further, contrasted to those who delight in the blood that flows in bullfights or the battle of cock against cock, what delights the American is:

> the careful assessment of force against force and idea against idea. The games he loves are full of pauses of deliberation of strategic moves. All this makes baseball and football seem boring to the uninitiated European (103:115).

These ball fans, Von Zahn noted, are descendants of immigrants who broke their ties with the Old World and sought groups with whom to identify: "The colors and emblems of their clubs have the same kind of symbolic meaning as the coat of arms and banners did for their fathers" (103:115).

In light of some happenings, Von Zahn's evaluation may be accurate. Melvin Durslag reported that when CBS began televising a game called soccer, the national sport of more than 200 countries, the game "fell on its bladder here," and the losses were not light (24:30). Observers said that the reason the American public seemed disenchanted with the game of soccer when it was introduced on television is that the sport was foreign and the players were mostly foreigners. It was not a matter of prejudice, but Americans wanted Americans, just as Brazilians would want Brazilians.

Some evidence that baseball in America has aroused sectional pride and national passion in a kind of desperate determination to beat the other guy includes these examples: The dedication of the raucous Chicago Cub fans, formally known as the "Left Field Bleacher Bums," is such that "they throw back any homer an opposing player hits into the bleachers." They have a president, vice-president, treasurer, a travelling secretary, and a bullpen cheerleader—former Cub pitcher Dick Selma—to whom the "Bums are tremendous." Whether they are sport enthusiasts or just "attention getters" did not seem to matter to Selma, who declared:

> It's really something to be in a crucial situation and hear 25,000 people behind you. It gives you a strength you never knew you had (9:18).

The subtle pleasures of baseball watching seem to prevail even when the team consistently loses. Even when the Mets were the most ludicrously losing team in the chronicle of baseball (in their first seven seasons they lost 737 games), the fans were behind them and they drew huge crowds. *New York Post* columnist James Wechsler wrote:

> The Mets are a symbol. They embody the furtive hopes and desperate dreams of every underdog and lost soul in the universe . . . of every philosopher who sees man capable of rising above his seeming limitations (100b:51).

When the New York Mets won the 1969 World Series, one announcer declared that "sociologically speaking the Mets brought New York back together again."

When the Washington Senators clinched a pennant "after being safely removed to Minnesota," a "capitol-wise" columnist for the *New York Times,* in a tongue-in-cheek article, disclosed why winning has no place in the Washingtonian's thinking. Baseball at D. C. Stadium, according to Russell Baker, "is what the tea ceremony is to the Japanese, what cricket at Lord's is to the Englishman, what Wagner at Bayreuth is to the opera lover, what *Swan Lake* at the Bolshoi is to the Muscovite"

(3:40). With the attitude of a purist who savors "the ingenious methods the Senators devise to lose," the Washingtonian "knows that the Senators will lose, just as the Wagner devotee knows that Tristan and Isolde will die in the last act. What interests both are style and quality of performance" (3:40-41).

Typical of the attitude about baseball's common persuasion is a comment made by Red Barber who gave this reason for the sag in game attendance:

> No longer does a fan feel loyalty to the home team. Today the club owner is usually a corporation or a tycoon who looks at the game as more a big business than a sport, and will move the team elsewhere at the drop of a few million dollars (4:155).

If the baseball fan's spirit is sinking in America (and there is evidence to the contrary), the spirit of the Montreal fan is not, according to *Time*. Although neither baseball nor big crowds are new to Montreal, a new high in fan delirium was reached with the Canadian invasion of major league baseball. Despite the still incomplete seating increase in the park from 3,000 to 30,000, and, although right up to game time ushers were setting up 6,000 folding chairs, 29,184 fans turned out for the opening day. Reportedly, one group of delirious fans excitedly waved a sign that read, "Expos—World Series Or Bust!" (100:56).

Similarly, the Caribbean countries have a great passion for *beisbol*, which "rates ahead of politics any day." Robert H. Boyle related this story as typical of the Latin enthusiasm: One night after curfew in Santo Domingo where warring troops patrolled the streets, a caravan of cars of the negotiating team of the Organization of American States was leaving the rebel zone, when the following happened:

> Suddenly, out of the darkness, a rebel civilian, brandishing a rifle, stopped a correspondent. The reporter stepped back nervously, but the rebel was insistent. "Tell me," he demanded, "how did Marichal do today in the All-Star Game?" (11:24).

What baseball is to the United States, *soccer* seems to be to most other parts of the world. It has a fan following also distinguished for its ardent devotion. It was reported that in England only a very thick fog or deep snow causes postponement of a game. In fact, "soccer contests continued right through the Battle of Britain, and air wardens reluctantly called games when sirens wailed" (72:109).

Another article reported that in Spain, each Sunday some 600,000 spectators watch soccer games somewhere in the country and a million more watch them during the rest of the week.

> The game is a national sport as well as a national distraction and dominates conversation in a way that bullfighting never has done (2:36).

A *hockey* puck may be to some people no different than a piece of coal, but the Minnesota North Stars are said to be "blessed with a hockey-mad populace that simultaneously learned to walk and skate and believed that basketball was played by giraffes." According to this writer, although the spectator at the Met, like the fan at the Forum in Montreal or the Maple Leaf Gardens in Toronto "inspects a game intelligently," just about everyone connected with the Minnesota Amateur Hockey Association is some type of hockey fanatic:

> The 10¢ fans and the tea-and-crumpet set . . . have made Minnesota the hockey capital of the United States during the last 10 years (57:28).

Basketball is considered by some to be more of a game of group identity than any other sport. In a color essay on basketball which appeared in *Sports Illustrated* (October 23, 1967) it was stated:

> In its simplicity and its setting, all is in the open, nothing is hidden, and the fan is so close he can see and hear everything.

In some ways *football* more than any other sport in America seems to evoke local pride, patriotism, love, and "fight for the team." The legendary hold of football on Ohio State University in its golden age has been depicted in the writings of some of its graduates—James Thurber, Milton Caniff, and Joel Sayre. Among Thurber's recollections of his days at Ohio State, depicted in *My Life and Hard Times*, is the description of an economics professor's struggle to get Bolenciewcz to answer just one question so that he could be given a grade and thus be eligible to play in the Illinois game. According to one article, Caniff, who created the comic strip *Terry and the Pirates,* managed, in a famous poem, "to link football with school spirit, brotherhood, love of country and the civic pride of Columbus" (13:102). In an article entitled "Frenzied Football," Sayre, who grew up in Columbus, satirized the fierce, affectionate loyalty of local fans with such comments as "when Ohio State loses, something extra seems to happen to Columbus." Robert Cantwell reported that an Ohio State University historian pointed out that the stadium built in 1920, to which Columbus citizens contributed, "gave Columbus a proprietary interest." In this same article, he went on to describe the year Ohio lost to Michigan 40-0, 1940, as the year when "trading in the bonds of the Columbus Railway Power and Light Company actually was suspended on the New York Stock Exchange." And, although Cantwell's contention was that football's dominance on the Ohio State campus was over, he stated:

> Without a flicker of hesitation, residents call Columbus the football capital of the U.S. . . . a community possessiveness of football still characterizes Columbus where, as one professor put it, "Football here is an important cultural event" (13:101).

As to whether football's dominance on the Ohio State campus is over, one can only speculate. The discontent with college football in general which has appeared more forcibly within recent years could cause difficulty, but right now Ohio State seems to have the kind of problem a college can enjoy. The August 1969 issue of *Sports Illustrated* pointed out the ease with which the big stadium (it seats 81,455) is sold out each year. By June 12, 1969, every available ticket had been sold, and:

> A howl of anguish immediately went up from almost 10,000 applicants who had been shut out, even though they had sent their applications in well before deadline (93:8).

Ohio is not the only football-fevered state. During football season the 86,000 or so citizens of Green Bay, Wisconsin reportedly "live and breathe football."

> Indeed, a prominent feature of many wills is the disposition of the decedent's season tickets (71:88).

When Alabama beat Nebraska in the Sugar Bowl in 1966, but was not selected for the national rankings by the best-known award givers, the loyal fans of Alabama were reported to have put on the licenses of their cars: "To Hell with AP and UPI, Alabama is still No. 1" (34:30).

A 1969 CBS television special called "Football—100 Years Old and Still Kicking" seemed to sum up the idea that football is more than a game in America. It is like America. The passions and furies of America are mirrored in the passions and furies of football, which was portrayed and described as a ritual as old as the prayer meeting and the side show—America builds temples to their football gods and worships there every weekend. And, as the program pointed out, football is a kind of extension of our lives. It represents organizational men, who, like us, are part of a machine. It is a game described as a mixture of Sanskrit, algebra, and infantry tactics. Television, which has now made football a personal experience for its viewers, confirmed in this program that "in football Americans find what they expect from their country—a sense of infinite possibility."

HERO WORSHIP

No small part of a community's source of unity and pride is found in the feats of its dazzling sport figures. For that matter, in the annals of heroes and leaders, few persons are more highly esteemed than favored sport stalwarts. Homer's *Iliad* and other Greek literature of antiquity suggested that "champion athletes were taken to the hearts of people more enthusiastically than philosophers or statesmen"(8). A winner at Olympia could have "a statue of himself erected in the sacred grove where the temples stood." Now, as then, the reputations of sport heroes are inviolate and an appreciative citizenry cannot do enough to honor them. In fact, heroes no longer have to erect their own statues.

Among those who have reached statue-stardom in the United States is baseball's Stan Musial. In his honor a group of St. Louis businessmen paid $50,000 for a bronze statue of him to be placed in front of the Busch Memorial Stadium. It is 10 feet tall, weighs a ton, and stands on an eight-foot granite pedestal. It was done in the studio of sculptor Carl Christian Mose, a baseball devotee who played as a semipro in Chicago in the early 1920's.

Numerous stories attest to the adulation and high recognition accorded sport heroes. Some are noted later in Chapter 5, "Sport: A Pursuit of Nations." A few illustrations follow here.

In *Esquire's* thirty-fifth anniversary issue, F. Scott Fitzgerald wrote about his generation, the thirties, in which he declared that:

> The most beautiful thing in the world was a football captain killed in battle . . . Match me, Tommy Hitchcock or Bill Tilden for sheer power of survival as champions . . . Dempsey, scarred in reverse by the war, was becoming the brave of his day, while Tunney bided his time (26:119-121).

Frank Conroy wrote of his generation, the fifties, that:

> Our heroes were not of our own age group. For the most part they were athletes—Jackie Robinson, Joe DiMaggio, Sugar Ray Robinson . . . we are aware of the poverty of our history. We have generation envy. Fitzgerald's people believed in their world—it really mattered who won the Princeton-Harvard game (18:126).

Although some writers may contend that today's younger generation dismisses the sport hero as "bourgeois" or of little consequence, others confirm the notion that "heroes reaffirm the American idea of itself as a nation dedicated not to power but to ideals" (98:32).

When the New York Yankees retired Mickey Mantle's uniform, No. 7, and sent it to the Baseball Hall of Fame to join Babe Ruth's No. 3, Lou Gehrig's No. 4, and Joe DiMaggio's No. 5, over 60,000 devoted fans turned out to salute the 37 year old ex-slugger and capped their affection with an ovation that lasted six minutes. Reportedly, there was "nostalgia oozing from every corner of proud old Yankee Stadium . . . and hardly a dry eye in the stadium" (68:21).

Despite Jim Brosnan's perceptive analysis, "The Fantasy World of Baseball," in which he contended that today's major league ballplayer "contributes to the desecration of his image as a special sort of folk hero" by his preoccupation with security, business contracts, retirement pensions, and promotion of merchandise (11b:69), Mickey Mantle's response to his devoted fans provides some counter thought:

I've always wondered how a man who knew he was going to die [Lou Gehrig in 1939] could have stood here and said he was the luckiest man in the world. Now I know (68:21).

The fans of Arnold Palmer, one of the great barons of golf, have been called his "dyed-in-the-Alpaca army." About Palmer many praises have been sung, but perhaps this statement epitomizes most:

Palmer was a man whom the masses could both marvel at and identify with (104:27).

Around the world, the story appears to be very much the same. When Carlos Arruza, the greatest matador in the history of Mexico and number one to many people of the Spanish-speaking world, died in an automobile accident, homage was paid to him by thousands of mourners as his coffin was borne through the streets of Mexico City. Several books have been written about him, and, at the time of his death, a movie based on his life was being filmed (17:44).

Manuel Santana's tennis victories in the Davis Cup matches thrilled the nation of Spain. He received one of the highest medals that Spain can bestow upon a citizen—the Isabel la Católica—and was known as Ilustrísimo by the personal decree of Generalissimo Franco. Of Santana was written:

No athlete in the world is so revered by his countrymen and no defeat will alter this feeling (22:28).

In 1959, when Maria Bueno, the graceful Brazilian tennis player won at Wimbledon, President Kubitschek had her flown home in a special plane. Motorcades in Rio, a special mass at the cathedral in São Paulo, and a new medal of sporting merit coined in her honor were among the tributes paid to the young heroine. Later in 1959, following her triumphant winning of the U.S. National Championships, a bronze statue of her, two meters high, was placed at the main entrance of the Clube de Regatas in São Paulo (105:32).

Eric Tabarly, the 37-year-old French adventurer who singlehandedly sailed yachts across oceans, has received the *Légion d'Honneur*, dined at the Elysée Palace with Charles de Gaulle, and was hailed in France as the "magician of the sea" (60:86).

In a cover story about Italy which appeared in *Time*, the opening paragraph began as follows:

In the land of Michelangelo, Garibaldi and the Medicis there reigns a vast and unusual variety of contemporary heroes. The Italians idolize Grand Prix drivers, artists, novelists and occasionally Sicilian banditi. They fall barely short of adoring Nino Benvenuti, the boxing champion (99:58).

In Canada, the popularity of Elaine Tanner, world record swimmer, was analyzed by a Winnipeg bank executive in this way:

If we could bottle Elaine Tanner, we could make a million . . . Everybody identifies with her. Everbody will say 10 years from now they saw her do it. Nothing like this ever happened to Winnipeg before (102:23).

Frederick Exley's book, *A Fan's Notes,* was one of only five books published in 1968 that was nominated for a National Book Award in fiction. The following passage from it perhaps best sums up the memorable and wordless enthusiasm of the fan who is hooked on sport and its heroes:

> Where I could not, with syntax, give shape to my fancies, Gifford (Frank) could . . . I cheered for him with such inordinate enthusiasm, my yearning became so involved with his desire to escape life's bleak anonymity, that after a time he became my alter ego, that part of me which had its being in the competitive world of men; I came . . . to believe that I was . . . an actual instrument of his success. Each time I heard the roar of the crowd, it roared in my ears as much for me as him; that roar was not only a promise of my fame, it was its unequivocal assurance (25:134).

What motivates the fan, whether it be the desire to escape the boredom of everyday life or to reach out to a larger existence, is part of the story told in Part I. An extension of the idea that part of that motivation for the participant is derived from social factors is the contention of Chapter 4.

CHAPTER 4

Sport: A Vehicle of Integration, Assimilation, Status

A COMMON GENEALOGY

Steinbeck wrote about America that it was "rooted in all races, stained and tinted with all colors." In this sense sport may be likened to America. In sport there seems to be no more racial identity than in a blood corpuscle. If skin color separates the nation in civil rights, sport may be said to tend to unite the nation because it harbors an aristocracy of virtue that transcends ethnic categories. "Thus sport functions," as Günther Lüschen wrote, "as a means of integration, not only for the actual participants, but also for the representative members of such a system" (51:11).

Just as the relationship between sport and society in general is complex, so is the relationship of sport to racial integration complex. There is some evidence that contradicts the idea that sport achieves good will in racial concerns. In 1910, when the first Negro heavyweight, Jack Johnson, defeated Jim Jeffries, the white ex-champion, the incident touched off race riots that resulted in six deaths. In 1968, several findings of a study published by the Center for Urban Education, as summarized by Richard Kraus, suggested that the many assumptions regarding sport as a means of solving racial prejudices and discrimination were invalid. In large measure, according to Kraus, sports as carried on in public recreation programs, "are seen by recreation administrators as an incitement to racial antagonism and hostility." Kraus also stated the following

Many Negroes claim that the progress made is a facade which conceals the reality of continued racial discriminatory attitudes and practices. Black athletes say that sport status is something the white man can always snatch away, as witness the loss of the heavyweight title by Cassius Clay. Many are convinced that blacks usually make less money than whites of comparable talent, in salary as well as outside endorsements for the professional athlete, in jobs for the man who remains an amateur (42:32).

Sports Illustrated's series of articles called "The Black Athlete: A Shameful Story," pointed to such highly questionable practices toward the college Negro athlete as physical and mental abuse, restrictions concerning dating of whites, quotas (limiting number of Negroes on a team), stacking (playing Negroes in a few positions only), difficulties getting jobs, and so forth (61).

Despite these findings, however, numerous instances testify that sport has both deified and defied status and that it has represented for some persons the proof that "class tells" rather than race restricts.

The meaning of sport to the success saga in Negro life is portrayed in various sources. Jesse Owens in the book *Blackthink: My Life As Black Man and White Man* (1970) tells the story of his struggle through racial hatred to understanding and athletic success made possible by the first white man he ever knew, Charles Riley, a physical education teacher (62b). A. S. Young's book *Negro Firsts in Sports* (1963), pointing to the notable achievements of Roy Campanella, Jackie Robinson, Satchel Paige, Willie Mays, Rafer Johnson, Jesse Owens, Joe Louis, Hank and Tommy Aaron, Wilt Chamberlain, Don Newcombe, Maury Wills, Charles Sifford, Althea Gibson, Arthur Ashe, to name a few, is illustrative of the idea that, in the world of sport more than any other facet of American life, Negroes approach closer to the democratic ideal (107).

Wilhelmena S. Robinson's *International Library of Negro Life and History: Historical Negro Biographies* (1967) also provides biographical sketches of Negro notables in the sport world (66b). Other brief accounts, "Sports As An Integrator" in *Saturday Review* (100c), "Blacks on the Green," about Negro professional golfers, appearing in *Time* (99b), and "In Black and White," about athletic scholarships given to Negro students, in *Sports Illustrated* (94b), are illustrative of the dramatic changes of the status of the Negro in the sport world.

At the same time, perhaps sport has provided a rare advantage to the social scientist for assessing the progress of racial integration as well as for taking a stand against discrimination. And, as one reads the literature of the day, much of which postures as a parable of man in some generic crises or other, certain questions are raised: Is it too much to expect sport to clean up society in general—education, housing, ghettos, delinquency—or is it enough in sport if simple excellence is celebrated? Has sport used the individual or has the individual used sport to gain ends not as easily achieved in other facets of society? Does sport provide opportunities for justice, equality, assimilation; or do discrepancies between deed and action exist more because of sport? Does sport threaten a country's stability with social dissolution or help maintain its social health?

The excerpts provided in the following section may help the reader decide for himself suitable answers to some of the questions raised above.

According to Robert H. Boyle, Negro participation in baseball goes back to 1860 when Bud Fowler, the first Negro professional, began playing. After a player on the White Stocking team balked at playing against Fleet Walker (Negro catcher) and George Stovey (Negro pitcher), who were known as the "Mulatto Battery," the color line had been drawn (10:102). The most singular dramatic case of racial integration in the sport world occurred when Jackie Robinson was brought up from the minor leagues to play baseball for the Brooklyn Dodgers. This breaking of the color line represented a revolution in the thinking of many people and the story is documented in several sources (23b). Although the tremendous influx of Latin Americans into major league baseball followed the Jackie Robinson breakthrough in 1946, historically this influx was reported to have "started in 1911 when the late Clark Griffith, then manager of the Cincinnati Reds, imported a white Cuban third baseman, Rafael Almeida, for a tryout" (11:25). The great appeal of baseball to the Latin, like any other man, appeared to be the "individuality" in the game and "the chance to show himself" (11:26).

Basketball's prominent Negro athlete, Bill Russell, when he was appointed coach of the Boston Celtics, contended that the world of professional sport was one of the few worlds in which a man is judged on his talent, not on his skin.

> the other players accepted me with no antagonism at all . . . respected my ability as a player and my knowledge of the game . . . played as hard for me as they used to play for Red Auerbach . . . Out in the real world the prejudice seems to be growing stronger and the threat of violence closer (67:21).

Some Negro athletes, said to be bitter and caustic critics of the schools (*Sports Illustrated*, February 12, 1968), agreed to conduct clinics and physical education classes for children age 6 to 14 at Berkeley, Richmond, and Oakland playgrounds under a program sponsored by the University of California. Among the athlete-instructors was basketball star Bob Presley, who was reported to have said:

> I feel now that I am a Cal man, in the sense of belonging. The university has shown that it respects me as a human, and I respect the university. It's a trade, and a fair one, I think (90:8).

In 1967, three all-Negro high schools, Beach and Carver in Georgia and Gibbs in Florida, became the first in the deep South to play in white tournaments. Coach of Beach, Russell Ellington, explaining why Negro teams excel, had this to say:

> Most of our boys don't have anything else to do . . . Basketball gives them something physical and something good to do . . . and we're proud of our record (85:8).

In 1969, Thomas Paine became the first Negro to sign a letter of intent to play basketball at the University of Kentucky. Coach Adolph Rupp commented of Paine's signing that "race has nothing to do with it at all, we're just so happy to at last get the big boy we've wanted for so long" (69:C3). About Kentucky, Paine said he chose it for the educational program it afforded and because he thought Coach Rupp could help bring out his potential.

When Olympian basketball player Spencer Haywood returned to Detroit, his coach Bob Calihan saw his exposure to the Olympics as a great thing for Haywood culturally and commented that Haywood was very proud of his association with the Olympic team and what he did for the United States. Of himself, Haywood commented that in 1964, when he was shuttling between his mother's home in Mississippi and relatives in Chicago and Detroit,

> I was headed the wrong way. I was, you know, a thug. All I wanted to do was rob, man, or hustle a pool game, whatever it took to make some money (64:40).

By the conclusion of the 1970 American basketball season, Spencer Haywood was being paid in excess of a quarter of a million dollars by the Denver Rockets for his basketball talents.

Ed Emory, football coach in a high school in Wadesboro, North Carolina was confronted with this situation: Five Negroes wanted to resign from the team because one of their teammates had announced he was joining the Ku Klux Klan. Emory told the boy he had the choice of joining the Klan or staying on the team. He chose the team. The boy's father and some 20 fellow Klansmen told Emory he had violated the boy's civil right, to which Emory replied:

> There aren't any civil rights in football . . . when they put on their uniforms they're all the same . . . I just play the boy who can get things done . . . Chinese or Jewish, Negro or white. If he can't get the job done I don't care (84:14).

In Dallas, where social segregation still appeared to be "the way," Don Meredith, white quarterback, and Don Perkins, Negro fullback, commented that they could not point to any case of racial friction among the Cowboys. Perkins, although stating that conditions in Dallas forced the Negro and white players to separate when they leave the practice field, stated:

> On the football field, we've always, in my opinion, gotten along well, and been close as a team (45:83).

Melvin Durslag, describing how the Globetrotters have done more than play basketball in the last 43 years, quoted Inman Jackson, who, bristling at the charges that certain Negro groups had accused them of perpetuating the Uncle Tom image, pointed to the Globetrotters social triumphs:

> We started out going up the fire escapes of hotels and wound up going in the front door. We pioneered . . . integrated seating . . . broke down racial barriers . . . What have our critics done except talk? (24b:21).

On many campuses throughout the United States, Negro scholarship athletes entered in a series of demands that seemed to open an area of racial discontent. Accusations included: subjecting blacks to derogatory comments because of appearance, leaving them to fend for themselves in finding housing, giving them poor academic counseling, asserting that they malingered over injuries, assigning them to inferior summer jobs, treating them as paid employees. At issue, however, seemed to be not so much the question of race as "the college-perpetuated myth that such athletes are students first," as one writer put it. Citing the example of Bob Presley, Negro basketball player at Berkeley, this writer pointed out that Presley was expelled from three Detroit high schools, then imported to a California school for one semester where his grades were, for the most part, below average, and attended two junior colleges and another high school before going to Berkeley.

> This is the same kind of disadvantaged background shared by many athletes on college teams (87:9).

The series "The Black Athlete: A Shameful Story" produced a greater reader response than any other in the magazine's history, eliciting some 1000 letters. Although the response was overwhelmingly favorable toward correction of some of the abuses to which black athletes have been subjected, as the editorial pointed out, the bulk of dissenting mail came from those who believed that all scholarship athletes (black or white) suffer the same disabilities. Some readers acted quickly to form organizations with missions to help disadvantaged Negro students. Furthermore, the editorial asserted, if sport was unable to clean up the country surely it could clean up its own house. A noted impediment to the reforms was that reforms would cost money, of course, but:

> Sport has increased the opportunities for the Negro to go to college. It must now make certain that what is inside that open door is more than a basketball court, a football play-book—and a fast exit to oblivion (78:9).

Whether or not sport can or should meet such an obligation is a debatable point; nonetheless, what is inside the open door of the educational institution, insofar as athletics is concerned, will be discussed in Part IV.

Just as sport did not seem to be the real issue in the instances just cited, neither did it seem to be the issue at Grambling, a predominantly Negro college in Louisiana. When a six-day protest involving 1,200 demonstrators was fomented by advocates of Black Power, "with athletics being used to attract attention and sympathy," as the report stated, one Grambling official declared:

> This is part of a calculated plan to discredit Negro colleges. This is the only way the Black Power people can make inroads into the middle-class Negro community and hope to establish themselves (86:12).

The report also contained the dour observation that whatever the basis of the protest, the demonstrators showed up en masse to cheer loudly at the homecoming football game.

Perhaps the whole issue of integration in sport is capped by this comment from the promotion director of the Harlem Globetrotters. After seeing LSU's Pete Maravich, who is white, the director declared: "He's so fantastic we'd integrate to get him" (94:14).

A LADDER TO SUCCESS AND PASSPORT TO A BETTER LIFE

Often it has been said that sport opens many doors and provides opportunities that lead to other successful careers. John W. Loy, while pointing to the limited empirical data supportive of the "rags to riches myth," cited several studies which suggest ways in which college sports might facilitate upward mobility—provide entry into professional sports, enhance educational attainment, lead to various forms of social and occupational success, foster leadership and occupational skills (48b). Various organizations appear to be grounded in a similar conviction. Examples include The National Football Foundation and Hall of Fame, which began honoring electees to the Hall of Fame in 1951, and the *Sports Illustrated* Silver Anniversary Awards to former college lettermen "who prove beyond any doubt that football can be the forerunner of a useful, productive life of achievement and service to one's community" (81:4). The groups so honored have provided substantial evidence that sport has been one of the makers of men. And, although Benjamin Franklin was obviously recognized for reasons other than his natatorial accomplishments, he too was among the 15 persons recently elected to the International Swimming Hall of Fame which honored him as a swimmer, swimming teacher, and the first to write about swimming (he wrote *The Art of Swimming in the 18th Century*) (83:50).

Sometimes earning power is equated with success. Bryant Cratty, presenting research findings in psychology concerning the interaction of competition and aspiration level, indicated that individuals in lower economic groups work hard at competitive athletics because they may consider this avenue as one of the few by which they could raise their economic position in society (20b:187). Ralph Andreano, in his book *No Joy in Mudville*, exploring the question of money and the folk hero, pointed out that, although today's major league baseball player has many more income-producing possibilities and tends to be better educated than players of other eras, most of them do not view baseball primarily as a ladder to social and economic success (2b). On the other hand, O. J. Simpson, USC's all-America back, Heisman Trophy winner, and pro football's number one draft choice for the 1968 season, was reported as saying:

> Money means everything to the ghetto kids . . . I want to do youth work. If I can show that I got something material from sports, they'll respect me, but if I was a track star and wound up in recreation work in the parks with nothing much, they wouldn't . . . Willie Mays was my hero, not just because he was a good baseball player, but because he had a big house to show for it (91:7).

For those who equate money with "the better life," this may be an interesting statistic: The 1969 baseball season reportedly showed nine players who made $100,000 that year. Perhaps the most telling part of this statistic, because it is somewhat a contradiction of some assertions reported in the previous section, is that of those nine players, four were Negro and two were Latin.

The evidence that big money is available to outstanding sport performers is presented in several studies; for example, a study by Weinberg and Arond showed that many professional boxers recruited from low socioeconomic backgrounds ascended the economic ladder quickly at a young age (104b). Further evidence of the economic stature of professional sportsmen is presented in Chapter 7. The fact that sport may be responsible for providing a passport to a better life for reasons other than money is acknowledged by variously expressive individuals whose words are presented in the following passages.

Some statistics attest to the fact that sport provides a kind of transportation system which moves some Negroes out of the ghettos and into the colleges. A study from the Department of Health, Education and Welfare conducted in 1968 revealed that of 796,709 students registered in 59 colleges, 12,699, or one and one half percent, were Negro. The schools granted 10,698 athletic scholarships, of which 634, or about six percent went to Negroes (88:10). Apparently, the percentage of athletic scholarships granted to Negroes is greater than the percentage of the total student population represented by Negroes.

Writing about what he called the "Underground Railroad of the 20th Century," William Johnson described it as the "mysterious but highly efficient network operating for Negro athletes who want to play college-level sports but simply do not have the grades, or the intelligence, or the disposition to meet the academic requirements." Johnson was highlighting the abuses of the Negro and the cold opportunism in college recruiting, but in this article, Negro Will Robinson, coach at an almost all-white high school in Detroit, was quoted as saying:

> If we can get a boy one year of college, it's better than no years at all. Once in a while one stays long enough to catch the message, and anything is better than letting them go off the deep end when they drop out of high school (35:53).

Other persons appear to share Will Robinson's conviction. Bob Teague, who was raised in a ghetto, asserted that his passport to a better life was football. His "miracle," as he called it, and a good high school academic record won him a scholarship to the University of Wisconsin. There he became a star halfback and made the All-Big-Ten-Team. The Green Bay Packers and three other professional teams reportedly were ready to give him a tryout, although he chose a career in journalism instead. His nightly newscasts on NBC were reported to be viewed by nearly four million people in the New York area (97:55).

Negro Paul Robinson, who was Rookie of the Year in 1968 in the American Football League and was receiving a salary over $70,000 in only his second pro season, declared he had to be dragged to classes at Marana High School because "I was mainly going to school to eat and play sports" (63).

Willie Davenport, Olympic gold medalist in hurdling in 1969, who, during his student teaching, advised young people of the need to set goals for themselves. He stated:

> You see, I didn't have any [goals] for myself until . . . I got interested in running track. Up until then I was wild. What would have happened to me if there hadn't been track? Well, I don't know. But it is something interesting to think about (58:42).

Ivory Crockett, who scored a suprising upset over John Carlos in the 100-yard dash in the 1969 National AAU Track and Field Championships, appraised his success in these words:

> Track gave me an opportunity to go to college. I never would have made it any other way. It turned my life around when I was in high school . . . when I learned that running fast could get me to college I started studying (27:62).

Recently, Jackie Robinson was reported to have charged that big league club owners were shortchanging black American athletes once their playing days were over and that the front offices had not grown the way the rest of the country had in terms of the contribution of black America to baseball. Bob Feller "fired the brushback" in these comments:

> I think professional baseball and professional sports have done more for what you may call the underpriveleged or those in minority groups than all the politicians, all the welfare, and all the other programs combined (28:37).

Whether or not baseball is "dragging its feet" in terms of better race relations, Robinson acknowledged that "in my book baseball will always be No. 1."

Sport has been used by other ethnic groups and persons in lower socio-economic levels as a means to educate and elevate. The Jesuit fathers and Franciscan sisters of St. Stephen's Mission in Wyoming used sport to wage a battle for the education of their Indians. What the mission tried to do about the problems and conditions of the about 2,200 Arapaho and 1,600 Shoshoni Indians who shared the Wind River Reservation was explained by the mission teams. In order to overcome "almost an ethnic despair" which rarely summoned "the spirit for a sustained try at anything," the fathers reportedly had to find something to lure the children into an education. The lure was basketball, a sport which already existed as a "disorganized passion" among the Indians. Father Zumach was quoted as saying:

> The basketball court is really the only place where the boys will take a scolding . . . They love it too much to quit. That's important—if they go out and get jobs (30:70).

The mission appeared to have succeeded when boys drifted in from all over the reservation to play.

Poor when he was young, French-Canadian Bernard Geoffrion (nicknamed "Boom Boom" because of his slap shot that rocketed a puck from his stick into the boards at 128 m.p.h.), who was coach of the pro hockey New York Rangers, declared:

> If they had more arenas to skate, you wouldn't see all the trash going around the world, hanging around restaurants and all that jazz . . . I'm a lucky man. Where would I be if not for hockey? (46:82).

When Orville Moody, ex-career army sergeant, won the 1969 U.S. Open Golf championship, he was reported to have said the highlight of the day was this congratulatory telephone message from President Nixon:

> It was a nice thing that someone from the middle-class, not the elite, won a tournament . . . It's always nice when someone comes out of the Army to win (70).

The evidence of sport providing opportunities that lead to other successful careers also is convincing. A few examples may serve to illustrate: In his column "Dateline America," David Snell, a senior editor of *Life,* dealt with sport heroes in the business world. He pointed out that "there's nothing like a career in big-time sports to help a fellow succeed in business without really trying." Athletes whose "hero voltage" and "natural competitiveness" had been drawn upon for the hard-nosed business world included: corporation executives Whitey Ford, former pitching star of the New York Yankees; Jim Katcavage of the New York football Giants; Dick Lynch, former all-pro defensive back of the Giants; Pat Summerall, Giant placekicker—turned broadcaster; and Ellis E.

"Woody" Erdman, play-by-play voice of the Giant radio network. The hero status of Dick Lynch, as Snell also pointed out "has helped generate another status: he is more visible and better paid in retirement than he ever was on the NFL playing fields" (74:85).

And, Jackie Robinson, whose "breaking the color line" was mentioned earlier in this chapter, might be considered as the person to provide an appropriate conclusion to the thesis that sport provides a ladder to success. At the time of this writing he was an assistant to New York's Governor Rockefeller.

CHAPTER 5

Sport: A Pursuit of Nations

The sporting brand of nationalism has a long-honored tradition, dating back to the time of the Greek Olympic Games in which small villages vied with one another in sport as well as in politics. Now as then, in the words of Sir Arnold Lunn, "games which bulk so largely in the life of individuals cannot be neglected in studying the life of nations" (49).

National slogans, whether it be America's *E Pluribus Unum* or Kenya's *Harambie* (let's all pull together), seem to take on more meaning and intensity in the arena of world sport. Even the parade preceding the Olympic Games is a kind of study in national tastes and dress.

Sport is equipped too with symbols that are used and understood across national and cultural boundaries. Lewis Mumford in his book, *The Myth of the Machine,* made the point that in the absence of language, man's first communications were made by bodily actions. In this sense one may conclude that the very strangeness of remote lands has been domesticated by sport as one form of bodily communication. A kind of international understanding echoes across the arena of sport at the same time that expressions of national virility, pride and patriotism ricochet off the international scoreboard.

And, it seems that if sport is a binding force in humanity, so too has it inflamed nations with a kind of explosive determination to beat the other guy. Whether or not sport should be dominated by nations and whether or not nationalism and internationalism are incompatible, desirable, or inevitable, sport may be seen in the following sections as a preoccupation of nations. In some instances it may function as a national symbolic ritual or help to maintain national solidarity, or it may be used by nations—emerged or emerging—as a showcase of virility, a symbol of political status, an ambassador in international diplomacy, or simply a mother tongue of communication.

72

THE AMERICAN WAY

Celeste Ulrich, describing the different kinds of sport as one of the most significant indices of the character and personality of America, declared that "they portray the genius of its people and set the stage for cultural formation" (101:109). "Athletic America" to General Douglas MacArthur represented a talismanic phrase:

> It arouses national pride and kindles anew the national spirt . . . Nothing has been more characteristic of the genius of the American people than is their genius for athletics . . . If I were required to indicate today that element of American life which is most characteristic of our nationality, my finger would unerringly point to our athletic escutcheon (52:27).

Although General MacArthur wrote that statement in 1928 at the time of the Ninth Olympic Games held in Amsterdam, still today sport seems to stand at the exact center of the American personality. That the American "melody lingers on" in sport contests abroad is a fact one can hardly deny. "Almost the only tune heard in Winnipeg," said one reporter at the time of the 1967 Pan-American Games, "was the 'Star Spangled Banner!'" On the basis of the number of gold medals won, the United States locked up its fourth Pan-American game that year. One Canadian matron, perhaps expressing the opinion of the many, was reported to have "flounced huffily" and said: "I swear, if I hear The Star Spangled Banner just one more time, I shall scream" (62:20).

Despite the Black Power boycott publicity at the time of the Olympic Games in Mexico City, there remained considerable evidence that the national pride of Americans was heard from. American heavyweight boxer and Negro, George Forman, for example, after winning the Olympic gold medal, "joined in the singing of the National Anthem and then grabbed a little American flag and marched around the ring with it" (75:66). This spirit that characterized Americans both in particular regions of this country and at international contests, regardless of all the background mutterings and rivalries, needs no documentation for those who have witnessed such events. Part of the picture of personality and passion of the American fan is presented in Chapter 3 and will not be amplified further in this section except for one further observation which may be needed to complete a consideration of American sport. It comes by way of Gregory P. Stone, who sensed a loss of dignity and value in sport when sports are contrived with the audience in mind. Stone, proposing the idea of "play and dis-play" as an antinomy, placed emphasis upon the "tension between the morality of the game and the amorality of the spectator (immoral in its consequences)" (95). However, Stone showed the importance of spectatorship in American sport in promoting food for conversation, in providing mutual accessibility to anonymous members, in promoting solidarity in various relations such as work and family, and in the development of team loyalties and self-concepts, and so forth (96).

Whether or not the spectator constitutes an "agent of destruction," to use Stone's phrase, the spirit of nationalism characterizes nations around the world. The next few pages are devoted to such an overview.

THE WAY OF THE WORLD

Soccer, a game originating in the hamlets and villages of England nearly 18 centuries ago, is considered to be the world's most established sport. For some countries it pulsates more exuberantly as a national pastime than for others. In *Brazil*, it (called futebol) is by far the most popular mass spectator sport. Although some 30 years ago it was played only by members of the upper classes and strictly on an amateur basis, today, like baseball and football in the United States, it is considered to be a big business. Players who are said to be "all shades from white to jet black," now rank among the best in the world, and important matches are said to:

> generate an excitement that borders on the hysterical . . . the population of every small village will be out watching the local futebol teams . . . It is also a common sight to see the local washerwoman's line hung with the jerseys of one team, sweaters striped like wasps (44:117).

When the Brazilian team won the world title in Sweden in 1958 and again in 1962, they were "tumultuously welcomed back to Rio."

In *Spain*, the importance of soccer is also considered to be a startling phenomenon—"New Passion of A Proud People," as Gordon Ackerman called it. Like bullfighting, soccer has achieved a kind of mysticism and the players, like the best matadors, are the highest-paid citizens. There are even far fewer bull rings than the 3,600 soccer stadiums (Barcelona alone has four stadiums that hold 300,000 spectators), and, whereas "in bullfighting the Spaniards have found an expression for their sense of tragedy and bravery; in soccer they have found an expression for loyalty, duty, brotherhood." Soccer attracts professors, esthetes, intellectuals, and the mass of Spanish citizens alike.

> Learned treatises are devoted to the art of the game; it has been seriously proposed that Spanish university students study soccer strategy as students once studied Napoleonic battle tactics (2:36).

Kenya and Ghana in *Africa* have a long history of soccer, but, more recently interest in other sports, particularly track and field, has grown. In Kenya, which has a population of nearly 10 million representing different tribes and four main language groups with various dialects in each group, the idea of national unity, according to one author, has been advanced through the help of sport and John Velzian, the English coach of the Kenya National Track Team. Reportedly Velzian, who was ridiculed at first for suggesting that the African would work for the intrinsic value of sport, said:

> The willingness of the African to compete and to work for the glory of it is now established . . . there are athletes who go out and train for the sheer joy . . . and the knowledge that possibly one day they will represent Kenya (38:80).

Lest the reader be tempted to assume that African nations are using sport for reasons other than a facet of life "as unique, perhaps as it was in Athens before the first Olympics," another writer pointed out the contrary as being the case. The track team was not given money, except by the coach, to buy even a javelin and a Kenya government official was reported as saying that "sport is no instrument of international politics for us . . . the feel for sport must grow upward or it will not last" (77:56).

In *Ireland,* the sport of hurling certainly may be said to have grown upward. A wide-open, high-scoring, free-wheeling and slashing sport, hurling is considered to be the most purely native game and "much more than a game to fervent Irish patriots." Uniquely Irish in style with a long and romantic history, it is "intensely nationalistic." And the All-Ireland hurling championship played annually in Dublin, Joseph Carroll wrote:

> sets loose a hullaballoo very much like that of the World Series and the pleasant noise crosses the ocean to the little Irelands of the Western Hemisphere (14:40).

In New York, where some 22 hurling clubs (named for the Irish counties from which their players came) compete at Gaelic Park, it is said that "a spirit beyond games hovers over the place. It is . . . an Irishness never far below the American surfaces" (14:40).

In *Australia* kangaroos may be symbolic, and it may be horses that the Australians love ("Horse racing is more than a sport; it's a national frenzy," declared a news commentator), but Australia is touted as an all-round "sports-playing, sports-watching, altogether sports-minded country such as the world has never known before." When one considers Australia's numerous sport clubs, the wonder athletes who have made the country's reputation indomitable, their production of records in track, tennis, cricket, swimming (not to mention a basic swimming stroke itself, the Australian crawl), it is not astonishing to learn what Herbert Warren Wind said:

> I was hard put to recall any conversation in which sport was not the accepted subject or did not inevitably intrude and take over . . . Australians will talk sport almost as if they existed for nothing else (106:84).

In *Japan,* among other sports "Sumo," the ancient form of wrestling, has regained popularity through the influence of television. It is said, however, of the newly affluent Japanese, with more leisure than their fathers knew and a vigor that demands outlet that "whatever the sport, the Japanese attack it with a fearsome determination to be *dai-ichi*—the very best" (29). Perhaps the Japanese lunge into sport may be characterized by the statement, "Rough Creed: 'There's No Success Without Suffering,'" adopted by taskmaster Coach Hirofumi Daimatsu in leading the Japanese girls of the Nichibo team to repeated world volleyball championships. The "exercise in mass masochism," as Lee Griggs called it, was evaluated by one of the players in these words:

> There are no dances or dates for us. But there is something much more important—the pride of bringing some sporting glory to the company and our nation (29:34).

The game that the Japanese en masse seemingly have chosen for themselves is baseball, learned from the missionaries and teachers who used to play it in their spare time. Baseball in Japan is said to be played with complete seriousness and to have replaced the Army and Navy in attracting the rugged youth who were drawn into the military in former days (16:73). National honor seemed to be at stake when the Japanese people viewed the 1964 Olympic Games as "an opportunity to show off their nation's talents . . . maturity as a modern state . . . respectability after the dark years of militarism" (15:38).

In *Mexico*, when Felipe Munoz won the 200-meter breaststroke for Mexico in the 1968 Olympic Games, it was an emotion-packed evening. One observer wrote that

> it seemed like everyone . . . sang the Mexican national anthem at the top of their lungs, and Munoz was carried out on the shoulders of his countrymen . . . far into the night, the cheers and car honking went on . . . it was their big night (36:74).

When Rafael Osuna led Mexico's Davis Cup team to its historic upset of Australia in 1969, his countrymen carried him from the court on their shoulders. At the time of his untimely death ten days later, many expressions of sadness revealed Mexico's pride and loss. One writer said that "wherever he went, Osuna captivated the crowds . . . but he was always Mexico's. No athlete ever meant more to his country . . . By Osuna's death, an entire nation is bereft" (92:10).

Soviet Russia has given "attention and subsidation to athletes by the millions" stated Yuri Mashin. Contrasted to the 126,000 sportsmen in 1923, Russia boasted that in 1966, 50,528,000 people, every fifth person, trained regularly and competed in sport. This is aside from the many millions of sport participants who do not compete. The mass sport movement and high standards of athletes indicated to Mashin that

> Russia has been following the right track the past half century . . . Our sports movement has widespread international ties . . . one of the best ways of strengthening cooperation and friendship among nations (53).

Whether or not international sport contests are ways of strengthening cooperation and friendship among nations is discussed in the next section.

THE INTERNATIONAL WAY

An editorial raising the question, "Why Not Wave the Flag?" pointed out that "like sex, you can't make nationalism unpopular . . . Spectators and athletes have regarded themselves as belonging to nations" (80:12). In international contests, nationalism does not appear to be unpopular even though nations at times seem to be less than popular. One might hope for the benefits ascribed to sport by Konrad Lorenz who, in his book *On Aggression,* stated:

> Sporting contests between nations are beneficial not only because they provide an outlet for the collective militant enthusiasms of nations, but also because they have two other effects that counter the danger of war: they promote personal acquaintances between people of different nations . . . and they unite, in enthusiasm for a common cause, people who otherwise would have little in common (47:282).

There are numerous incidents that testify to the fact that sport is an ambassador of good will and international diplomacy. A few illustrative examples follow: In the World Series in soccer held in Rio de Janeiro in 1959, Brazil and England were choices as finalists and the United States a unanimous choice for the consolation prize. The United States beat the British 1-0 and, although Chile beat the United States, an embassy man was reported to have said:

> The performance of the United States team did as much to further United States-Brazil relations as all the good-will missions combined (72:111).

When the United States basketball team played the Russians in Hungary in the 1965 World University Games, it was reported by Paul Ress that the American athlete was "nearly suffocated with adulation." In his welcoming speech to athletes from 35 countries and to the 60,000 spectators at the opening ceremony, Hungarian Premier Gyula Kallai was reported to have directed his affection toward the Americans with these words:

> Sports are not only physical education but also one of the means of rapprochement and friendship between countries . . . I hope that you will find an opportunity to see some of the sights and the life of the people of Budapest (65:21).

On that occasion Paul Ress reported that "politics were left to the politician, and no one seemed inclined to bring up the war in Vietnam." Nor did the Hungarians bring up Negro civil rights and the Los Angeles riots.

> The most articulate answer was the playmaking and togetherness of the U.S. basketball players, white and Negro, Northern and Southern. In Budapest you could not miss them (65:21).

As part of the Olympics Cultural Program "Advertising in the Service of Peace," billboards with the legend, *Todo es Posible en la Paz* (Everything is Possible With Peace), were a prominent part of the 1968 Olympiad in Mexico City. In addition, the symbolic dove of peace appeared in opening ceremonies, electric lights, store windows, automobile stickers, billboards and banners everywhere. Said Lloyd C. Arnold:

> More importantly it seemed to appear symbolically in the hearts and minds of the athletes, spectators and local citizens (36:66).

The Olympic Games in Mexico were even credited by some with bringing a temporary halt to the student riots. And, those great moments of mass silence as well as those tidal waves of exuberant cheers for the excellence of performers regardless of nationality seemed to reflect what Avery Brundage had in mind when he declared that "the Olympics are the most important social force in the world today" (36:70).

Perhaps the best illustrations of the positive outcomes accruing from sport on an international scale occur either among the contestants themselves in the Olympic Games or among competitors in international events that are staged apart from the Olympic spectacular. One such example is provided by the Masters Golf Tournament. When it began in 1934 it was very much an Anglo-American game. Today the foreign professional golfer is no longer a rarity. In 1967, twenty-three outlanders competed in the Masters and the sport of golf has now been taken to six continents. Bobby Jones was credited by one author with "weaving many distinguished foreigners into the very fabric of this event, enhancing not only the tournament itself but the image of world golf as well" (76).

Tennis, too, still appears to be a game of benevolent amiability on the international scale. The professional players' tour was described by one writer as having "more foreign performers than any enterprise since the Lipizzan horses crossed the sea" (21:62). When Arthur Ashe played tennis in Lynchburg, Virginia on the occasion of an Appreciation Day for Dr. Walter Johnson, who helped develop young Negro tennis players, it was planned for him to bring his own opponent. At the last minute, Dennis Ralston, who had been scheduled to play with Ashe, had to decline. Who stepped off the plane in Lynchburg with Ashe?

> None other than Manuel Santana, who had just beaten the Americans in Spain. Because of the international goodwill among tennis players, Santana had agreed to accompany Ashe to Lynchburg . . . Incidentally, Santana won the match (82:98).

When the World Wrestling Championships for the junior-age division, held in Boulder, Colorado in 1969, brought together young athletes from a dozen nations, these observations were made:

they started exchanging team shirts . . . everyone who attended the champion-ships sensed the comradeship that developed . . . Certainly it was worth it when Youri Statsura, the personable freestyle coach from the Soviet Union, congratulated the American team when it won the trophy by one point over his own squad in a warm show of friendship (56:39).

Still, an unhappy consequence of international sport is that one nation or another grows to dominate a particular event or events which, in turn results in international contests becoming a kind of tour de force of world politics. Seemingly, as Dan Jenkins put it, "trend-spotters agree that sport is now likeliest to develop explosively in the direction of inter-national competition. Partly this is due to pressures exerted by the gov-ernments . . . that see victory in sport as an important political status symbol; partly and simply by increased prosperity, leisure and facilities for global travel" (33:26).

There have been many summations of the political dissent existing during the Olympic Games which suggest that the spirit of the Games does not rise above the politics of the times. In the 1924 Olympics, when Hungary lost to Egypt in soccer, it was reported that the Hungarian players were threatened in their national press and that many of them never returned home again (72:111).

Since that day, some national and international affairs have not improved. Wilhelm Pollmans, technical director of the West Germans at the 1960 Olympics, was reported to have said this about the West and East Germans being teamed up:

We may speak one language and compete under one flag, but there is no way to make us a team (39:33).

When Russia lost to Czechoslovakia in ice hockey in the world championships at Stockholm in 1969, reportedly the whole Czech nation erupted, and,

The celebration rapidly became a bitter political protest . . . In Prague's Wenceslas Square, a mob sacked the office of Aeroflot, the Soviet airline . . . as rumors of possible Soviet armed reprisals swept across the country, their (Czechs) hockey team lost to the Swedes, and, the Russians won the world championship after all (43:93).

The question of whether America should quit international sport has more than piqued the curiosity of many serious-minded observers of the world scene. At the same time, as Dan Jenkins put it, "The rest of the world has a new game. It is called 'Beat America First,' and just about everybody is doing it." According to Jenkins, not only is the prestige of the United States "going down faster than the *Titanic*," but,

By excelling at games that we either invented ourselves or dominated for years, foreigners are walking off with our money and trophies, and as they gleefully stomp Uncle Sam they are also openly asking whether we try very hard anymore (32:13).

Some speculate that America does not try very hard, that the true reasons behind the erosion of America's sport supremacy are softness lack of tenacity, loss of killer's instinct, and so forth. Some proffer the idea that other nations seem to have an edge because no one seems to agree precisely on what constitutes an amateur. Still others point to America as having some of the best athletes in the world in baseball basketball, and football and ask the somewhat rhetorical question: "Do they get to compete? Not on your life . . . instead we have kayak rowing Greco-Roman wrestling, you name it" (37:8). Thus, Roger Kahn, whose perceptive commentaries on sport have appeared in publications ranging from *The American Scholar* to *Sports Illustrated,* made a strong plea for the United States to pull out of the Olympics because the games "serve the dictators, the propagandists, the manipulators, but not the U.S." He remembered (as did the historian Sir Arnold Lunn [50]) that the International Olympic Committee awarded the 1936 games to Germany, a gesture which sanctioned Hitler as a "dandy sportsman" and a member of the civilized community. Although believing that "the theory of certain somber sportsmen that World War III will begin at an Olympiad" may be an extreme point of view, Kahn declared that:

> The brutal quality of Olympic events brings out the worst in most nations and the combative in all . . . The Olympic Games are not just merely ludicrous or merely anachronistic . . . Inevitably they become a political tool . . . struggles for national prestige and propaganda . . . We should quit this corruptive mess, this sweaty hypocrisy, before the damage to our spirit becomes irremediable (37:8).

Following the 1968 Olympics, one person in an official United States government and education capacity sounded warnings similar to those of Kahn. In a talk given at a National (DGWS) Sport Leadership Conference for Women, this official delegate to the Olympiad of 1968 presented such information as the following: Traditionally the United States has looked upon summer Olympic competition as a swimming track and field, basketball, and perhaps boxing contest. In Mexico City in 1968, of the 107 medals won by the United States, 86 were in swimming and track and field. Yet, it was very difficult for other countries especially the "emerging nations," to understand why the United States if it is really the great nation it purports to be, did not excel in all areas of competition. They wondered why the government does not "promote" cycling, canoeing, soccer, equestrian events, volleyball, water polo, weight lifting, and wrestling for the political reasons that seem so obvious to many other parts of the world. Even those persons who do understand a system which permits contestants the freedom of choice of events in which to compete and who understand the necessity of athletes having to support themselves while training and competing still told the Americans, with whom they became friendly, that the United States was either very foolish or very blind to the possible implications. They also revealed that many of the countries receiving financial assistance from the United States were using that money to prepare their Olympic and World Championship teams in order to defeat the United States. Furthermore, it was reported that, in at least one country, employees of U.S. governmental agencies who were living and working in that country had to prove their athletic ability before they were given the opportunity to have diplomatic conferences with official government representatives of that nation (55).

Contrary to these warnings, however, are those of observers who have claimed that they preferred a more dignified concept of national honor than either defeat in Olympic competition or refusal to compete with countries which do not subscribe to the political principles of the United States. As one observer argued:

> The notion that we should become dropouts if someone does not do things the way we do them contradicts the democratic spirit (89:9).

Still a larger question appears to be what help or harm do the Olympic Games bring to the free world in general. Visitors to China, for example, reported astounding enthusiasm for sports, yet warned about a drive for athletic supremacy.

> Woe to the world's best athletes when the Chinese sports colossus gets into real stride . . . Red China quit major international competition in 1958, ostensibly in protest over recognition of Nationalist China teams. It may forget its pique when it has enough potential winners to conquer the rest of the world, communist as well as capitalist (79:27, 29).

Perhaps the solution to the present dilemma, or at least a fitting conclusion to this chapter, however tentative, is the idea of the play-element in civilization offered by Huizinga. Concluding that true play knows no propaganda, Huizinga wrote:

> real civilization cannot exist in the absence of a certain play-element . . . To be a sound culture-creating force this play element must be pure . . . It must not be a false seeming, a masking of political purposes behind the illusion of genuine play forms (31:211).

REFERENCES

1. Abernathy, Ruth. "Sociology and Physical Education," *Report,* Western Society for Physical Education of College Women, November, 1962, pp. 29-39.
2. Ackerman, Gordon. "New Passion of a Proud People," *Sports Illustrated,* July 3, 1961, pp. 35-36.
2b. Andreano, Ralph. *No Joy In Mudville.* Cambridge, Massachusetts: Schenkman Publishing Company, 1965.
3. Baker, Russell. "We Were Eyeball to Eyeball With Victory," *Sports Illustrated,* October 11, 1965, pp. 40-41.

4

4. Barber, Red. "Can Baseball Be Saved?" *Reader's Digest,* April, 1969, pp 155-160.
5. Barzun, Jacques. *Science: The Glorious Entertainment.* New York: Harper & Row, 1964.
6. Beisser, Arnold R. *The Madness In Sports.* New York: Appleton-Century Crofts, 1967.
7. Betts, John Richards. "The Technological Revolution and The Rise of Sport 1850-1900." *Mississippi Valley Historical Review,* XL, 1953, pp. 231-256 (Reprinted in Loy and Kenyon, *Sport, Culture, and Society.* New York: The Macmillan Company, 1969, pp. 145-166.)
8. Bloch, Raymond. "The Origins of the Olympic Games," *Scientific American* August, 1968, pp. 79-85.
9. Boyle, Robert H. "Leo's Bums Rap For The Cubs," *Sports Illustrated,* June 30, 1969, pp. 14-19.
10. Boyle, Robert H. *Sport—Mirror of American Life.* Boston: Little, Brown and Company, 1963.
11. Boyle, Robert H. "The Latins Storm Las Grandes Ligas," *Sports Illustrated* August 9, 1965, pp. 24-30.
11b. Brosnan, Jim. "The Fantasy World of Baseball," *Atlantic Monthly,* April 1964, p. 69.
12. Caillois, Roger. *Man, Play, and Games.* New York: The Free Press of Glencoe Inc., 1961.
13. Cantwell, Robert. "Say It Isn't So, Woody," *Sports Illustrated,* September 11 1967, pp. 98-118.
14. Carroll, Joseph. "The Gentle Irish," *Sports Illustrated,* August 28, 1967, pp 40-51.
15. Connery, Donald S. "Tokyo Changes Face For Asia's First Olympics," *Sport Illustrated,* May 8, 1961.
16. Connery, Donald S. "Yank In Japan," *Sports Illustrated,* June 25, 1962, pp 60-73.
17. Conrad, Barnaby. "Homage to a Peerless Matador," *Sports Illustrated,* August 1, 1966, pp. 44-52.
18. Conroy, Frank. "My Generation," *Esquire,* October, 1968, pp. 124-126.
19. Cooley, Charles H. *Social Organization.* New York: Charles Scribner's Sons 1920.
20. Cozens, Frederick W., and Stumpf, Florence. "American Sports From The Sidelines," *Journal of Health, Physical Education, and Recreation,* November 1952, pp. 12-13, 56-57.
20b. Cratty, Bryant J. *Psychology and Physical Activity.* Englewood Cliffs, New Jersey: Prentice-Hall, Inc., 1968.
21. Deford, Frank. "A Man To Lead The Pros Out of Darkness," *Sports Illustrated* June 20, 1966, pp. 58-62.
22. Deford, Frank. "The Reign In Spain of King Manolo," *Sports Illustrated* July 3, 1967, pp. 26-29.
23. Dichter, Ernest. "Should You Be A Fan?" A Uniroyal Advertisement, *The Reader's Digest,* May, 1968, pp. 158-160.
23b. Dodson, Dan W. "The Integration of Negroes In Baseball," *Journal of Educational Sociology,* Vol. 28, October, 1954, pp. 73-82.
24. Durslag, Melvin. "TV Turns To The Boys In The Underwear," *TV Guide,* July 5-11, 1969, pp. 30-31.
24b. Durslag, Melvin. "From Back Alleys to Ballrooms," *TV Guide,* January 24 1970, pp. 20-21.
25. Exley, Frederick. *A Fan's Notes.* New York: Harper & Row, 1968.
26. Fitzgerald, F. Scott. "My Generation," *Esquire,* October, 1968, pp. 119-121.
27. Glick, Shav. "Ivory Floats Into Stardom," *The Denver Post (Los Angeles Times),* July 17, 1969, p. F62.
28. Graham, Jim. "Jackie, Feller In Fiery Duel," *The Denver Post (Los Angeles Times),* July 23, 1969, p. 37.

29. Griggs, Lee. "Frantic Lunge Into Sport," (photographs by Larry Burrows), *Life*, September 11, 1964, pp. 34-42.
30. Heilman, Barbara. "Farewell to Shannon Brown," *Sports Illustrated*, April 3, 1969, pp. 70-82.
31. Huizinga, Johan. *Homo Ludens: A Study of the Play-Element In Culture.* Boston: The Beacon Press, 1950.
32. Jenkins, Dan. "O.K., Everybody: Beat America," *Sports Illustrated*, July 26, 1965, pp. 12-17.
33. Jenkins, Dan. "Stop the World, the U.S. Is On," *Sports Illustrated*, May 2, 1966, pp. 26-29.
34. Jenkins, Dan. "This Year the Fight Will be In The Open," *Sports Illustrated*, September 11, 1967, pp. 28-34.
35. Johnson, William. "Collision On The New Underground Railroad," *Sports Illustrated*, February 12, 1968, pp. 52-53.
36. *Journal of Physical Education.* Yellowstone, Ohio: Physical Education Society of the YMCA's of North America, January-February, 1969.
37. Kahn, Roger. "Let's Pull Out Of The Olympics," *Saturday Evening Post*, October 10, 1964, pp. 8-10.
38. Kane, Martin. "A Very Welcome Redcoat," *Sports Illustrated*, December 19, 1966, pp. 79-82.
39. Kane, Martin. "Olympic Roman Holiday," *Sports Illustrated*, August 15, 1960, pp. 14-16, 33.
40. Kenyon, Gerald S. (editor). *Aspects of Contemporary Sport Sociology.* Proceedings of C.I.C. Symposium on the Sociology of Sport, University of Wisconsin, 1968. Chicago: The Athletic Institute, 1969.
40b. Kenyon, Gerald S., and Grogg, Tom M. (editors). *Contemporary Psychology of Sport.* Proceedings of Second International Congress of Sport Psychology, Washington, D.C., 1968. Chicago: The Athletic Institute, 1970.
41. Kenyon, Gerald S., and Loy, John W., Jr. "Toward A Sociology of Sport," *Journal of Health, Physical Education, and Recreation*, May, 1965, pp. 24-25, 68-69.
42. Kraus, Richard. "Race and Sports, the Challenge to Public Recreation," *Journal of Health, Physical Education, and Recreation*, April, 1969, pp. 32-34.
43. *Life*, "The Russians Lose a Pair and set off 100,000 Czechs," April 11, 1969, pp. 93-94.
44. *Life World Library: Brazil* (Chapter 8, pp. 113-125, "A Changing Social Scene"). New York: Time Incorporated, 1967.
45. *Look*, Interviews by Gerald Astor. "The Black and White Cowboys," January 7, 1969, p. 83.
46. *Look*, Gerald Astor (photographs by Bob Lerner). "The Rangers Go Boom," February 4, 1969, pp. 80-82.
47. Lorenz, Konrad. *On Aggression* (translated by Marjorie Kerr Wilson). New York: Harcourt, Brace and World, Inc., 1966.
48. Loy, John W., Jr., and Kenyon, Gerald S. (editors). *Sport, Culture, and Society.* Toronto: The Macmillan Company, 1969.
48b. Loy, John W., Jr. "The Study of Sport and Social Mobility," *Aspects of Contemporary Sport Sociology*, Gerald S. Kenyon (editor), Proceedings of C.I.C. Symposium on the Sociology of Sport, University of Wisconsin, 1968. Chicago: The Athletic Institute, 1969, pp. 101-119.
49. Lunn, Sir Arnold. *A History of Skiing.* London: Eyre and Spottiswoode, 1952.
50. Lunn, Sir Arnold. "Sport In Politics," *Quest*, Monograph I, December, 1963, pp. 33-36.
51. Lüschen, Günther. "The Interdependence of Sport and Culture," Paper presented at the National AAHPER Meeting, 1967.
52. MacArthur, Douglas. "Athletic America," Excerpts from a *Report to President Coolidge on American Participation in the Ninth Olympic Games.* Amsterdam, August 22, 1928.

53. Mashin, Yuri. "Athletes By The Millions," *Soviet Life*, 1706 18th Stree N.W. Washington, D.C., 1966, pp. 58-60.
54. McIntosh, Peter C. *Sport In Society*. London: C. A. Watts Company, 196
55. Merrick, Roswell. "The Sports Continuum," A Panel Discussion presented the National Conference of the Division for Girls and Women's Sports, Est Park, Colorado, June 21-27, 1969.
56. Moss, Irv. "Mat Tourney Was Worth It," *The Denver Post*, July 23, 196 p. 39.
57. Mulvoy, Mark. "If You Love Me Tell Me So," *Sports Illustrated*, February 2 1968, pp. 28-32.
58. Myslenski, Skip. "The Woes of Wee Willie Wisp," *Sports Illustrated*, Marc 17, 1969, pp. 42-49.
59. Natan, Alex. *Sport and Society*. London: Bowes & Bowes Ltd., 1958.
60. *Newsweek*, "The Solo Breed," March 31, 1969, p. 86.
61. Olsen, Jack. "The Black Athlete: A Shameful Story," *Sports Illustrated*, Ju 1, 8, 15, 22, 29, 1968.
62. Ottum, Bob. "And The Melody Lingers On," *Sports Illustrated*, August 1 1967, pp. 18-21.
62b. Owens, Jesse, and Neimark, Paul G. *Blackthink: My Life As Black Man ar White Man*. New York: William Morrow & Co., Inc., 1970.
63. Porter, Carl. *The Tucson Daily Citizen*, February 19, 1969, p. 29.
64. Reed, William. "A Would-be Dunker With Soul," *Sports Illustrated*, Janua 6, 1969, pp. 40-41.
65. Ress, Paul Evan. "Yankee Dandies on the Danube," *Sports Illustrated*, Se tember 6, 1965, pp. 20-21.
66. Riesman, David, and Denney, Reuel. "Football In America: A Study In Cultu Diffusion," *American Quarterly*, 3:309-319, 1951.
66b. Robinson, Wilhelmena S. *International Library of Negro Life and Histor Historical Negro Biographies*. New York: Publishers Company, Inc., 196
67. Russell, Bill, with Tex Maule. "I Am Not Worried About Ali," *Sports Ill strated*, June 19, 1967, pp. 19-21.
67b. Sage, George H. *Sport and American Society: Selected Readings*. Readin Massachusetts: Addison-Wesley Publishing Company, 1970.
68. *Salt Lake Tribune* (from New York AP), "Wet Eyes at Yankee Stadium June 9, 1969, p. 21.
69. *Salt Lake Tribune* (Louisville, Ky. AP), "Negro Cager Signs to Play at Ke tucky," June 10, 1969, p. C3.
70. *Salt Lake Tribune*, June 16, 1969.
71. Sanders, Jacquin. "Bart Starr: Nice Guy Finishes First," *Reader's Dige September, 1968, pp. 87-91.
72. Shane, Ted. "The World's Most Popular Game" (condensed from *La Prensa The Reader's Digest*, March, 1951, pp. 109-111.
73. Slusher, Howard S. *Man, Sport, And Existence*. Philadelphia: Lea & Febige 1967.
74. Snell, David. "Dateline America—All-Pro Miniconglomerate," *Life*, May 2 1969, pp. 85-86.
75. *Sport Annual*, produced by *Sport* magazine, "American Boxers Do Well 1969, p. 66.
76. *Sports Illustrated*, "A Week The World Comes to Augusta," April 10, 196 pp. 44-49.
77. *Sports Illustrated*, "Africa: Sport In The Emerging Nations," (photographs Jay Maisel and Marvin E. Newman), December 19, 1966, pp. 56-58.
78. *Sports Illustrated*, "The Black Athlete: An Editorial," August 5, 1968, p.
79. *Sports Illustrated*, "By The Numbers Red China Gets Into Shape," June 1 1961, pp. 26-31.
80. *Sports Illustrated*, "Editorial: Why Not Wave the Flag," August 15, 196 p. 12.
81. *Sports Illustrated*, "Memo From The Publisher," October 20, 1958, p. 4.

82. *Sports Illustrated*, "19th Hole," October 4, 1965, p. 98.
83. *Sports Illustrated*, "People," April 22, 1968, p. 50.
84. *Sports Illustrated*, "Scorecard," October 3, 1966, p. 14.
85. *Sports Illustrated*, "Scorecard," March 27, 1967, p. 8.
86. *Sports Illustrated*, "Scorecard," November 13, 1967, p. 12.
87. *Sports Illustrated*, "Scorecard," February 5, 1968, p. 9.
88. *Sports Illustrated*, "Scorecard," February 19, 1968, p. 10.
89. *Sports Illustrated*, "Scorecard," February 26, 1968, p. 9.
90. *Sports Illustrated*, "Scorecard," September 2, 1968, p. 8.
91. *Sports Illustrated*, "Scorecard," April 28, 1969, p. 7.
92. *Sports Illustrated*, "Scorecard," June 16, 1969, p. 10.
93. *Sports Illustrated*, "Scorecard," August 11, 1969, p. 8.
94. *Sports Illustrated*, "They Said It," March 17, 1969, p. 14.
94b. *Sports Illustrated*, "In Black and White," February 19, 1968, p. 10.
95. Stone, Gregory P. "American Sports: Play and Dis-Play," *Chicago Review*, University of Chicago Press, Fall, 1955, pp. 83-100.
96. Stone, Gregory P. "Some Meanings of American Sport," *60th Annual Proceedings*, College Physical Education Association, 1957, pp. 6-19.
97. Teague, Bob. *Letters to a Black Boy.* New York: Walker & Company, 1968. (from excerpts appearing in *Redbook*, January 1969, pp. 55-62.)
98. *Time*, "On The Difficulty of Being A Contemporary Hero," June 24, 1966, pp. 32-33.
99. *Time*, January 17, 1969, p. 58.
99b. *Time*, "Blacks on the Green," February 14, 1969, p. 56.
00. *Time*, "Au Jeu," April 25, 1969, p. 56.
00b. *Time*, "The Little Team That Can," September 5, 1969, pp. 49-53.
00c. Tobin, Richard L. "Sports as an Integrator," *Saturday Review*, January 21, 1967, p. 32.
01. Ulrich, Celeste. *The Social Matrix of Physical Education.* Englewood Cliffs, New Jersey: Prentice-Hall, Inc., 1968.
02. Underwood, John. "The Winning Ways of Winnipeg," *Sports Illustrated*, August 7, 1967, pp. 20-25.
03. Von Zahn, Peter. "The Busy Search For Leisure," Chapter 6, *Life World Library, The United States.* New York: Time Incorporated, 1965, pp. 113-131.
04. Ward-Thomas, Pat. "Around The World In 80-Strokes," The Professional Golfers' Association *Book of Golf*, 1968, p. 27.
04b. Weinberg, S. K., and Arond, H. "The Occupational Culture of the Boxer," *American Journal of Sociology*, March, 57:460-469, 1952.
05. Wind, Herbert Warren. "Mucho Bueno From São Paulo," *Sports Illustrated*, September 5, 1960, pp. 32, 64.
06. Wind, Herbert Warren. "Over the Rainbow," *Sports Illustrated*, May 16, 1960, pp. 84-97.
07. Young, Andrew S. *Negro Firsts in Sports.* Chicago: Johnson Publishing Company, 1963.

PART III

Sport is Cultural

*"The cultural pattern of any civilization makes use of . . .
the great arc of potential human purposes and motivations."*

— — —RUTH BENEDICT

The works of René Maheu and Günther Lüschen, among others whose
works were cited in Part I and Part II, provide cogent observations
and suggest hypotheses either tested or worthy of testing regarding
the relationship of sport and culture. Maheu, although suggesting that
there were few cultural works with sport as their basis, related and
attempted to elevate sport to all cultural pursuits which spring from
the same source, that of leisure. Lüschen proposed that sport be described
as an activity in interaction with the organic, personality, social, and
cultural systems. He added, however, that the relationships of sport to
"higher" culture are weak.

Apparently this viewpoint may be shared, at least in part, by some
surveyors of the contemporary cultural scene. For example, in a special
issue of *Harper's Bazaar: Comment On Culture U.S.A.*, this country was
regarded as having produced "not one culture, but a multiplicity." Yet,
in such an assessment, in which a "hooked rug is culture," as is The
Jefferson Airplane and *Hair*, and in which culture may be equated with
money ("Americans are spending five billion dollars a year getting
cultured"), one might expect to find sport to be among the listings. Sport,
however, was conspicuously absent in that report. Perhaps it was not
considered to meet the definition of culture that was provided from
Webster—"the enlightenment and refinement of taste acquired by intellectual and aesthetic training" (17:2).

Among the views countervailing the idea that sport is opposite the

87

intellectual life, however, is one by John McCormick, a professor of comparative literature at Rutgers University. Assessing the sweep of events on today's college campuses, he asserted that "the question of sport versus the intellectual life does not arise anymore." He sensed the changed attitude toward sport by a large variegated public from such evidence as the wider selection of people attending sport events today, the use of sport in such serious dramatic works as *The Great White Hope,* the play which explores basic attitudes toward sport and society, and in it the welcome addition to dinner party discussions ("it is now possible to talk not only shop, gossip, politics and war, but also sport"). One may conclude with McCormick, therefore, that it is "safe to say that we are seeing the coming of age of sport within the framework of our society" (36:46-59).

Or, one may conclude that, if the "artist in every field is the spokesman for this intellectual elite," as *Harper's* report put it, some communication surely must be regarded as stemming from the domain of sport. The National Art Museum of Sport in New York's Madison Square Garden is dedicated to the proposition that there is a close relationship between sport and the arts. The fact that these exhibits have received widespread viewing throughout the United States and Canada demonstrates that sport is a vehicle of communication (20). But, sport itself does have another language, however silent, that stops people and has them listening. And, if one listens carefully he will find words of expression that belong to the most eloquent literature of any culture—words such as beauty, the aesthetic experience, imagination, freedom, self-expression, creativity. As for the relationship between culture and civilization itself, one may subscribe to the notion of Nikos Kazantzakis, author of *Zorba the Greek,* that "civilization begins at the moment sport begins."

Nor can one deny the significance of sport in transforming the American industrial and entertainment world. Although explanations as to the "why" of it may be missing, there is the compelling fact that the great outpouring of people and money at numerous sport events is in numerical figures which other cultural events do not approach, to say nothing of those various social phenomena such as parties, reunions and the like which surround such events. Then, too, there are those spotlighted and exclusive subcultures (boxers, skiers, surfers, youth—to name a few) who similarly offer a rich bonanza for art, literature, photography, and the business and entertainment world. One such subculture which is a facet of the larger general culture—the subculture of women—may indeed be considered as flourishing or floundering in emancipation on the sport scene.

The sections which follow, therefore, are based on the postulation that sport is not in a vacuum removed from culture—higher or lower—

but that it is part of the parcel called culture, and that as such, it has not only developed within the culture but also has helped to shape such facets of culture as literature, the arts, entertainment, and the *raison d'être* of some subcultural groups.

No attempt is made to examine the history or influence of the prominent social institutions on sport. For such literature and for that on ethnic cultures and comparative perspectives, one may wish to consult the excellent source of material provided by Loy and Kenyon (31). The examples provided in the ensuing sections are once again only illustrative of those appearing in current popular literature for the most part and are not intended to be all-inclusive.

CHAPTER 6

Sport and the Arts

René Maheu, although declaring that sport has inspired few works of merit in the arts—the theatre, literature, the plastic arts—regarded sport as a parallel and comparable phenomenon to culture in that, like the arts, sport has its origin in leisure, the audience is involved in its drama, and it is a creator of myths and of beauty (33). Günther Lüschen stated that "one can hardly deny that sport indeed has some impact on 'higher' culture, as may be shown by symbolic elements from sport to be found in script and language," although he added that the appearance of sport in communication media, language, poetry and the arts tells us little about the interdependence of sport with general culture (32:3).

Long ago Plato declared that "God, I should say, has given men the two arts, music and gymnastic. Only incidentally do they serve soul and body. Their purpose is to tune these two elements into harmony with one another by slackening or tightening, till the proper pitch be reached" (37).

The presence of sport, both in the arts and as an art, is the theme of the ensuing section; wherein, one may find that sport inspires a lyric, a picture, a satirical parody, a poem or a single word, and it may, as Plato stated, tune the two elements of the soul, "the spirited and the philosophic," as man finds in it a fundamental form of human expression.

SPORT IN ART FORMS

Sculpture and Painting

The human figure in sport has long served as subject matter for the sculptor and painter. The Olympic Games of ancient Greece inspired some of the best artists of the time and enabled them to record a moment for the pages of history.

Like a sculptor of ancient Hellas, R. Tait McKenzie, an athlete, surgeon and artist of world-wide fame, has exerted a wide and lasting appeal on sport and art within modern times by his athletic sculptures. His *Masks of Expression* displayed scientifically the facial reactions of violent *effort, breathlessness, fatigue,* and *exhaustion.* His figures *The Sprinter, The Athlete, The Competitor, The Supple Juggler, The Relay, The Boxer* (to name only a few), and his relief plaques such as *The Joy of Effort* at once achieved artistic success and became a living testimony of the beauty of the human form (21).

The recently developed National Art Museum of Sport also displays some of the sport figures of outstanding sculptors. Among such works are *Athlete,* a bronze by Auguste Rodin, and *Bob Cousy in Action,* a bronze by Stanley Martineau (20). The American Association for Health, Physical Education, and Recreation has produced an interpretive film-strip, *Art and Sport,* which illuminated the bond between the two. Among the more than 50 color slides or art works depicting athletes and sport activities are the 2,000-year-old Greek amphora decorated with sport scenes, Andrew Wyeth's *The Hunter,* Winslow Homer's *Skating in Central Park,* and R. Tait McKenzie's *The Plunger.*

Geometrically conceived figurative sculptures, however, as Gene Logan pointed out, "offer little in terms of expression of movement" (30:44). With regard to the attempt to depict movement, the twentieth century has introduced marked changes; and, sportive activity has been used as one of the vehicles to deliver a graphic message of movement or to construct a new visual form which attracts attention. One example may be found in the works of Leo Jensen, an avant-garde sculptor who also has been a rodeo performer and high school football, baseball, and track star. Sport is one of the recurrent themes of his works of art which are also said to "do something" and to have become "the darling of the sophisticates." Some of his works were: *The Lure of the Turf, The Zipster* (auto racing), *Football Machine, King of Clubs* (boxing), *Champions' Choice* (baseball and breakfast food) (65:7-8).

In painting more than 40 years ago, Picasso made artful use of distortion to convey a feeling of movement. Of his painting, *The Race,* one writer said:

> The arms and legs whip out like banners in the wind, the breasts float free as if helium-filled and the necks are stretched so the racers can drink of sunlight. The sense of buoyant speed is so powerful that we half expect the girls will run off the canvas (28:20).

Picasso's runner in the painting, *By the Sea,* the writer described as "charged with power and strength, as if she were a sister to the cranelik player winding up for the pitch" (28:20).

Sometimes the painter may use sport and the movement of the body to construct a new visual form which attracts attention, intensifies a idea, or which visibly transmits to the world the anxieties of the times. Picasso, in this connection, was an expert in what one writer called "the iconography of anguish." His painting of welterweight Kid Gavilan getting his jaw mashed in by Sugar Ray Robinson in 1948 gave a "visceral shock."

> The wrench of stress and violence that cry out in the face of Gavilan . . . depict the outward states of woe and the inward states of mind behind the woe (28:22).

Similar impressions of the force, speed, and energy of movement, as well as the excitement and emotion of the event, are to be found in the paintings of artists whose works have been commissioned by *Sports Illustrated*. Bob Stanley did a portfolio of paintings of the Indianapolis 500 car race. Stanley included on his canvases glimpses of racers in battle, the mechanical splatter of a smashup, and the means by which drivers and pit men communicate in the attempt to "find a maximum emotion in stark color and economy of form" (60:74-78). These scenes from the Indianapolis 500 continue to be shown as paintings in private homes and museums. Stanley also did a series of paintings about ice hockey in which he depicted the contrast between "the coldness, the transparency of the ice and the heated human conflict above it" (64: 42-47).

Artist Bernie Fuchs also did a portfolio on the Indianapolis 500 as well as the Masters and the U.S. Open Golf tournaments and baseball. His paintings of the U.S. Open, entitled "A Horror to Play In But Great to Watch," portrayed some of its difficulties as well as its theatrics (54: 32-37). Fuchs recorded in paintings baseball's "3 and 2" situation (bases loaded, two men out and a full count on the batter), which he considered to be baseball's most dramatic moment (84:42-48). Fuchs' paintings of tennis tournament play provided an aesthetic look at the changing spectrum of strategy, strokes, and style (72:30-35).

The more ordinary life (the towns, motels, the dull gray look of dressing rooms and lockers) behind the dazzling existence of the big men who play basketball appeared in paintings by Cliff Condak (57: 40-45). And the men who play professional football, and the thunder of their conflict on the field were brought to life in close-up color paintings by Bob Peak. These paintings revealed football as "a ballet of bulky elephants—bruising, yet curiously graceful and always expressively serious" (77:36-45).

Paintings of crew by Harvey Schmidt were intended to express meanings of the word "cadence" to the oarsman and the layman (74: 42-50). Glimpses of spring and players captured in watercolors, by Robert Andrew Parker, reflected the hopeful mood of the Masters Golf Tournament (70:28-35).

Artist Jim Jonson, a sometime vaulter and hurdler himself, looked "beneath the mechanical perfection of the track and field athlete" to find determination, fury and even fear in the man. His paintings expressed, in semiabstract style, "the unique marriage of dynamic motion and emotion that only such fierce competition can produce" (59:48-55).

The din, color and mood of track were also captured on canvas by artist Jerome Martin. His paintings showed the hurdler "hampered by a heavily bandaged thigh," shotputters "with ponderous dignity, like elephants," a pole vaulter who "stares up into the endlessness of height." Everything was pictured as "smaller, closer, more intense . . . more violence . . . brassy, circuslike atmosphere . . . the action is continuous" (75:34-39).

Other gifted artists have used sport as subject matter to express satirical ideas about mankind and the unpredictable, funny circumstances in which man finds himself. Again, *Sports Illustrated* has commissioned such artists to put their impressions on canvas. One such example is the satirist André François, a Frenchman, known for his posters, cartoons and caricatures and his "sharply pointed style and uninhibited palette." François did several paintings called "A Wry Glimpse of Wimbledon," about the tennis championships held there each year (56:28-32). In similar style he also captured the bold lines and flashing colors of hockey (78:32-37). Another is Jean-Jacques Sempé, who did several cartoon essays on professional bicycle racing and skiing (55:38-43). Artist Ronald Searle took a distinctive look at baseball's spring training in Arizona and California in paintings depicting the leisurely pace and easy living, the autograph hounds and the fans reaching for a foul ball "which looks as good in March as in July" (63:16-23).

Photography

Perhaps one needs only to be reminded that the first commercial motion picture ever shown on a screen was a six-round boxing bout in May, 1895 to realize that photographers, ever since the inception of this art, have found a constant challenge in the beauty, motion and emotion that sport generates. In fact, prior to that time, in 1872 Eadweard Muybridge made the first successful attempt "to secure an illusion of motion by photography" when he photographed the movements of a trotting horse, thereby proving that at one point in its gait all four hooves of the horse were off the ground (3:160-161). Since that time a host of experimenters and photographers have developed techniques of photography by means of sport and in order to illustrate sport, and, with the simplest of commentary have managed to expose the creative approach underlying successful sport performance.

Sometimes the pictorial account of a champion or an event, or the superior dramatic action of the game is its own spectacle. *The Spectacle of Sport,* composed entirely of photographs and articles which appeared originally in *Sports Illustrated,* offers a most striking presentation of color photographs of the very essence of sport this magazine has celebrated (90). One book published as an international record of the Olympic Games, first produced at the time of the Tokyo Olympiad, includes photographs of performances, drawings, and the written record of some of the world's greatest sports writers.

On other occasions, photographers interpret a given sport as their own imaginations dictate by telling a story with visual images. Like the painter, the photographer may deliver a graphic message through the artful use of distorted images. Freakish shapes of a runner and the exaggerated wind-up of a pitcher in order to give the viewer a vivid sensation of speed and energy have become standard photography fare. A few examples may serve to direct the reader's attention to the numerous techniques used to develop rich, rare, expressive pictures.

"Solarization of color," a process of taking color film, reexposing it and getting a negative image, fogging it with color filters and gelatins and then continuing the normal developing process was used imaginatively by John G. Zimmerman to produce a new way of photographing baseball and to reproduce in an almost psychedelic manner the mood and fire of the game (69:26-31). The arc of a curved putt etched in a morning dew, the exploding earth from a deep-grooved-wedge pitch shot, the magnified magic moment as a ball is teed up offered Art Kane the subjects for photographs of "the pristine joys of golf" (81:30-38).

Photographers may ingeniously mount cameras on the performer and on his equipment, or they may themselves become involved in dangerous and uncomfortable situations in an effort to provide a jolting, sharp awareness of the action in sport. For example, John G. Zimmerman satisfied both the impulses of being a participant in the sport and a photographer of the action. He strapped cameras to skiers' legs, chest or back and tripped the shutter with a remote-control button as they hurdled down the slopes. The result was a dramatic portfolio of photographs that show how it feels to ski a steep mountain (61:44-51). Another portfolio showed the perils of skiing in deep powder snow (79:52-60).

Through the miracles of photography an otherwise transient skill or a feeling may be frozen in a moment of time forever. Photographs of lacrosse by Arthur Rickerby which appeared in *Life* were said to have captured "with all the elegant savagery of an Indian war dance" the thunder, hard knocks, and skillful stick work of the game (29:49-56). The turmoil and beauty created by the swimmer were re-created in photographs taken by Coles Phinizy and Jerry Cooke for *Sports Illustrated*. They provided a unique look at both of the competitive swimmer's worlds—above and below the surface (83:24-33). Photographs by Zimmerman captured forever the movement in time of the flashy acrobatics and shiny trail of the water skier (68:56-63).

In "The Longest 90 Feet in Baseball," the race to the bases between man and ball was viewed in an unusual manner and from interesting angles in photographs by Neil Leiffer (76:32-36). The race against the ball had also provided a theme for the skills of photography in an earlier portfolio (82:28-37).

Design and Architecture

Sporting goods designing and the architecture of sport facilities have become a kind of art form. Even the paraphernalia of sport tends to be described in aesthetic terms—the clean grace of a sailboat, the delicate balance of a tennis racket and so forth. The Museum of Modern Art, which spent a year examining the artifacts of sport, considered a baseball "beautiful even on the shelf."

> Every handsome element of a baseball's design is there for a reason. Nothing is extraneous. Everything works . . . A ball is one of sport's simplest expressions of the form-follows-function credo (53:47).

In the above article, Fred R. Smith pointed out that "the pursuit of excellence has a refining influence on the equipment of sport as well as on men." This relationship between the potential in a piece of equipment and the potential in the performer "is a very close and personal one, indeed more personal than that of a consumer to a product in any other field." Arthur Drexler of the Museum of Modern Art stated that the best designs for sport also display a second important attribute, "the mark of a designer's individual taste;" and a third, less tangible force also motivates good design in sport:

> It embodies a classical concept of the Greeks—that winning the race is not so important as running it well (53:47).

Sport clothes, too, have become part of the mosaic of modern art forms. Mike Micheli of Milwaukee, for example, who calls his firm Motivational Design, designed basketball uniforms with broad bands of bold color "which are consonant with power basketball . . . match the pace of the game . . . move an audience" (67:13).

Sport facilities have opened up a vast and ever new realm of artistic activity for architects. The plush elegance of the Houston Astrodome, the fourth Madison Square Garden (the first was built in 1874) rising from New York's old Pennsylvania Station, the Spectrum in Philadelphia, the Forum in Los Angeles, to name only a few of the indoor stadiums constructed in the past few years, testify to the fact that architects and builders alike have been challenged to create works of art as well as to solve problems that range from "indoor smog to the fact that ladies' heels often become clenched in the teeth of escalators" (58:36). Some of the stadium structures of the 1960's, although they are still disliked by some fans, were described and pictured in one article as architectural wonders:

> Round as circus tents or shaped like amoebas, America's newest palaces of sport boast symmetrical baseball fields, mighty candlepower and cantilevered upper decks that remove the need for view-blocking pillars . . . already rich with memories of great catches, key hits and gobbled hot dogs (71:30).

Whatever the future may hold regarding use, convenience, and cost of such super stadia, the creative architecture found in sport seems not only to reflect the times but to inspire architectural ideas and guidelines for use in developing other public and private structures (51b).

Golf course architects are also finding as one article title stated, "New Twists for an Old Art." Golf architect Desmond Muirhead declared:

> Architects are going to have to be familiar with the great paintings and sculptures. They will have to learn, through art, to solve the problems of the site and create something imaginative (5:52-53).

One example describing part of the demanding and elaborate work of golf course architecture may be illustrative. The publishers of *Sports Illustrated*, with the idea in mind that "golfers are forever talking about tactics—how to handle this tree, that bunker, this swale, that mound— all things that dictate how they play a hole," decided to build what amounted to a sand table for the four crucial holes at the Olympic Country Club in New York. Completion of this project required the efforts and talents of aerial mapping photographers, topography experts, golf pro Ken Venturi, art director Richard Gangel, and artist Asdur Takakjian. Takakjian (himself not a golfer) made multicolored four-foot dimensional models which he and Gangel gradually stylized down to essentials and from which Takakjian constructed the final models pictured in *Sports Illustrated* (88).

The preceding sections have brought together as many examples as appeared necessary to make the point that sport is used by and in other art forms. These illustrations do not exhaust the examples available— the exhibitions that link sport and art, the private and public collections, and so forth. In fact, at the time of this writing *The Athletic Institute* was preparing three different loop films on selected sports in art pictures. The reader's thoughts may lead him to further illustrations.

Literature

The natural inquiry into the relationship between sport and art might well be expected to be addressed to the arts of sculpture, painting, photography, design, and architecture. As Plotinus declared, "Beauty addresses itself chiefly to sight," but he also acknowledged the beauty in certain combinations of words. In the following section, therefore, consideration is given to some of the literature of sport on the premise that the end of this art, too, is to extend imagination and feeling. At any rate, it may be said that the circumstance of sport has contributed to the general character of a work whether it be poetic or merely expository in nature.

The development of interest in sport literature and the impact of the technological revolution on the expansion of sport publications is authoritatively chronicled in various sources. Percy Knauth took the tradition of sport literature back at least 2,500 years in describing how a Greek historian (Xenophon), a Holy Roman Emperor (Frederich II), a French count (Gaston de Foix), and an English duke (Edward Plantagenet) shaped the art of writing about sport (25:34-43). John Richard Betts pointed to the enlarged format and greater circulation achieved in early America by numerous inventions which revolutionized the printing process. In the 1800's sport fiction writers appeared on the scene and some of their adventurous tales not only helped them achieve literary reputations but did much to extend enthusiasm for sport. Notable among such works, as listed by Betts, were: Mark Sibley Severance (*Hammer-Smith: His Harvard Days*), Noah Brooks (*Our Baseball Club*), Thomas Hughes' English classics (*Tom Brown at Rugby* and *Tom Brown at Oxford*), and of course the "voluminous outpouring" of Gilbert Patten's Frank Merriwell's heroic sporting achievements (3:155). Robert H. Boyle's chronicle, *The Bizarre History of American Sport,* notes that William T. Porter began publishing the sports sheet, "Spirit of the Times," and employed Henry William Herbert who, using the pen name of Frank Forester, became the first writer in America to earn a living writing about horses and hunting (4:54-63).

Percy H. Tannenbaum and James E. Noah, in their article "Sportugese: A Study of Sports Page Communication," as presented in Loy and Kenyon, discussed the "slightly tarnished silver age of sports writing" that arose in the twenties, which spawned contemporary sport language (86:327-336). Whether or not this *"patois—'Sportugese',"* as Tannenbaum and Noah called it, is an integral part of the sportswriter's "kit-bag," apparently the writer of today, like the artist and photographer, uses sport both as a media to express his literary talent and to portray the temper of the times in which he lives. Many of these writings not only combine literary quality with a sound knowledge of sport, but provide clinically penetrating insights into why people participate in sports or watch them. Eric Berne even views people's behavior, as his book title shows, as *Games People Play* (2). A number of essays, research studies, and books stemming from the psychosocial aspect of sport has been cited elsewhere in this book. No further attempt will be made in this chapter to describe this substantial literary subject matter. Rather, the following section is intended to give a brief overview of the sport literature that has come from the pens and minds of those contemporary writers who have varied experience as sports participants, news reporters, journalists, and novelists.

Since one of the pleasures of sport literature is to be found in the savor it gives to magazines and newspapers, a brief aside is made to these sources. How many millions of people read the daily sport pages of their newspapers is difficult to ascertain. The fact that the sport pages occupy a large and separate section of every paper obviously attests to reader interest. And, one-tenth of the *World Almanac* is devoted to sport, a greater volume than is devoted to other areas of cultural interest such as politics, science, or business. When *Sports Illustrated* started publishing in 1954, its circulation was 450,000. In May, 1967, circulation hit one and a quarter million and conservative estimates at that time for 1968 were reported to be 1,450,000. When Rick Mount appeared on the cover of one issue, 7,300 newsstand copies were sold in Lebanon, Indiana alone—where the population was 9,523 at the time. Bob Cowin, circulation director, recalled that:

> most people in the business predicted *Sports Illustrated* would be a flop. There was a feeling that interest in sport was only expressed in areas of individual preference, and that anything else—a larger umbrella—just wouldn't work (62:4).

The authors of this book, having depended heavily upon *Sports Illustrated*, can attest to the fact that at most newsstands the magazine was sold out on the day it arrived. Perhaps history will suggest an important part of the answer for the growing reader interest in sport literature. No doubt John McCormick's conclusion that sport is attaining a rightful place within the framework of society will be a part of that answer. At any rate, one may be inclined to concur with McCormick's statement:

> People who once faulted Hemingway for writing about baseball in *The Old Man and the Sea* may still fault him, but not on that ground. Ring Lardner's baseball stories are held in new esteem, while Bernard Malamud's *The Natural* is over-praised simply because it deals with baseball (36:55).

Meanwhile, the task of this section is to chronicle some of the sport literature which appears to be part of the contemporary art forms, and which in turn has provided writers with at least a part of their reputations.

Sportswriters. Among those who have made their reputations as sportswriters are such household names as Grantland Rice, Red Barber, Paul Gallico, Red Smith, and the eminently readable Jim Murray, who, believing that sport "has its entire poke riding on journalism," stated clearly that in a large sense sport heroes "live off the talents of a long line of skilled story-tellers." Nonetheless, Murray declared:

> There is a story in every man . . . No one cares what you and I have for breakfast. But what Mickey Mantle has for breakfast moves on the A wire (39:xiii).

With an irrepressible and provocative humor in the "exaggerated idiom of Ring and John Lardner," Murray jabs Little League baseball as a "tribal ritual," the pro football habit he calls "about as exciting as twin beds," the racetrack crowd is "the greatest floating fund of misinformation this side of the pages of *Pravda*," and baseball is not a sport anymore, "it's a multiplication table with base lines."

Red Barber, one of the well-known sport announcers, is the author of *The Rhubarb Patch* and *Rhubarb In the Catbird Seat* (with Robert Creamer) (1). The phrase "catbird seat," which means in a position of advantage, is part of Barber's contribution to the special lingo of baseball. George Plimpton expanded his series of articles for *Sports Illustrated* into the best-selling book, *Paper Lion*, which is an account of his excruciating experiences as an amateur NFL quarterback (44). After his football fling and despite an 18 handicap he pitted himself against big-time golfers and, in the book *The Bogey Man* wrote, once again in an amusing yet poignant tone, of his travails as a golfer, the big swingers and caddies in the world of golf (45).

Baseball Lingo, edited by Zander Hollander, sportswriter, author of *Yankee Batboy* and co-author of *The Home Run Story*, happens to be another amusing book worthy of attention in this listing because it expressed much of the lore of baseball in terms unique to the sport. In it, cartoonist Jerry Schlamp added his own graphic definitions of baseball's special lingo (18).

Still other writers gather and chronicle the technical facts of sport which are of particular interest to and cherished by those who may be described as "superfans" or "genuine nuts." Some of these writings are enriched with a detail and color of sport not found elsewhere. Among some of the most recent writings of this type are: James O. Dunaway's *The Four Minute Mile 1954-1967*, a compilation of all the statistical milestones in track's "showcase event," the sub-four-minute mile (10); *The World of Professional Golf—1968*, edited by Mark H. McCormack, which goes beyond the catalogued statistics and presents interesting information on foreign tournaments, players, and their performance (35); *How To Talk Car* by John Lawlor, which is an authoritative as well as humorous dictionary of car racing terms (27); *The Official Encyclopedia of Football* by Roger Lamporte Treat, ex-sports columnist, which is a carefully assembled and catalogued maze of statistics, names, numbers and "juicy little would-you-believe-its" (87).

Some writers turn to biographies of sport figures. Exemplary of such writings is the book *Arnie,* written by Mark H. McCormack, Arnold Palmer's friend, advisor, partner, and manager. It presents many facets of Arnold Palmer and his doggedly devoted fans (Arnie's "Army") as well as many facets of the complex world in which the pro golfer moves (34).

Whether sportswriters, columnists, and biographers "tell it like it is" has been a point debated by some sports participants who may be inclined to agree with Bill Russell, who said that the toughest part of sport is "talking to a sportswriter after the game."

Player-Manager-Writers. Numerous books have been written, for one purpose or another, by those who have become champions or have well-known names in the sports world. In the eighteenth century, Benjamin Franklin, an accomplished swimmer and teacher, wrote *The Art of Swimming,* the first instructional text to be printed in the United States. Since that time, "how to play" books in all sports, from archery to wrestling, have been numerous and some have attained best-seller status. One such recent book may serve to illustrate the many. It is a book of tips on golf, *My 55 Ways to Lower Your Score* by Jack Nicklaus. It alone has sold more than 80,000 copies and is available in three languages.

Notable contributions to the literature of sport as well as to the history of baseball include Ty Cobb's *My Life In Baseball—The True Record* (8) and Jimmie Dykes' *You Can't Steal First Base* (11). In this autobiography full of its free advice, Jimmie Dykes, "one of baseball's most peripatetic managers," wrote of his restless path, wives who spell trouble, and the good old days when players didn't have "air-conditioned clubhouses with wall-to-wall carpeting."

Instant Replay, edited by Dick Schaap and written by Jerry Kramer, is about Kramer's "love-hate relationship with his remarkable coach, Vince Lombardi; about the delicately calibrated anatomy of a pro football team, about the rituals and rewards of playing the game; and about himself and his drive toward excellence." A bestseller, this book may be considered artistic in yet another way—Kramer talked into a tape recorder, and the tapes were then typed into transcripts—it became an "electronic diary" (26).

Distinguished Literary Figures. Lawrence S. Ritter, a professor of economics, in his book *The Glory of Their Times,* used the technique of tape-recorded accounts of 22 eminent baseball players in discussing baseball lore (48). Among the world's most accomplished writers—William Saroyan, Bill Mauldin, Budd Schulberg, and William Faulkner, to name a few—were some who prepared the text for a four-pound volume called *The Spectacle of Sport* (90). Other talented literary figures such as Damon Runyon, John Updike, Jack London, and Alistair Cooke are among those who have recaptured in the book *Great Sports Reporting* some of the feats and excitement evoked by numerous sport heroes (23). *The Realm of Sport,* edited by Herbert Warren Wind, is a classic collection of great sporting events and personalities recorded by distinguished writing that ranges from the humor of Robert Benchley and James Thurber to classic pieces by William Hazlitt, Robert Louis Stevenson and Joseph Conrad (89). *More Than a Game* is a collection of unforgettable stories from the world of sport immortalized through the emotions and words of talented writers who saw what took place. Paul Gallico's "Farewell to the Babe" may be a story of particular interest to women (19).

Stephen Potter, one of Great Britain's foremost humorists, has written three books (*Gamesmanship, Lifemanship,* and *Golfmanship*), all of which detailed in a humorous vein the latest snide gambits and treacherous plays which, if followed assiduously, are guaranteed to destroy an opponent. *Gamesmanship,* in fact, has become a household word to the sport world (47).

Poetry. Some poets, too, have found in sport a medium for the expression of their talents. Perhaps the most classic example is provided by Ernest Lawrence Thayer, a New England philosopher who had runaway success with his poem *Casey At The Bat,* which was written in 1888. Although hardly anyone may be able to quote the poem, it is considered so well-known as to be on the tip of everyone's tongue. It has had many "imitations, sequels and parodies," and two silent motion pictures have been based on it (14:m3–m4).

The famous and feared double-play combination, from Joe Tinker (shortstop) to Johnny Evers (second baseman) to Frank Chance (first baseman), which helped the Chicago Cubs win three straight pennants in 1906, 1907, and 1908, inspired Franklin P. Adams to immortalize them in an equally immortal poem: "Baseball's Sad Lexicon" (18:43). More recently, Ogden Nash, poet laureate and ardent fan of the Baltimore Colts, wrote a poem to that team, "My Colts," which appeared in *Life* magazine (40:75-81).

Perhaps more significant than the fact that poets write of sport is the fact that some poets have found in sport a subtle link with the art of poetry. Yevgeny Yevtushenko too likened art to sport despite the possibility that the comparison may "seem somewhat crude to literary snobs." Both art and sport, he asserted, are "a combat, and above all, a combat with oneself. Real art, too, needs strong muscles." He quoted the poet Blok, who said of writing his poem "Retribution":

All the movement and development of the poem became closely linked for me with the development of my muscular system . . . this rhythmic and gradual growth of muscles became the rhythm of the whole poem (92:114, 117).

Of himself Yevtushenko said:

When I write verse there is an element of mountain climbing in it . . . in the frightening resistance of the thematic material there is an element of freestyle wrestling, the question of who's going to be thrown—I or the theme . . . Allegorical verses are like dribbling and feinting at football, a ruse to lead the defenders astray so that you can kick the ball into the rival's goal (92:117).

An article called "The Poet and the Boxer," prefaced by Robert Cantwell, is an interesting story about the eminent French poet, Jean Cocteau, and his "bizarre avocation," that of managing a world champion prizefighter, Alphonso Theo Brown. In this article, Cocteau's own words describe an unusual relationship between poetry and the boxer.

I took an interest in the destiny of the boxer because for me he was a kind of poet, a kind of mime or magician who brought to the ring the perfect expression of one of the human enigmas: the marvel of presence. Al was a poem in black ink, a paean to spiritual strength in its victory over mere physical force (80:62-72).

James Dickey, poet and National Book Award winner, gave poetry a similar perspective and one which takes the reader to the concept presented in the next section. He said simply: "I think a track meet is as poetic as anything you can get."

SPORT AS AN ART FORM

"Sports belong with the arts of humanity," as Cozens and Stumpf stated, "because they are as fundamental a form of human expression as music, poetry, and painting" (9:1). Obviously sport dispenses with canvas, paint, and the other accouterments of the typical arts. And, it may be regarded as a perishable work in the sense that collectors cannot buy it, museums cannot show it, it cannot be displayed on a wall. Nonetheless, there are numerous patrons of the art form of sport and it satisfies their demands of being visible.

Sport has been considered for centuries to be a kind of applied art—a formal, classical art form. "Formality, however," as Friedenberg noted, "does not make sport inexpressive; by limiting and channeling expression to previously established modes it makes expression more forceful" (52). With his body, equipment, courts and implements the performer creates a picture—the graceful postures of a gymnast, the supple stretch of a golfer, the delicate discipline of a skater, the fluid thrusts of a fencer, the harmonious control of a rider, the rhythmic burst of a hurdler, the crescendo coil of a javelin thrower, the synchronized swirls of a canoeist—

all these and more may become a kind of flawless execution in which the viewer may see the beauty Emerson described when he wrote: "Beauty rests on necessities . . . the result of perfect economy." In such beauty the viewer may see, as did Michelangelo, "the purgation of superfluities," or he may see in such activities as track and field or surfing, as Friedenberg stated, "the rules that govern what may be done like those that govern classical ballet, grow out of the function of the human body in relation to the task" (52).

Sport also may be considered a creative art form in the sense that it exists only for itself, is enclosed in itself, and the experience is art. The sportsman is then considered as pursuing art for its own sake, finding, as Kaelin put it, "a vehicle of creative physical activity akin to that expended in the production and experience of any bona fide work of art" (22:19). As Friedenberg put it, "the inner glow from this experience is an important part of erotic attractiveness" (52). Those eclectic lovers of sport who hold that all sport is beautiful may find such beauty in the spectator appeal, in a player's imagination for the game, in the intensity and steadiness of a champion, in the perfectionist's zeal, or perhaps even in the briefest shorts on some coordinated gamin.

In the following brief passages, then, are the words and works of some persons who see in sport one form of art or another.

Painting a Picture in Skill and Words

For Paul Gallico, a veteran sports reporter, moments of beauty were remembered inseparably with athletes performing in the arenas. There were:

> the gleam in the eyes of Helen Wills looking up at a tennis ball in the air during her service . . . the smooth swiveling of Dempsey's shoulders . . . Maxie Hebert and Ernst Bair skating in a snowfall that made the scene resemble an old print . . . the six-round bout between Jimmy Slattery and Jack Delaney, the most graceful prizefight ever boxed . . . Dorothy Poynton's magnificent and graceful swan dive in which for a moment she became an exquisite white bird poised on some unseen current of air . . . Jesse Owens running, not on the track, but over the top of it (13:6).

For centuries writers, photographers and artists have pictured "the bold and fluid beauty of the human form." In the twisting acrobatics of a diver, for example, one photographer saw "a sort of visual music, a melding of precise parts and different tempos into a single fluid expression" (73).

Numerous other examples are cited in the previous sections which, like the striking presentation of color photographs and their captions in the book *The Spectacle of Sport*, from *Sports Illustrated* (90), testify to the fact that the human body is the medium for an artistic creation. Some of the titles in this particular book are illustrative of the many:

Grace In A Dive," "Track Night At the Garden," "The Look of Febru-
ry" (hockey), "The First Pitch," "Patterns on Hardwood" (basketball),
nd many more. Still others write in various expressive ways about the
rt they find in the body or its skillful use.

A physicist who never tired of pondering on the mysterious phenomena
f archery wrote as follows:

> the writhing of a shaft past the bow and its flight through fields of potent
> but unseen forces are so puzzling even while so beautiful. All that is artistic
> within us responds to the grace of a bending bow. Our strength of body may
> be taxed to exhilaration by a powerful weapon, or we may be charmed by the
> sprightly response of one contrived more delicately (12).

Gene Mauch, when he was manager of the Philadelphia Phillies, paid
tribute to the artistry of Sandy Koufax, describing it this way:

> Sandy . . . kicks at the mound until it is absolutely perfect. This is part of
> Koufax the true artist, and sitting on the bench you realize he is getting
> ready to paint a picture that only he wants to look at (66:13).

The game of golf is considered to be more than swings and scores.
To some, it is "pleasing postures and graceful maneuvers repeated again
nd again in a ritual that excites the senses." Arnold Palmer stated:

> What other people may find in poetry or art museums I find in the flight
> of a good drive—the white ball sailing . . . into that blue sky, growing
> smaller . . . suddenly reaching its apex, curving, falling . . . finally dropping
> to the turf to roll some more, just the way I planned it (42:29).

Of Eric Tabarly, French long-distance yachting adventurer, an old
cquaintance reportedly said:

> On land he is like an awkward albatross, but when he sails he has infinite
> grace. He steers his boat like a choreographer directs a ballet (41:86).

Even football teams have been described artistically by Ogden Nash
s "the best trained repertory companies in the country—everybody is so
vell-rehearsed and everybody is perfectly cast" (40:75-81).

Arthur Steinhaus, in defending "spectatoritis," described how in a
ootball, basketball or baseball game, the players

> paint a picture for hundreds of thousands of people, in which the theme moves
> constantly and each second the scene changes completely. They are creating
> a picture of the highest form of Art, neuro-muscular control . . . Every game
> is different (85:32).

'urthermore, all the knowledge which gives substance to this art form
compares with anything one can talk about in the fields of music or
rchitecture."

The concepts of physical beauty and of aesthetic expression have
ecome more varied, however, particularly through the viewpoint of the
xistentialists. It is to this aspect of sport as an art form that the following
ection is devoted.

The Sport Experience as Art

The following section digresses somewhat from the general pattern of this book in order to sketch, in barest outline, some theories of man's search for meaning (a term in vogue), particularly as related to sport. This brief exposition is not intended to summarize what is known or being investigated in the many-sided search for meaning in movement forms by thinkers in widely diverse fields of knowledge. Its purpose is first, to suggest some of the kinds of resources available that are related to the construction of theory in sport and other related forms of human movement; and, second, to point to the relationship between sport and other arts as forms of human expression. In neither instance is the discussion all inclusive. Nor is it conclusive in the sense that any one theory of sport as an art form or as an aesthetic experience may be considered as having won the day.

Ernst Cassirer in his *Essay on Man* stated that "beauty is part and parcel of human experience" (6:137). Taking their lead from Cassirer's general *Philosophy of Symbolic Forms* (7), numerous investigators have become interested in the search for symbolic meaning inherent in man's movement experiences.

Philip H. Phenix, in his book *Realms of Meaning*, made a cogent case for the "arts of movement" in the curriculum for general education, by stating that:

> Of all the arts, the arts of movement best exemplify . . . immediacy, since the person's own body is the instrument of expression and response . . . Thus, the meanings communicated . . . interpret the life of persons at the very wellsprings of organic being (43:167).

Drawing upon Huizinga's classic treatment of the philosophy of play, Phenix noted that the element of play is a factor of great importance in the arts of movement:

> Whether or not particular play activities fall within the province of the arts as such, the typical meanings inherent in play belong to the esthetic realm (43:173).

"Here, in body movement, is one of the keys that will unlock the doors of imagined conception," Harold Rugg stated in his book *Imagination* (50). And, many persons have been exploring such a concept in a search for the meaning in body movement. They became interested in the fact of expression, not just in the mode of performance. Dance, sport, and other forms of human movement, like art or music, were purported to be understood not merely in the sense of symmetry of form or the architecture of the human body. Rather, if one stepped beyond the bound of the analogies to the "body beautiful" a more subjective character could be ascribed to sport.

The search for meaning in movement forms yielded encouraging results in the field of physical education. Eleanor Metheny, building upon the works of Ernst Cassirer, Susanne Langer, Harold Rugg, and others, pointed to the wider possibilities of expression provided by the arts of movement. In her book *Connotations of Movement in Sport and Dance,* she asserted that although man may not be able to verbalize the meanings he finds in moving, he can formulate his deepest feelings in movement experiences. Furthermore, man creates sport and other movement patterns in the same way and for the same reasons he creates works of art or music.

> We play tennis for the same reason that men paint pictures, sing, play musical instruments, devise and solve algebraic equations, and fly aeroplanes . . . because it satisfies our human need to use our human abilities, to experience ourselves as significant, creative, and, therefore, personalized beings in an impersonal world (38:104).

The field of investigation in which extensive conceptual schemes for the interpretation of the meanings inherent in sport generally has been that of "personal knowledge" characteristic of the existentialist view as developed among such philosophers as Martin Heidegger, Karl Jaspers, Jean Paul Sartre, Martin Buber, Paul Tillich, Frederich Nietzsche, and such existential psychologists as Rollo May.

Howard Slusher, in his book *Man, Sport and Existence,* drew upon existential psychology and the phenomenologic principle of bringing to the experience openness and acceptance rather than predetermined judgments and evaluations in the attempt to probe the meaning of man's involvement in sport. Slusher affirmed that sport "can be an arena for the location of a meaningful existence rather than a hell of conquest and survival" (52:216). However, Slusher declared that in contrast to literature, architecture, music, dance, sculpture, painting, and other forms of human expression, in which men center their efforts on the creation of the new, sport has not broken away from the known images of the culture.

> Influenced by the material culture sport serves to preserve the present . . . Its product is maintenance of form rather than creation. Its instrument is rational rather than emotional (52:107).

Ellen W. Gerber, in an article entitled "Identity, Relation and Sport," approached the question of what meanings are found in sport by the following hypotheses:

> When people are engaged in the act of competing in a sport they are . . . engaged in a dialogue between themselves and the other players. The relationship . . . is basically an I-Thou relationship, thus making sport a medium for self-definition and the creation of man's essential being (or being of essence) (15:90).

An examination of the attributes of this special I-Thou relationship led Gerber to uncover the elements of mutuality, directness, presentness, intensity, and ineffability (15:97).

In a mode of phenomenologic interpretation, other investigators have inquired into the nature of spectator sport. Like the artist, who believes as does Logan, "that in order for the feeling to be successfully expressed and for empathy to be successfully evoked, the viewer must intensely perceive or experience the action" (30:45), the spectator in sport is not left to merely a passive role. As Cassirer remarked that "like the process of speech the artistic process is a dialogical and dialectual one" (6).

E. F. Kaelin, professor of philosophy, inquiring into the nature of spectator sports in American culture, developed a phenomenologic interpretation of aesthetic experiences in sport. Pointing out that the well-played game is the aesthetic ideal of sporting events, he examined the conditions under which memorable games have achieved this aesthetic character. The first consideration for understanding aesthetic quality in sporting events is that

> although the winning or losing of the game is aesthetically irrelevant, the desire to win is never aesthetically irrelevant . . . the game is made an aesthetic event by the opposition of strength in the wills to win (22:23).

Thus, fans can only be disappointed aesthetically by a calculated decision to accept a tie game. A second consideration taken from general aesthetic theory by Kaelin is that the competitive sport is "controlled violence," aesthetically recognizable for the manner in which it creates a qualitatively unique experience "in which pressure is built up from moment to moment, sustained through continuous opposition, until the climax of victory or defeat" (22:25). Sudden death play-offs or extra-inning games, therefore, may be as close as the sport may come to achieving this aesthetic ideal. Kaelin's observations of spectator sport led him to point out that football is a more dramatic game and has greater spectator appeal than baseball. Football is "continuous, tightly structured, and usually climaxing," while baseball is "diffuse, badly articulated, and rarely climaxing" (22:19).

Seymour Kleinman questioned the appropriateness of theory development in sport in the same manner in which Morris Weitz had addressed himself to the appropriateness of theory development in aesthetics. He contended that asking the question, "What is sport?" is essentially as pointless and meaningless as asking the question, "What is art?" While acknowledging the value inherent in every theory in that attention is given to elements of sport deserving consideration, Kleinman suggested that phenomenologic and logical description have "openendedness," "disclaim philosophical theorizing in the sense of constructing definitions," and "adhere to a 'look and see' approach as a means of understanding"

(24:31). Emphasizing the virtue of faithful description in the phenomenologic approach, he concluded:

Phenomenology . . . maintains that experiential description gets closer to the heart of the matter by revealing the essence of sport which transcends both quantitative analysis and linguistic utility (24:34).

Many of the experiential descriptions from the realm of sport which have been abstracted from the words of actual performers and spectators of sport and which appear in various sections throughout this book might be regarded as appropriately belonging to phenomenologic description, or as at least supportive of the idea that no theory of sport can capture the significance of the experience for the individual. These descriptions will not be repeated here, but the reader is urged to re-read those personal descriptions, particularly in Part I, in the light of the foregoing theoretical discussion. A few further descriptions are added here, principally to emphasize the focus of this particular section—that of the sport experience itself as an art form.

Edward Rutkowski, declaring that "it is the task of the arts to drive home a point of reality by abstracting it in a meaningful way for all those who are involved in the experience," called football an art form.

Its aim is the experience one receives as a participant in the game or as a fan watching the contests . . . As an art form, its acceptance or rejection stems from preferences of personal taste (51:31).

George Plimpton likened watching a sporting event to seeing any dramatic art wherein one can identify with the hero and hiss the villain.

In, say, a football game there is a beginning, a middle, and an end, and within a defined time period you watch villains and heroes playing out a drama; there are extraordinary feats to be seen . . . and all of that is very much an art form, like a play (46:299).

Writing to the point that the use of drugs is a sure way to despoil sport, Bil Gilbert presented the idea that sport is an art form because it measures men's weaknesses, virtues, skill, and character. What is sporting about sport, he declared, is not the demonstration or the spectacle. For sport to be of interest—emotionally, artistically, commercially—no contestant must have an artificial advantage, such as by the use of drugs, over another.

The mystery and drama of sport, for both participants and spectators, has always been the unfolding action that occurs when men match these intangible elements of their characters. It is the thing that elevates sport to an art form, perhaps our oldest (16:32).

Another illustration comes by way of Jay Wright, poet and playwright, who was once a catcher for Mexicali in the Arizona-Texas Baseball League. In an article entitled, "A Diamond-Bright Art Form," he reflected on the sport of baseball and concluded that for him the game is an art that is completely enclosed in its own esthetic.

> I could think of baseball as the realization, the summit of . . . an esthetic, which, as in the highest art, summarizes a man's life, sets him in a historical context where he measures himself against the highest achievement and where he feels that he is perpetuating the spirit of the best of his chosen work . . . the ballplayer still tries to transcend, by the perfection of his craft, the limitations that are inherent in it, and in himself (91:33, 39).

Sport Language as An Art?

In the realm of language sport may be said to keep company with the arts in the sense that it is a form of nondiscursive, symbolic communication. The object of language is communication, and, as a form of communication, the visual language of sport is almost universally intelligible. As noted in previous sections, sport is something one communicates with no less articulately than through a microphone or a poem or a story. And the language of sport serves as a common denominator in the sense that it is equipped with symbols that are used and understood throughout a range of activities and across cultural boundaries. What could be more symbolic of the language of sport as universal than the American astronauts' use of the single phrase, "about the size of a football field," to describe their site on the moon.

This silent though coherent language of sport is not the concern of this section, however. Rather, it is to point out that the spoken language of sport is understood and used across diverse professions and at the same time is a rather secretive binding force in some subcultural groupings. Again, the examples provided are intended only to be illustrative of the fact that the language of sport is a cultural, if not an aesthetic, invention.

Some sport terms are rather conventional, a kind of trade talk which is not only a part of the sport idiom but which also has common meaning in business, religion, politics and so forth. Examples of words and phrases taken into general language from sport are: "Keep your eye on the ball," "team spirit," "take a rain check," "that's not cricket," "knowing the score," "farmed out," "out in left field," "bully for you," "touché," "boner," "clutch," "sent to the shower," "seventh-inning stretch," and "struck out." In circles other than those of sport, top executives are referred to as "quarterbacks," "team captains," "lead off men," even "pinch-hitters." Among the spate of clichés in sport which are commonly understood in other professions are these: "We play these games one at a time"; "I'd ride the bench if it would help the team"; "They put their pants on one leg at a time like everybody else." One might say that even the advertisement, "Vitalis is for athletic hair," conveys a commonly understood meaning.

Then again, some sports have their own lexicon and, although it appears to be unintelligible in the proper sense of the King's English, the meanings are quite clear—at least among those who follow the sport. Surfing jargon, for example, includes such terms as the following: "stoked" (very enthusiastic or wound up); "jazzed" (more or less the same as "stoked"); "bitchin" (good, as in "a bitchin wave"), and a raft more (49:98,100).

In racing, hot rodders must master a large vocabulary of terms if they are to communicate. Henry Gregor Felsen, who provided a foreword to John Lawlor's book, *How to Talk Car*, called sports car terminology the "most exciting and lively language" (27). A few examples are as follows: a "hog" (a big luxurious Cadillac or Imperial), a "sewing machine" (a Volkswagen), a "hot dog" (a top-performing driver), a "springy thingy" (a dragster) a "tube steak" (a hot dog), "the oasis" (a refreshment stand), and a "weekend warrior," "flyboy," or a "Joe Log Bolt" (one who competes in drag racing only on weekends). And one will remain a "nerd" (not in the know) at the race track unless further profitable reading time is spent with Lawlor's dictionary of racing terms.

Some of the expressive jargon in the game of golf is described by George Plimpton in his book, *The Bogey Man*. Some of the lingo which follows attests to the color and lively patois of the sport of golf: "chilly-dipping" (to flub the ball or not put any "noise" on it); "crashed and burned" (player who had a bad round); "snipes" or "blue darters" (hooks); "tall and uncut," "the asparagus," "the cabbage," "the zucchini," "the lettuce," "Marlboro country" (expressions for the rough); "cat box," "silicone," "on the beach," "bogey dust" (expressions for being in the sand trap); "a frozen rope" (long, low drive); "field goal," "gobbler," "snake" (a successfully sunk long putt); "knee-knocker" (short putt); "career shot" (a great shot hit at the right time); "knocked stony" or "you hit that one adjacent" (a good approach shot). Some of the transitions which are more involved include: "scratch off the blues" (could refer to nice weather); "18 off the reds" (could refer to a blizzard) (45).

And, if one is to adapt effectively to the colorful and sometimes baffling language of even that all-American game, baseball, Zander Hollander's *Baseball Lingo* provides some cues (18). With this informal dictionary one can "tee off" (hit a hard ball) or get an "Annie Oakley" (free ticket to first base), get "aboard" (on base) with stops at "keystone" (second base) and the "hot corner" (third base). On the way one may meet a "leather man" (outstanding fielder), "junk man" (pitcher who uses off-speed pitches, "long man" (an early relief pitcher), a "jockey" (player who taunts the opposition), or a "pheenom" (highly touted rookie). Of course, if one gets the "collar" (goes through an entire game without a hit) or "pulls a rock" (makes a boner or mental error), he may be a "castoff" (discarded player). Oh well, there's the possibility for a "rain check" (ticket stub for future admission).

Such, in brief outline, is the evidence that sport is used by other art forms to convey meanings and to create new forms of experience, and is itself a distinctive art form, with its own mode of expression and imaginative use. Hence the argument that the richness of culture and the level of civilization achieved are the consequence, in part, of sport

The following chapter serves to illustrate the point that the sub cultural group called women also consider sport, with art and other cultural activities, as important parts of their world.

REFERENCES

1. Barber, Walter Lanier (Red), and Creamer, Robert. *Rhubarb In The Catbird Seat.* Garden City, New Jersey: Doubleday and Company, 1968.
2. Berne, Eric. *Games People Play.* New York: Grove Press, 1964.
3. Betts, John Richard. "The Technological Revolution and the Rise of Sports 1850-1900," *Mississippi Valley Historical Review,* XL, 1953, pp. 231-256. (Reprinted in Loy and Kenyon [editors], *Sport, Culture, and Society.* The Macmillan Company, 1969.)
4. Boyle, Robert H. "The Bizarre History of American Sport," *Sports Illustrated* January 8, 1962, pp. 54-63.
5. Brown, Gwilym S. "New Twists For An Old Art," *Sports Illustrated,* February 20, 1967, pp. 52-53.
6. Cassirer, Ernst. *An Essay On Man.* New Haven, Connecticut: Yale University Press, 1944.
7. Cassirer, Ernst. *Philosophy of Symbolic Forms.* New Haven, Connecticut: Yale University Press. Vol. 1 (1953), Vol. 2 (1955), Vol. 3 (1957).
8. Cobb, Ty. *My Life In Baseball—The True Record.* New York: Doubleday and Company, 1961.
9. Cozens, F. W., and Stumpf, F. S. *Sports In American Life.* Chicago: University of Chicago Press, 1953.
10. Dunaway, James O. *The Four Minute Mile, 1954-1967.* Available from the author, 239 East 79th Street, New York City 10021, 1967.
11. Dykes, Jimmie. *You Can't Steal First Base.* Philadelphia: J. B. Lippincott Company, 1967.
12. Elmer, Robert P. *Archery.* Philadelphia: The Penn Publishing Company, 1933.
13. Gallico, Paul. *Farewell To Sport.* New York: Alfred A. Knopf, 1937.
14. Gardner, Martin. "Yesterday: The Harvard Man Who Put The Ease In Casey Manner," *Sports Illustrated,* August 2, 1965, pp. m3-m4.
15. Gerber, Ellen W. "Identity, Relation and Sport," *Quest,* Monograph VIII May, 1967, pp. 90-97.
16. Gilbert, Bil. "Drugs In Sport: Part 3, High Time To Make Some Rules," *Sports Illustrated,* July 7, 1969, pp. 30-35.
17. *Harper's Bazaar Spot Check Comment On Culture—U.S.A.,* Special Supplement by Eastern Airlines, 1967.
18. Hollander, Zander (editor). *Baseball Lingo.* New York: W. W. Norton and Company, Inc., 1967.
19. Holmes, A. Lawrence (compiled by). *More Than A Game.* New York: The Macmillan Company, 1967.
20. Hough, Gordon L. "Art Museum of Sport," *Parks and Recreation.* April, 1968, pp. 30-32.
21. Hussey, Christopher. *Tait McKenzie: A Sculptor of Youth.* Philadelphia: J. B. Lippincott Company, 1930.

22. Kaelin, E. F. "The Well-Played Game: Notes Toward an Aesthetics of Sport," *Quest*, Monograph X, May, 1968, pp. 16-28.
23. Kirchner, Allen (editor). *Great Sports Reporting*. New York: Dell Publishing Company, Inc., 1969.
24. Kleinman, Seymour. "Toward a Non-Theory of Sport," *Quest*, Monograph X, May, 1968, pp. 29-34.
25. Knauth, Percy. "Makers of the Sports Page," *Sports Illustrated*, September 16, 1963, pp. 34-43.
26. Kramer, Jerry and Schaap, Dick. (editor). *Instant Replay*. New York: The New American Library, 1969.
27. Lawlor, John. *How To Talk Car*. Chicago, Illinois: Topaz/Felsen, 1966.
28. *Life*, paintings by Picasso, December 27, 1968, pp. 20-22.
29. *Life*, "The Little Brother of War," photographs by Arthur Rickerby, April 18, 1969, pp. 49-56.
30. Logan, Gene. "Movement in Art," *Quest*, Monograph II, April, 1964, pp. 43-45.
31. Loy, John W., Jr., and Kenyon, Gerald S. (editors). *Sport, Culture, and Society*. Toronto: The Macmillan Company, 1969.
32. Lüschen, Günther. "The Interdependence of Sport and Culture," Paper presented at the National Meeting AAHPER, 1967.
33. Maheu, René. "Sport and Culture," *International Journal of Adult and Youth Education*, UNESCO, XIV, No. 1962, p. 169. (Also see *Journal of American Association for Health, Physical Education and Recreation*, October 1963, pp. 30-32.)
34. McCormack, Mark H. *Arnie*. New York: Simon and Schuster, 1967.
35. McCormack, Mark H. *The World of Professional Golf*. New York: World Publishing Company, 1968.
36. McCormick, John. "Score One for Today's Students," *Sports Illustrated*, May 20, 1968, pp. 46-59.
37. McIntosh, Peter J., Dixon, G., Munroe, A. D., and Willetts, R. F. *Landmarks in the History of Physical Education*. London: Routledge & Gegan Paul, 1957.
38. Metheny, Eleanor. *Connotations of Movement In Sport and Dance*. Dubuque, Iowa: William C. Brown Company, 1965.
39. Murray, James. *The Best of Jim Murray*. New York: Doubleday and Company, Inc., 1965.
40. Nash, Ogden. "My Colts," *Life*, December 13, 1968, pp. 75-81.
41. *Newsweek*, "The Solo Breed," March 31, 1969, p. 86.
42. Palmer, Arnold. "My Game and Yours," *Sports Illustrated*, July 15, 1963, pp. 28-42.
43. Phenix, Philip H. *Realms of Meaning*. New York: McGraw-Hill Book Company, 1964.
44. Plimpton, George. *The Paper Lion*. New York: Harper & Row, 1966.
45. Plimpton, George. *The Bogey Man*. New York: Harper & Row, 1968.
46. Plimpton, George. "Does A Woman Need Sports Appeal?" *Mademoiselle*, April, 1968, pp. 196-197, 294-299.
47. Potter, Stephen. *Golfmanship*. New York: McGraw Hill Book Company, 1968.
48. Ritter, Lawrence S. *The Glory of Their Times*. New York: The Macmillan Company, 1966.
49. Rogin, Gilbert. "An Odd Sport—And An Unusual Champion," *Sports Illustrated*, October 18, 1965, pp. 94-104.
50. Rugg, Harold. *Imagination*. New York: Harper & Row, 1963.
51. Rutkowski, Edward. "What Is Football?" *Journal of Health, Physical Education, and Recreation*, September, 1967, pp. 30-31.
51b. Schleppi, J. R. "Architecture and Sport," *The Physical Educator*, October, 1966, pp. 123-125.
52. Slusher, Howard S. *Man, Sport and Existence*. Philadelphia: Lea & Febiger, 1967.
53. Smith, Fred R. "Design For Sport, Challenge of Form," *Sports Illustrated*, January 2, 1967, pp. 46-60.

5

54. *Sports Illustrated,* "A Horror To Play In But Great To Watch," paintings by Bernie Fuchs, June 15, 1964, pp. 32-37.
55. *Sports Illustrated,* "As Sempé Sees The Olympics," paintings by Jean-Jacque Sempé, February 12, 1968, pp. 38-43.
56. *Sports Illustrated,* "A Wry Glimpse of Wimbledon," paintings by André François, June 25, 1962, pp. 28-32.
57. *Sports Illustrated,* "Big Men On The Move," paintings by Cliff Condak, October 28, 1963, pp. 40-45.
58. *Sports Illustrated,* "Design For Sport, A Garden Built For Tomorrow," January 2, 1967, pp. 36-37.
59. *Sports Illustrated,* "Emotion In Motion," paintings by Jim Jonson, May 23, 1966 pp. 48-55.
60. *Sports Illustrated,* "500-Mile Journey Into An Artist's Eye," paintings by Bob Stanley, May 29, 1967, pp. 74-78.
61. *Sports Illustrated,* "Just Once Like Stein," photographs by John G. Zimmerman, December 4, 1961, pp. 44-51.
62. *Sports Illustrated,* "Letter From the Publisher," May 8, 1967, p. 4.
63. *Sports Illustrated,* "Out In The Sun Again," paintings by Ronald Searle, March 2, 1964, pp. 16-23.
64. *Sports Illustrated,* "Passion In A Cold Climate," paintings by Bob Stanley, December 16, 1968, pp. 42-47.
65. *Sports Illustrated,* "Scorecard," February 17, 1964, pp. 7-8.
66. *Sports Illustrated,* "Scorecard," November 28, 1966, p. 13.
67. *Sports Illustrated,* "Scorecard," March 27, 1967, p. 13.
68. *Sports Illustrated,* "Skier's Shiny Trail," photographs by John G. Zimmerman, May 21, 1962, pp. 56-63.
69. *Sports Illustrated,* "Splash of Strange Hues In Baseball's Most Frantic Week," photographs by John G. Zimmerman, October 9, 1967, pp. 26-31.
70. *Sports Illustrated,* "Spring Sets The Mood of The Masters," paintings by Robert Andrew Parker, April 2, 1962, pp. 28-35.
71. *Sports Illustrated,* "Stadiums of the '60's," photographs by Neil Leiffer, July 10 1967, pp. 30-37.
72. *Sports Illustrated,* "Strategy, Strokes and Style," paintings by Bernard Fuchs, September 4, 1961, pp. 30-35.
73. *Sports Illustrated,* "The Bold and Fluid Beauty of the Human Form," photographs by Tony Triolo and Coles Phinizy, July 29, 1963, pp. 32-36.
74. *Sports Illustrated,* "The Cadences of Crew," paintings by Harvey Schmidt, June 10, 1963, pp. 42-50.
75. *Sports Illustrated,* "The Din, The Color, The Mood of Indoor Track," painting by Jerome Martin, February 24, 1964, pp. 34-39.
76. *Sports Illustrated,* "The Longest 90 Feet In Baseball," photographs by Neil Leiffer, June 22, 1964, pp. 32-36.
77. *Sports Illustrated,* "The Men," paintings by Bob Peak, September 9, 1963 pp. 36-45.
78. *Sports Illustrated,* "The Most Beautiful Game of All," paintings by André François, February 20, 1961, pp. 32-37.
79. *Sports Illustrated,* "The Perils of the Deep Powder," photographs by John G. Zimmerman, November 15, 1965, pp. 52-60.
80. *Sports Illustrated,* "The Poet and The Boxer," preface by Robert Cantwell paintings by Jean Cocteau, March 2, 1964, pp. 62-72.
81. *Sports Illustrated,* "The Pristine Joys of Golf," photographs by Art Kane, July 15, 1963, pp. 30-38.
82. *Sports Illustrated,* "The Race Against The Ball," July 31, 1961, pp. 28-37.
83. *Sports Illustrated,* "Traveler In Two Different Worlds," photographs by Jerry Cooke and Coles Phinizy, July 3, 1961, pp. 24-33.
84. *Sports Illustrated,* "When It's 3 and 2," paintings by Bernie Fuchs, April 13 1964, pp. 42-48.

85. Steinhaus, Arthur H. *Toward An Understanding of Health and Physical Education.* Dubuque, Iowa: William C. Brown Company, 1963.
86. Tannenbaum, Percy H., and Noah, James E. "Sportugese: A Study of Sports Page Communication," in Loy and Kenyon (editors), *Sport, Culture, and Society,* pp. 327-336. New York: The Macmillan Company, 1969.
87. Treat, Roger Lamporte. *The Official Encyclopedia of Football.* New York: A. S. Barnes and Company, 1968.
88. Venturi, Ken. "The Shakes In Quakes Corner," photographs by Richard Jeffery, models by Asdur Takakjian, *Sports Illustrated,* June 13, 1966, pp. 56-64.
89. Wind, Herbert Warren (editor), *The Realm of Sport.* New York: Simon and Schuster, 1966.
90. Wood, Norton (editor). *The Spectacle of Sport* (from *Sports Illustrated*). Englewood Cliffs, New Jersey: Prentice-Hall, Inc., 1957.
91. Wright, Jay. "A Diamond-Bright Art Form," *Sports Illustrated,* June 23, 1969, pp. 32-39.
92. Yevtushenko, Yevgeny. "A Poet Against the Destroyers," *Sports Illustrated,* December 19, 1966, pp. 104-128.

CHAPTER 7

Sport and Women

The material presented in Part II emphasized the relationship between sport and such large social collectives as ethnic, local, regional, national, and international groups. In this section (Part III, Sport Is Cultural), the material is descriptive of some of sport's relationships with and influences upon other large general aspects of culture—art forms, entertainment, and business.

By contrast, this chapter is focused upon what sociologists would label as a microcosm of the larger society—women in sport. The topic of women in sport is included in this section because women may be considered subcultural within the concepts provided by Milton Gordon in that they are "composed of a combination of factorable social situations . . . but forming in their combination a functioning unity which has an integrated impact upon the participating individual" (11b:40).

Although the effectiveness with which women have functioned in sport and the impact of sport upon them as participating individuals are of theoretical as well as practical concern, it seems interesting and surprising that philosophers, psychologists, and sociologists as well as physical educators have not given more attention to the cultural significance of women in sport in America. Numerous observations and scholarly studies have been made of such subcultural groups as boxers, surfers, skiers, and the "man on the horse." As far as women are concerned, however, assessments of their function and role as a consequential force in the world of sport have been largely a matter of a few scholarly investigations, some speculation, and considerable hearsay. Regardless of whether this chapter will add to one or the other of these assessments, its intent here, as throughout the book, is to report what has been happening with women in the sport world, both as they see it and as those who see them see it.

PARADOXES AND PROBLEMS

"One of the more ancient chestnuts, concerning the mixture of women and sports," related Gary Valk, "is the story about the pretty young thing who turns to her escort in the first inning of the second game of a double-header and asks, 'Honey, isn't this where we came in?' " (43:4). For many Americans, however, the idea of women in sport is one which results in numerous and serious paradoxes and problems. (Among such paradoxes, and consequently the problems, are those of femininity versus masculinity, equality versus inequality, ability versus fragility, and woman's place versus man's place.)

The reasons for sheltering women from sport competition have included such time-honored beliefs as: first, the belief that female athletes are tough-looking muscle molls; and second, the belief that they aren't tough enough physiologically or psychologically to provide or withstand strenuous competition. As the Reverend Thomas Boslooper said, "Women have three basic rights. The first is political and the second professional . . . Now women are fighting for the most basic of their rights, the physical right, the right to play, to be fit, to compete in sports, and we're hearing the same arguments again" (21). "The same arguments" refers to the fact that when women won the vote and when they began working alongside men, it was said they would lose their femininity.

Paul Gallico sized up the "muscle molls" of the 1920's and 1930's with such phrases as:

> tennis ladies . . . Look at the shoulders . . . forearms . . . Those legs! . . . Never saw a good lady swimmer with small feet . . . Track athletes . . . Flat chested . . . close-cropped hair . . . and those legs . . . The freaks bring up the rear guard . . . ballplayers . . . toughies and exhibitionists. For the most part they have ugly bodies, hard faces, cheap minds (7:234-236).

Although Gallico acknowledged that the muscle molls were not all sexless and unattractive ("they have definite glamour . . . a strong physical attraction") he added that "no matter how good they are, they can never be good enough, quite, to matter." And, according to Ernst Jokl, M.D., women have been told:

> that sports would produce a masculine type of woman, that exercise makes girls muscle-bound, that participation in competitive athletics would lead to difficulties in child birth, even rare developmental malformations were alleged to be caused through athletic training (14c:50).

Another more recent yet similar assessment by Brian Glanville appeared in an article in *Mademoiselle.*

> For women to compete with the same intensity as men must lead to imbalance, psychological stress, and sometimes physical distortion (10:166).

Yet, such arguments against sport participation and competition have been seriously challenged and even dispelled by a variety of persons including educators, physiologists, physicians, and theologians. Eleanor Metheny, using the context of the mythological images projected by the early Greek goddesses, declared that women in our own time, within the realm of sport competition,

> have found it possible to combine the sexually-based image of Aphrodite, Hera and Demeter with the personal powers of Athena, Artemis, and Hippolyta, without doing violence to either (24b: 56).

Physiologically speaking, superstition, rumor, and old wives' tales have slowly given way to scientific investigation and research regarding the effects of strenuous exercise and activity on the female systems of reproduction. Arthur Steinhaus, an exercise physiologist, in a paper prepared as early as 1932, reviewed the findings of several studies dealing with the possible effects of vigorous physical activity and/or sport participation on pregancy and child birth, position or displacement of the uterus (supposedly caused by jumping), and menstruation. The conclusions were that in normally healthy girls and women, strenuous exercise and active sport participation "do not militate against the chances of normal childbirth," that "any actual movement or strain on the uterus resulting from broad or high jumping would be insignificant in a normal, healthy woman," and that a large majority of the cases studied showed "that training was without effect on the character of the menstrual history." In fact, most of the girls and women mentioned in the study continued their activities during their menstrual cycle "without detriment to their health or performance ability" (55:147).

At the 1952 Olympics in Helsinki, Ernst Jokl and a team of investigators took a long look at the question of physiological capabilities of women under strenuous competitive situations. They concluded

> that biologically the female sex is more robust and more capable of adapting itself to the demands of environmental challenges than has so far been assumed. Physiologically, the woman is fully capable of active participation in the sports movement (14c:45, 50).

A survey reported in 1967 in *Today's Health,* published by the American Medical Association, confirmed the existence of certain "myths" that inhibit female participation in sports and further dispelled the validity of such myths. One study reported was that of Doctor Gyula J. Erdelyi who discovered that ease in childbirth and apparent immunity from back difficulties following pregnancy result from physical conditioning characteristic of female athletes. Further, at least six gold medals in the 1956 Olympics were won by women who were competing during their menstrual period (11c).

A Massachusetts physician who has long promoted the participation of girls and women in athletics, Clayton L. Thomas, was quoted as saying:

Women just aren't as fragile as society likes to think they are. The idea is a myth that has no scientific basis in anatomy or physiology. Any healthy person who has the desire and the patience to become conditioned for the sport should be able to do so (40:16).

Despite such evidence, many writers and thinkers still may share the conviction of Paul Weiss who, in *Sport: A Philosophic Inquiry,* emphasized the physiologic obstacles more than the cultural obstacles as the reasons for women's relative nonparticipation (62). Nonetheless, the cultural factors seem to come in for a greater share of attention in the popular communication media. The following is an example of one such cultural factor at work: Reverend Boslooper interviewed happy and well-adjusted women for twelve years in an attempt to gain insights which might help him in the counseling of unhappy parishioners. In a paper presented to the American Association for the Advancement of Science, he made the following observation: "In early childhood we admire the spirit and activity of little girls. We encourage them to run and to compete with boys, who are their equals until puberty. Then suddenly, at different ages for different women, we say, 'When are you going to grow up and be a lady?'" (21).

There may be several legitimate definitions of the word "lady." The definition alluded to by most writers may appear to require the abandonment of, or at least the camouflaging of, such basic human characteristics as strength, speed, endurance, and coordination. Of course, such qualities in women may be proper if it is strength for carrying out the washing, speed for keeping up with three children moving in three directions, endurance for completing spring house cleaning in a day, or coordination for the tasks of changing a diaper, ironing, and preparing a dinner simultaneously.

For some persons, sport participation seems to be acceptable only if it is connected with a "sexual preoccupation," or is an "object for the chase." Janet Coleman, a writer for numerous magazines, responded in *Mademoiselle* to the question "does a woman need sports appeal?" with the thesis that the active life is connected with sex. Some sports, she declared, can be "sexy, serviceable, and up-and-coming sport." In search of support of her thesis she turned to the *Playboy's* Playmates, in whom she saw this concept of the active life:

swims in a regular carefree sports-loving way . . . No fan-toothed competitor . . . Above all, she isn't stranglingly serious: bikini marks are proof that she only plans to play . . . No playmate is fanatical about horses. Too Freudian . . . Other eclectic, turned on sports are all right . . . approached with the right amount of nutty femininity (6:294).

A different point of view regarding a woman's need for action was presented by Reverend Boslooper, who found that quite common among happy and well-adjusted women was participation in physical activity, frequently performed in direct and successful competition with males. Such participation never seemed to pose a threat to either the woman's femininity or the man's masculinity. He added that far too frequently a woman's need for physical activity and exertion are repressed, often to the emotional disadvantage of the woman (21).

The material that follows is intended to present further the story of women in sport from the perspective of those who actually participate or who view the scene rather directly. The story is presented from the standpoint of such concerns as status and progress, glamour and femininity, ability and equality.

ON THE MOVE—AN AVALANCHE OF FEMALE ATHLETES

Despite one writer's description "that it is impossible to run like a girl and get anywhere, except to church on time," and despite the fact that many women (as well as many men) have been "deceived by the feminine prejudice that running is not ladylike" (59:34), an ever increasing number of American girls are running, and, as a few have done in the past, are running all the way to the victory stand in Olympic competition.

Public suspicion and objection to women running in competitive events have shown definite signs of disappearing. In fact, progress towards an expanded awareness of programs in women's track and field is evident. Slightly over a decade ago there were but 24 clubs sponsoring women's athletics; now the number exceeds 200 (59:35). For some time young girls have been encouraged through the President's National Fitness Program to run, to jump, and to throw. High schools and colleges slowly but surely are providing opportunities for girls to continue such activity beyond the novice stage, through track clubs and teams and through more knowledgeable leadership.

National championships in track and field for girls and women currently draw more than 500 participants. This number represents a significant improvement over the 200 to 300 entrants of just a few years ago and a most remarkable change from the days when Babe Didrikson Zaharias won the national championship team title single-handedly.

Will Stephens, coach of a California track club for girls which "specialized" in distance running, made an interesting observation regarding competition:

> Boys are under constant pressure to compete. Girls are not. As a result boys go out for a sport even when they don't want to, and they get discouraged. The girls expect less and stick with it (59:42).

Increased interest and participation in track and field programs has been shown by girls of all ages and the result has been a whole new image for track and field. For one such example, the readers are referred to Bil Gilbert's "Thank Heaven For . . .," in which the author shared his experiences as track coach for a group of 8 to 14 year old girls and in so doing painted a delightful illustration of athletic involvement by future "all-American girls" (*Sports Illustrated,* November 27, 1967). The National AAU Women's Cross-Country championship in its sixth year drew 542 girls and women as compared to 40 competitors just five years earlier (29b).

At the time of the Olympics in Mexico City, the United States' women's swimming team, by taking 75 percent of the gold medals and 60 percent of the total medals available to them, provided convincing evidence that:

> In the United States, it's socially acceptable for teenage girls to run around with short, wet hair and to spend several hours every day churning up and down swimming pools (61:73).

Because of this fact, "the United States completely dominated the swimming events in the 1968 Olympics . . . putting the United States' Olympic team in first place as far as medal-standings go (for the first time in 12 years)" (61:73). If any one swimmer could be singled out, the heroine according to one observer was the pert Miss Debbie Meyer, a high school junior whom the Russians had named "Athlete of the Year" in 1967. About Debbie it was said:

> When she was just 12 years old, her father gave her a stopwatch with "Mexico City 1968" inscribed on it. Mexico was on her mind from then on. She came away from the country of her dreams with three gold medals (41:49).

For every American girl who made the recent Olympic or Pan American swimming teams there were hundreds, even thousands of girls and women in the age-group swimming programs throughout the country who did not, but who have "Munich 1972" very much on their minds.

In women's gymnastics both the quantity of participants as well as the quality of the competition have increased quite markedly. In 1967, at the Pan American Games, the vastly improved American team won 11 gold medals, six of them by members of the women's team. In 1968 at the Mexico City Olympics, several of the American women gymnasts came very close to being among the top six performers in several of the events. Indicative of the growth and the interest in women's gymnastics at the college level is the fact that the first national collegiate championship was held in the spring of 1969 under the auspices of the Division of Girls and Women's Sports. Or, as Muriel Davis Grossfeld, as coach of the American women's gymnastic team, has been quoted as saying: "When I started competing a dozen years ago I knew every girl gymnast in the country. Now I couldn't begin to count them. There must be at least 10,000!" (11c:21).

When one speaks of high school basketball in many Iowa communities the residents immediately think of the game as the girls play it. Not only are there some 22,000 girls playing basketball in Iowa each year, but they also have a large gathering of fans and loyal supporters.

> Comes March and most of Iowa is in a frenzy over the State High School Basketball Finals—for girls. The young women pack the house in the capital city with their furious play, then depart as the boys take over—before fewer fans (24:34).

And, for very good reasons: Not only are the players attractive young women (tournament manager Wayne Cooley "demands that the girls measure up to high standards of appearance, competition, and responsibility") but also, they are skillful in the art of playing basketball (24:39). In 1968, the state championship game matched two teams that boasted top scorers with season averages of 59.4 and 62.7 points per game. During state tournament games Denise Long of Union-Whitten scored 93 points in a single game, hit 28 out of 30 field-goal attempts in another, and, in the championship game, led her team to the title by scoring 64 points. Meanwhile, Jeanette Olson, Everly's jump shooting senior, scored 76 points in that championship game, and during the course of her four tournament games, made 72 of 79 free throws, which is outstanding free throw shooting in any league (46).

It might be noted that, although these two girls are taller than the average woman, 5'11" and 5'10" respectively, they do not extend upward to within a few feet of the basket as has come to be the expectation for basketball players with similar scoring averages. Of additional interest might be the fact that the year Denise Long was graduated from high school, she was drafted by the San Francisco Warriors, becoming the first woman and perhaps the youngest player ever to be drafted by the National Basketball Association. The Warriors expected Miss Long to be the super-star of the recently organized four-team women's professional basketball league. At the time of this writing it was reported that there were 100 girls participating in tryouts for team berths (53b:12).

In the world of golf the increasing number of women has been felt from the community course all the way to the Ladies' Professional Golfers Association's struggle with the Professional Golfers' Association (P.G.A., the men's association) for the right to share in television money. It has been estimated that there are more than two million women golfers in the United States, representing a 400 percent increase in the past decade, and that the Junior Girls' Tournament divisions now boast about one million players (11). A recent survey of golf professionals revealed that women were taking four times as many lessons and spending twice as much money on golfing apparel as they did in 196 (32:63).

Although the *Golf Digest* suggested that a possible reaction to increased women's play may be the appearance of more all-men's golf clubs (11), another source described clubs formed for women only. In addition, a Long Island architect "cognizant of the female influence on the purse strings in most families," suggested that "shorter courses be built especially for women, and surrounded by new-home sites" (32: 64). It is doubtful that all-girl clubs really will become popular, thereby assuring that golf clubs will never again be retreats solely for men.

Another area within the world of golf which has yielded to the advancement of women is that of the teaching professionals at country clubs. The number of women teaching professionals has increased from few, if any, some twenty-five years ago to a present total of about 80. The Ladies' Professional Golfers Association presently stands as the greatest organization in all of professional sports for women. In addition to the teaching pros, there are the touring pros, who currently number about 100, and who annually play for approximately $500,000 in prize money. Reportedly, Susie Maxwell Berning, a touring pro, believes quite frankly that the average man can learn more golf from watching her play than by watching Arnold Palmer, Jack Nicklaus and Company.

> We play the way the men club members play. We don't hit a driver and then a wedge to the green all the time. Arnie and Jack are playing a different game (32:64).

Also it should be noted that, throughout the country, many good amateur tournaments have sprung up, thus giving large numbers of women opportunities for golf competition at local, regional and national levels in addition to serving as proving grounds for prospective tour players.

The world's largest women's sports organization, according to *The Woman Bowler*, is the Women's International Bowling Congress, which has seen its membership grow through its 52-year history from 40 members in 1916-1917 to a total of over 2,900,000 in 1969. In 1967, 6,094 teams, or more than 30,000 women, competed for $296,760 in prize money in the largest championship tournament ever held by the Women's International Bowling Congress (63b).

The presence of women as participants on the American sport scene has been recorded by *Sports Illustrated* since 1954, and admittedly, "from the start sportswomen have provided some of our most entertaining and engaging stories." The first issue contained a picture of diver Pat McCormick, and the following week, tennis champion Maureen Connolly was featured. The fourth issue carried its first full-length story on women athletes. Since that time, the publishers asserted:

We have covered blondes, brunettes, and red heads, with épées in their hands, crash helmets on their heads and aqualungs on their backs. We have covered them climbing mountains and skiing down them, flying jets and shooting pool (43:4).

By 1967 *Sports Illustrated* estimated that it had included more than 200 stories and articles on women athletes and had featured them on 44 covers.

Two women scored significant firsts in Mexico City in the Nineteenth Olympiad of modern times. The flag bearer of the American contingent of athletes for the opening ceremony was Mrs. Janice York Romary, the first American woman to be so selected. Mrs. Romary, a 40-year-old fencer, had been selected to participate in her sixth Olympic competition, another first. Accompanied by the cheers of some 80,000 persons, Enriqueta Basilio, the first woman ever selected to be the anchor runner of the team of runners carrying the flame, touched the torch to the urn high above the Olympic Stadium in Mexico City, signifying the official opening of the Summer Olympics. It might also be noted that more than 800 women competed in the 1968 Olympics, an increase of approximately 300 women since the 1960 Games in Rome.

Evidence of the inroads made by women in a wide variety of sports is ample indeed. Only a very brief portion has been presented here. Although the women are on the move in sport, there are reminders from time to time that their accomplishments are going unnoticed by a large portion of the sporting public:

> Doris Brown, [when] asked by a television sportscaster after she won the mile in the Seattle Invitational if she had ever run the distance before: "Yes, I hold the world's record" (51:10).

GLAMOUR—RESHAPING WOMEN'S SPORTS

"If you think the typical woman in sports is a zaftig Brundhilde—one of those large, spear-carrying opera singer types—take another look" (26:8A). Television coverage of women's athletic events in local, national and international competition in a variety of sports (swimming, track and field, ice-skating, skiing, tennis, golf, gymnastics, basketball and volleyball), in addition to the newspaper and magazine coverage are telling quite a different story. Although some women athletes have always been as concerned about their femininity as their athletic ability, as the public exposure of women in sport increased so did their concern for their public image and for the image of their sports. In many instances, increased television and newspaper coverage simply exposed for the public that which had always been—highly skilled but lovely girls and women providing technically difficult but graceful and beautiful performances. In other instances, there was a deliberate effort on the part of the competitor to retain a ladylike composure through the fiercest of competition, during the most strenuous of efforts of setting or breaking world records. They deigned to accomplish the most difficult and demanding physical feats of strength and endurance and coordination without appearing to contract a single muscle fiber, misplace a single strand from their hairdo, and until recently, to do so without producing a single drop of sweat. (It might be noted that the popular belief that it is not ladylike to sweat has for the most part been dispelled—a dance form called the "twist" took care of that notion.)

For whatever reasons, and no doubt there are many more than alluded to here, the question of whether there is femininity behind the athletic prowess of women athletes can no longer be answered by the example "about as feminine as a blacksmith."

"Blacksmith" certainly wasn't the word an enthusiastic reporter was searching for in attempting to describe Sharron Moran, a touring golf pro who, while still an amateur, was named "Most Beautiful Golfer" by *Golf Digest*. The reporter finally found this description:

> "She makes you think of a Greek goddess," an assessment that is only a slight slander against the good name and good looks of Aphrodite and Pallas Athene (38:30).

Sharron seemed to be well aware of public image, and, after appearing in *Golf Digest* performing exercises in a gold sweat suit, had been "consciously cultivating, as she calls it, 'the beauty bit' " (38:30).

Susie Maxwell Berning, 1968 U.S. Women's Open Golf Champion, explained that "most women in sports are very ladylike . . . In golf, especially during the last five years, the girls have been dressing more femininely" (26:8A).

Carol Mann, considered one of the best players on the women's pro tour for the past several years, rated femininity first, golf second. Carol, a 6′ 3″ "effervescent blonde" said her height made her self-conscious. Whether it did or not, she was careful about the selection of her wardrobe. Being one of few players to wear culottes on the course at all times gave her "a fine sense of femininity," and it was said that "her clothes tend to accentuate her size while at the same time complimenting it." Commenting about her appearance Carol stated:

> I know I have the longest legs in the whole world, but they're kind of nice legs. And I think the skirts look so much better than old shorts . . . We all should try to look more feminine out there. Being thought of as anything other than a woman absolutely frosts me (18:23).

Indications that concern and attention to dress and behavior did not go unnoticed or unappreciated by the viewing and reporting public were evident in such examples of reporting as:

There was Marlene Hagge, with her orange pigtails and her neat curves and most of the men in the gallery in her "army" (18:22).

There was the goddess, Sharron Moran, last year's Rookie of the Year, with her glowing teeth and her wide hats (18:22).

She [Carol Mann] is now the tour's leading money winner and certainly one of its most colorful personalities (18:23).

there are the ever-present elements of girlishness that can be most pleasant. Talking about her shot on 15, Miss Mann said, "I got goose bumps when I chipped in." One can hardly imagine Arnold Palmer saying that (3:23).

And when describing Donna Caponi, the 1969 U.S. Women's Open Golf Champion, Curry Kirkpatrick used the phrases, "a bubbly 24-year-old in a pink gingham . . . a crisp cutie in gingham" (16:54).

In speaking of the progress being made by the women's pro tour, Lennie Wirtz, the tour director, said:

The galleries are larger, and the whole tour is getting more attention. One reason is that the girls are taking an active part . . . We're not so obscure anymore, everyone is working on promotion and the girls are finally getting credit for being people rather than a bunch of Amazons (18:22).

In women's tennis circles, from amateur to professional and everything in between, the focus appears to be more and more on youth and glamour. The attempt to bring a special feminine glamour to the tennis courts already has had a rather "colorless" history. Dating from 1947, the two principal contenders in the battle over the direction of women's tennis fashions may be said to be Ted Tinling, a leading London fashion designer and creator of about two thirds of the tennis costumes which were worn in the 1969 women's competition at Wimbledon, and the Wimbledon Tournament Committee. "Tinling screams for color in tennis. Wimbledon insists on white." In his attempt "to shock the tournament committee out of its white rut," Tinling has sent to the courts: Joy Gannon with blue and pink hems, Gussie Moran with lace panties, Beverly Baker in the peekaboo suit, Maureen Connolly (his first "modeled" woman Wimbledon champion) in youthful dresses embroidered with tiny white-on-white kittens, butterflies, and poodles, Doris Hart in a classic pleated skirt, Italy's Lea Pericoli in a pink petticoat, Karol Fageros with lace-covered gold lamé tennis pants, and Maria Bueno with diamond-shaped petals of color decorating her skirt lining (2). Although the colorless decree at Wimbledon had not been abolished by 1969, most other courts provided glamorous proof that women's fashions in tennis were quite up to date.

An attempt to describe or to discuss the glamour and femininity in the sports of figure skating and gymnastics is perhaps an unnecessary one. Few, if any, would deny either the athletic ability or the classical beauty and graceful poise of Peggy Fleming. Miss Fleming, having won two

World Figure Skating titles and numerous United States titles, became for many the symbol of the beauty, the poise, and the athletic ability that women could bring to the sport world. In the 1968 Winter Olympics, Peggy performed a near flawless free skating routine—collecting 5.9 scores out of a possible 6.0 from all nine judges—to become the "darling of the Games" and only the fifth American woman ever to win a gold medal in the Winter Olympic competition. Recognition of the role of glamour and femininity in the sport of figure skating is, however, by no means recent. At the same time it has been apparent that public response to the delightful blend of the beautiful and the athletic took place in the sport of figure skating well in advance of similar appreciation in other forms of sport for women. As long as thirty to forty years ago American moviegoers, as well as the sport world, knew the name of Sonja Henie, Norwegian-born figure skating champion and later Hollywood movie queen. Other "queens" and "champions" who brought their own unique blend of athletic skill and womanly grace to this physically demanding sport include: Barbara Ann Scott, Tenley Albright, Carol Heiss, and of course, Peggy Fleming.

In women's gymnastic events as in women's figure skating competition, there has been an inherent demand within the sport itself that the "true champions" of these events possess and be able to demonstrate, without an obvious attempt at doing so, a feminine finesse and graceful flow of movement which completely belies the physical battle and enormous expenditure of energy occurring somewhere beneath the very composed surface. In figure skating, the woman competitor must perform leaps, turns, spins and a variety of balancing acts without a hint of hesitation or indication of effort. The woman gymnast must convince the judges that her Herculean tasks—press to a hand stand on the beam, her "Heck dismount" from the bars, her floor exercise routine complete with aerial cartwheel and full-twisting somersaults and her lay-out hand spring vault on the horse—are all performed without benefit of such physiologic prerequisites as cardio-respiratory fitness or muscular strength and endurance. Whereas men gymnasts are permitted, even expected, to "look strong" while performing on the horizontal bar, on the parallel bars, and in floor exercise routines, the women must look only "graceful" while performing similar skills on the uneven parallel bars, on the balance beam, and in floor exercise routines. As one article noted:

> Skill counts more than beauty in athletics, but both qualities are happily combined in the women's U.S. Gymnastic team (44:28).

In recent years, however, changes in gymnastics judging for women's events have placed still greater emphasis on the performer's appearance—poise, gracefulness, fluidity. Even facial expressions are to be judged in order to distinguish the artificial smiles from the sincere. In short, it is no longer sufficient simply to execute a given skill or stunt correctly; it must be performed with such effortless ease that most spectators are completely unaware of the extreme difficulty of the feats which they applaud. As Bob Ottum described when he observed the women gymnasts during pre-Olympic competition in Mexico City:

> all the girls are leggy, tiny-waisted creatures who uniformly manage to look strong and helpless at the same time (33:23).

By way of contrast, one might consider the development of the feminine and the glamorous in the world of track and field. Although the public seemed ready decades ago to accept a figure-skating female athlete, it seemed equally unprepared or unwilling, until recently, to accept female runners, hurdlers, high jumpers and discus throwers as feminine. Although the reasons may be numerous, perhaps there is one reason which stands out as one of the most significant. Pioneer women in track and field competition were no doubt very courageous, very dedicated, very skilled, but, in some instances, very unfeminine. This appeared to have led to a rather widely spread rumor that for a woman to be successful in track and field events she had to look like a "blacksmith." The rumor became a type of self-sustaining hypothesis: few women who by their appearance and manner might be considered "feminine" turned to track and field for competitive experiences. Other women who considered themselves unable to compete in the "feminine world," or who believed others viewed them as unfeminine because of body build and/or manner were drawn to the sport, perhaps in order to seek the recognition and sense of accomplishment they were denied, or thought they were denied, elsewhere. This is not to say that all women participating in track and field at all levels of competition before or during the emergence of the new image in women's track were of the "Brunhilde" or "blacksmith" type. But they were present in sufficient number, they captured enough headlines, and appeared in enough newsreels to have an effect on public opinion that is only recently being altered.

It is on this point that several questions might be raised. Has too much of the blame for the projection of such an image been placed at the doorstep of track and field competition or of any other sport in which such a hypothesis has been at work, or in truth, was it the sport of track and field which produced an undesirable image? Phrasing the question a bit differently: Is Wilt Chamberlain over seven feet tall BECAUSE he plays basketball or could it be he plays basketball because he is over seven feet tall?

Regardless of how one resolves such questions, to those who have observed the scene it has become increasingly apparent that the image, therefore the hypothesis, therefore the rumor, about track and field for women has and still is changing rather drastically.

In her own way Wilma Rudolph was for women's track and field what Sonja Henie, Barbara Scott and Carol Heiss had been for figure skating. In the 1960 Olympics in Rome, Miss Rudolph surprised the world as she sprinted to three gold medals, and in the process, won for herself a place in the hearts of the Italians and the world of sports, all without endangering her femininity. During the past decade, sport commentaries and news articles extolling the womanly qualities of American women track and field athletes have been almost as numerous as those reporting the remarkable progress in skill made by those same girls and women in national and international competition. From such articles it is possible to piece together part of the story of the emergence of track and field for women in the United States.

In the year or two following Wilma Rudolph's stunning Olympic victories the new found fervor over women's track apparently settled back to previous levels. Early in 1963 a German girl, Jutta Heine, who had competed against Wilma Rudolph in Rome came to the United States to run against the Olympic title holder. The appearance of the beautiful and talented Miss Heine again called attention to the sport of women's track. One article referred to her as a "dash of style for track and field" and claimed that her brief presence did more to promote the sport of track and field "than Perry O'Brien has done during his athletic life," even though she failed to finish first.

> German sprinter Jutta Heine, running for the first time in the United States, came in second in Los Angeles but did more for sport than an arena full of record breakers (56:13).

About the time Wilma Rudolph was considering retirement, and spurred on by the fact that there did not appear to be an immediate American successor to her Olympic titles, writers questioned the depth and quality of track and field programs for girls and women in this country.

> Pretty girls from all over the world are competing in track and field—and having fun. But where are the Americans? They are at home, demurely avoiding physical stress and missing out on a very good thing (54:54).

This same article went on to point out that

> the odd thing about all this is that emancipated American women have long since dropped the philosophy that playing fields are strictly for cheerleading and gymnasiums made only for sock hops . . . Our girls golf, swim, ski, skate and perform in most other sports, but they dodge track and field as though it were a combined course in weight lifting and wrestling (54:54).

Accompanying the article was a series of photographs of top European competitors and the article concluded that running has not diluted the natural loveliness of . . . and other European track stars any more than playing flanker back ever dulled Frank Gifford's handsome cast (54:54).

As though to highlight the "glamour bit," in 1964 *Sports Illustrated* brought the Texas Track Club to the attention of its readers in an article entitled "Flaming Mamie Ellison's Bouffant Belles of Abilene, Texas." One of the club members had been reported as saying:

Bouffant is easier to run in because the wind doesn't blow your hair in your face (43:4).

It was noted some years later, however, that the Texas Track Club appeared to be a team of young gals whose beauty and glamorous hairdos outdid their ability on the track.

Prior to the Tokyo Olympics, *Life,* in a pictorial section covering several track hopefuls, referred to "the classic grace of U.S. women athletes who are shooting for places on the Tokyo-bound team" (20:38). In the same article ReNae Bair, leading United States javelin thrower, was quoted as saying that "people expect you to be big and masculine, but they're surprised to find I'm different" (20:38).

Another article pointed out that following a rather surprising showing by many of the 168 participants in the 1964 Olympic tryouts, sports reporters as well as others had begun referring to the women's team as OUR girls rather than simply *the* girls, a fact of considerable significance (1b).

The Olympic sprint titles won by Wilma Rudolph did not leave America as many had feared was inevitable. Rather, this country sent to the 1964 Olympics not one but two outstanding women sprinters, Edith McGuire and Wyomia Tyus. Although the women's team had two Olympic champions the over all depth of the team was still insufficient for successful competition with European countries in dual meets.

Early in 1965, when America was suffering through another post-Olympic year sport slump, promoters of the national AAU indoor track meet to be held in New York decided to invite not only outstanding male athletes from foreign countries but female competitors as well. Or, as one article in *Newsweek* described the decision:

Panicky meet directors fired off a fusillade of invitations to other lands, where woman's proper place is not necessarily in a cocktail lounge (30:65).

The result was "a startling invasion of women" as over 200 women competitors took part in the meet, and as one reporter related the story:

Indoor track had never looked more fetching . . . New York fans were treated to the spectacle of lithe young women . . . in colorful selection of pants . . . blouses . . . shorts, leotards . . . bikini-short shorts. But if the variety of blossoming fashions was impressive, the exuberant athletes wearing them were even more so (42:19).

Later that same year, a track and field team composed of men and women prepared to go abroad for a series of dual meets. Sports reporters were prompted to recall that:

> The last time a big U.S. women's track team invaded Europe, the girls fell flatter than a bride's soufflé. The place was Moscow, and the tremors from that debacle were felt even in Washington (22:108).

This time, however, the results were somewhat different. The first stop was England and "for the first time, either indoors or out they (the women's team) won an international match" (22:108).

Then, a few days later, in West Germany, they were able to repeat the feat with another victory. The big test for the women's team was coming up later that same summer, however. After covering the 1965 National AAU championships and referring to the United States versus USSR dual track meet to be held in Russia, *Sports Illustrated* summed up the situation this way:

> Whether our girls have caught up with the Soviets will be disclosed at Kiev this month. But last week's AAU women's track and field meet produced a blend of talent and beauty that is hard to beat (12:20).

And, for the first time it appeared as though the dashes would not be our only hope for victory. From an article highlighting Marie Mulder and Janell Smith came this statement:

> Two strictly feminine teen-agers from towns and backgrounds widely separated are proving that running for distance is not so un-American after all (59:34).

And, again speaking of Marie and Janell, John Underwood referred to them as:

> girls full of expectancy and promise; girls who can run like boys with hardly an inhibition to clutter their way, and who can make the switch to the dance floor without missing a beat (59:35).

The summer of 1968 brought tryouts for another Olympic team. And it quickly became obvious that the long awaited development of depth was beginning to assert itself, making the 1968 women's track and field team the strongest ever.

> When it was all over, it was clear that something wonderful was happening to women's track and field in the U.S. Anyone . . . had to be surprised by this sudden burst of achievement, but those special fans . . . who follow the game closely had seen it coming all along (34:19).

Along with the improvement in performances the accompanying theme, that of the importance of the femininity image in women's track and field, was still being reported. For example, during pre-Olympic competition in Mexico City, Charlotte Cooke, American middle distance runner, was quoted as saying that "it is up to girl athletes to look as feminine on the track as off" (33:23). According to the reporter, Charlotte

Cooke, who had just won the 400 meters competition, had set an excellent example.

"Being a girl and an athlete goes hand in hand," said Mamie Rallins, the tiny-waisted hurdler on the American Olympic team. Ed Temple, women's track coach, called the American girls on the Olympic team more feminine than the swimmers, and another coach called the youthful touch of femininity in track "a great influx of pretty young things coming into the sport" (34:16). Calvin L. Brown, an announcer and follower of the development of track and field, made the observation that the girls in track find that "there can be a certain air of glamour in all this. For one thing, running does great things for the legs. It makes them shapelier" (34:19).

In 1969, another observer noted that "feminine charm and bright new faces come to the fore in the girls' and women's national AAU championships" as some 500 girls and women battled for the national title, and places on the United States national track and field team. As this writer stated:

> If the meet emphasized one thing, it was that a girl no longer has to look like a boy to compete in track and field, a development that becomes more obvious every year (60:20).

As Ken Foreman, coach and author in the area of track and field, reported:

> The women runners are tremendously sensitive people. They are an amazing transition from the typical brute, from the archetype that all those who don't know women's track claim them to be (29b:70).

One of the 500 participants in the meet was beauty queen, "Miss Tall Oregon," Tara Sheldon. Miss Sheldon had to bring to the meet not only her track equipment but also a suitcase with evening clothes since she was on her way to the "Miss Tall Universe" contest.

> "That's me," said Tara, the spirit of femininity. "Spiked shoes and stiletto heels" (60:22).

In 1965, John Underwood had reported:

> losing to Russian women is still accepted as a matter of course—no great disaster—though in deference to our own women we have quit calling the Russians "muscle molls" (59:35).

In July 1969, the American women scored their first track and field victory over the Russian women in eight attempts. The unexpected or, what some had called the impossible, had occurred. In the last event of the women's competition, John Davis, coach of the team, was reported to have summed up the victory by saying:

> We really wanted this one. We've waited 11 years for it. People have always looked at the Russians as the power in women's track. Now they will start looking towards us as well (29:38).

Morris A. Bealle in his book *The Softball Story* made a statement appropriate to the discussion of glamour and femininity in women's sports. He declared that many top-flight girl softball players "could enter any beauty contest in the land and finish in the upper brackets" (17:92). That was precisely what a first baseman from Kansas, Debra Dene Barnes, did and she became Miss America of 1968.

Curry Kirkpatrick, however, took exception to Bealle's comments and declared "as a matter of truth, there isn't much girl watching at a women's softball game," although he did concede that "the widely held theory that a girl softballer is less attractive than a lumberjack is a false one" (17:92).

Jane Anne Jayroe, Miss America of 1967, was another softball player who batted 1.000 in the beauty contest league. It was reported that to her a curve meant something in addition to its relationship to a beauty contest. Her pitch on opening day to Kansas City catcher Phil Roof was considered to be "better than most politicians'" (48:60).

Several years earlier, the parents of another Miss America, Marilyn Van Derbur, appraised the role of sports in their daughter's life. They were reported as saying that the thing that counts most in making a girl beautiful is participation in sports. They went on to say that Marilyn always had lovely blond hair and green eyes, "but her 35-25-36 figure didn't come by accident. She fought for it . . . by skiing, swimming, playing tennis, riding horseback. Sports gave her self-assurance, poise and vitality. Those qualities clinched the title for her" (35:6).

CUTE KIDS OR COMPETITORS—ARE THEY TOUGH ENOUGH?

As was mentioned earlier in this chapter, there have appeared to be two major objections to sports competition for women: one is the question of femininity; and the second relates to the physiologic and psychologic concerns. It is the purpose of this section to deal with the latter ones. Are American women athletes, especially the young participants in all areas of sports, simply "cute kids" or do they possess also the "toughness" qualities demanded of athletic competition?

Such questions obviously have been answered in the affirmative by American women swimmers year after year as they withstand all efforts from opposing teams and go calmly about the business of setting world records. In Winnipeg, Canada, during the Pan American Games, those persons fortunate enough to get tickets in the new swimming facility "watched in awe as American boys too young to shave and American girls too young to date set records, beginning for the U.S. what is sure to be the most extravagant accumulation of medals in the 16-year history of the games" (58:20).

Again, writing of the Pan American Games, one reporter confirmed the view that U.S. domination of the swimming events was complete:

> Launched in age-group programs before they could tie their shoes, the amazing U.S. kid swimmers included girls who had to tie strings across the straps of their suits to keep them up . . . kids, too, who were talking retirement before they were half through their teen years (58:23).

Of Debbie Meyer, who at the age of 14 had set a world record in the 400 meter, and had knocked 14 seconds off the world mark in the 800 meter, the report stated:

> Too young to hold hands but plenty old enough to swim the hours away, Debbie swam like there were two of her (58:23).

American women swimmers, however, do not have a complete monopoly on all world records. In 1965, when Karen Muir from South Africa was only 12 years old she set a world record in a backstroke event. At that time Karen was the youngest world record holder in any event in any major sport (49:10).

The success which has surrounded American swimmers has seemed to elude American women skiers. The best women skiers have come from France, Austria, and Canada. Speaking of skiing competition among the women just prior to the 1968 Winter Olympics one reporter observed that, while Canada's Nancy Greene rocked the European ski circuit by winning four big races and getting a fast start toward the new World Cup title,

> the U.S. girls contented themselves with the cute-kids awards. The main progress the Americans made was social. They looked cuter, smiled brighter, dressed better and danced sharper than any group before them (13:11).

Although those "cute kids" have come close to pulling off a few surprises, the big victories have not been theirs.

In speaking of one of the best women tennis players in the world, one reporter described her "type of toughness" in this way:

> On one side of the net was Billie Jean Moffitt King . . . the myopic pepper pot who is totally and absolutely dedicated to the proposition that Billie Jean Moffitt King is the No. 1 tennis player in the world, which she is (4:83).

Billie Jean made good use of that "toughness" as she won three consecutive Wimbledon singles titles and in 1967, at Wimbledon, she won the singles, doubles, and mixed doubles titles, thereby accomplishing the first "sweep" in sixteen years.

Peaches Bartkowicz at 15 became the youngest girl to win the Junior Wimbledon title. Her coach described her "toughness" on the court by saying that "she's mean, you hold up a racket and she'll knock it out of your hand from across the court. And if you hold it too tight, she'll break your wrist" (14:29).

Sport described its "teenage athlete of the month," tennis player Andrea Voikos, one of the finest teen-age girl tennis players in the country, by saying that "the thing that will get her to the top is fight. She wants to beat everybody that she plays . . . it means a lot to her to succeed' (5:84). Explaining that the raw climate of New England is far from ideal for developing tennis champions, experts believed her competitiveness would overcome that handicap.

> She plays tennis like it was a world war. Bad weather wouldn't dare interfere with her ambitions. She already has the most important ingredient—the desire to excel (5:84).

In the 1965 National Championship AAU Meet, Marie Mulder at the age of 15 surprised the world of women's track when, within the time of one and a half hours, she not only entered both the 880 and 1500 meters events in the women's division but also won both events. About such an accomplishment it was said:

> Her easy recovery seemed to smash forever the notion that females should not gasp their way more than twice around a quarter-mile track (12:20).

At the National Championships in 1969, Brooks Johnson, coach of track and field team for girls, talked about the "fresh and attractive faces" in the girls' division (ages 14 to 17):

> With so much talent and dedication in the girls' division, Americans can look forward with pleasure to the 1972 Olympics. "Our young girls are so serious about track that you have to watch out that they don't overtrain" (60:21).

In speaking of the "toughness" of the girls with whom he had been working, Johnson declared that "they can take pain much better than men" (60:20).

And, from Bil Gilbert, author of the article referred to previously, "Thank Heaven For—," came this appraisal:

> In the beginning the tendency around the pasture was to continue thinking of the girls as little squealers who were out for sort of an athletic party. However, it slowly became apparent that they were something far different, more than this. Whatever we did—jogged, sprinted, jumped—there were always half a dozen girls well up front, ahead of the boys. Furthermore, at the end of a two-hour practice session it was invariably a girl who wanted to know if she couldn't run some more (9:79).

When Mrs. Roberta Bingay not only started but completed the Boston Marathon (26 mile, 385 yard distance) at a clip fast enough (3 hours, 21 minutes) to finish ahead of 290 of the event's 415 male runners, a writer made this observation:

> How jarring an effect Mrs. Bingay's example of feminine endurance had on countless male egos can easily be guessed. But even if she fails to convince a single housewife that she is as capable as her husband of spading the garden, the performance should do much to phase out the old-fashioned notion that a female is too frail for distance running (1c:67).

It would be difficult to challenge the "toughness" of the twenty American girls who trained rigorously for berths on the United States cross-country ski racing team although they were described as stepping straight from the pages of Louisa May Alcott:

> cherry cheeks that need no rouge, complexions of outdoor children, the clear eyes of guileless girls; there is in all of them a delicacy of Little Womanhood . . . But do not be deceived . . . How they look and what they do are far different things (14b:72).

Training routine for one young hopeful included running 20 miles and then lifting weights, all before breakfast. For another it was wind sprints by the hour, up the steepest hills available. Still another bicycled 70 miles in a morning workout.

Perhaps the most talked-about girls in sports at the time of this writing were the girl jockeys. It all began when Kathy Kushner, a 1968 Olympic equestrienne, took her case to court when she was denied the right to ride horses professionally. The courts ruled that to refuse her application for a license simply on the grounds that she was a woman would be to deny her civil rights. Unfortunately for Kathy, shortly after receiving her long-fought-for license she broke her leg. But there were other girls who also were awaiting the court ruling and they rushed to complete license applications. After threatened and actual strikes and boycotts by the male jockeys, against whom the early female jockeys were scheduled to ride, Diane Crump finally became the first girl to ride in an all-male race. And on May 2, 1970 she was the first girl jockey to ride in the Kentucky Derby. Although girl jockeys had broken through the legal barriers, they had by no means seen the end of the resistance to their invasion of the traditionally male-oriented world of thoroughbred racing. Much of the resistance obviously came and continues to come from the men against whom they race. As *Time* reported it,

> The jockeys' complaint was that a fragile female simply could not handle 1000 pounds of race horse charging through the pack. There are hazards enough, they pointed out, without girl jockeys falling all over the track (57:73).

Some jockeys have said that so far, girls have been given all the advantages, but that "the physical and mental strain will get to them" because they aren't tough enough.

> Racing's too tough for women. Horse racing's a contact sport. They're (race tracks) using girls like a carnival act would use some odd person (25:1D).

Others said scornfully that "they'll find out how tough it is and then they'll give it up. Women are fragile, dumb, a menace to the track" (19:33). Despite such comments and feelings, Barbara Jo Rubin, Diane Crump, Tuesdee Testa, and Sandy Schlieffer have been racing and doing their share of winning. Seventeen-year-old Barbara Jo, who, by the end of March, 1969, had won on nine of her 18 mounts and was two for three at New York's Aqueduct Racetrack against the country's best jockeys (a record that is "almost beyond belief" for an apprentice girl), declared that she wanted to be more than just a novelty: "I want to get experience and take my chances, and prove myself like every other rider" (31:87). Sandy Schlieffer, the first woman ever to win a horse race in Colorado, "began carving a place for herself in the man's world of jockeys early in 1969" (36:19). Her first win was in Phoenix, Arizona in April of 1969 and by July she had ridden in more than 100 races, had won four and placed second in several. Jim Fuller, a well-known jockey tutor who held Sandy's contract as an apprentice jockey, said:

> She's the 26th apprentice I've had in 40 years. And at this stage of the game, Sandy's a far better prospect than any of the others have been. The track officials think she's good too (36:20).

Because of the comparatively recent entry of women into the circle of professional riders, it may be too early to judge whether lady jockeys are "cute kids or competitors"—whether or not they are "tough enough." The answer will become evident later.

EQUALITY OF OPPORTUNITY AND RIGHTS

According to current news coverage, women's liberation movements are bursting out all over. Although much of the publicity is given to the wayout manifestations of feminine power, women are most assuredly fighting for one of "the most basic of their rights"—to play, to be fit, to compete in sports. In the process, answers are being forged to questions regarding physiologic toughness, psychologic equilibrium, appropriate femininity, emerging glamour, and the reshaping of the image of the American sportswoman. But, even as records are broken, even as stories are written and questions are being answered, there appear to be factors which continue to be instrumental in the blockage of the growth of sport for women in the United States.

One factor frequently mentioned is the lack of opportunity for a great percentage of young American girls to participate and excel in sports during high school and college. Another factor considered as a toggle around the neck of growth of sport for women is the apparent objection to having women compete against men in noncontact sports.

A protesting father, explaining that his daughter was a promising young tennis player, said that "she cannot participate as a member of the high school boys' tennis team even though she could defeat at least half of its members" (45:67). He went on to explain that there was no team for girls because few in the school had the background to play at that competitive level.

The rules and regulations of most athletic leagues, conferences, and sport-governing bodies, at most levels of competition, prohibit men and women from competing directly against each other in most competitive athletics. Recently such regulations were challenged and there appeared to be sufficient precedent for such challenges. In most European countries, men, women, and children run races simultaneously although prizes are awarded separately. In the United States boys and men often run distance events together. One woman middle distance runner made these comments:

> where there are few women running, mixed competition would provide the only real competitive experience for girls with exceptional talent. As things stand now, a girl may never have had anyone . . . challenging her in a race until she reaches the national championships (47:100).

She went on to mention the respectable running times of women she has known who have entered the Boston Marathon, and concluded that there really weren't any good arguments for forbidding men and women to compete simultaneously even in distance events.

> Physically women are capable of running the distances, competitively they will benefit from it and personally they will enjoy it (47:100).

Rules preventing such competition between boys and girls and men and women have been and are being studied and challenged at both the high school and college level. At present a limited number of states allow boys and girls in high schools to compete together in interscholastic noncontact sports. A recent decision allowed New York school girls to compete with boys in some interscholastic sports on an experimental basis (many intramural sports have long been coeducational) (40:16).

The Southeastern Athletic Conference has allowed girls to compete with men in sports and to try out for places on men's athletic teams. A newspaper article reported the story of Linda Tuero who, at Tulane University in New Orleans, became the first female to receive a full athletic scholarship. After winning the number five spot on the tennis team, Linda declared that the boys on the team showed no resentment toward her. However, it was apparent that her presence on the team caused complications. In Tulane's opening match, no one wanted to play her. Other opponents scheduled to play Tulane informed the coach that their conference rules prohibited their players from competing with girls and that their schools had ordinances against women athletes. Linda Tuero spoke for many women in similar situations when she said:

> I'm just a girl. I don't see what they're so worried about . . . I'm not looking to embarrass a lot of men . . . They're just afraid to lose to a girl . . . and that doesn't say much for them (27:8A).

Due to instances such as this one the Southeastern Conference decided to reverse its decision to allow girls to compete with the men on their athletic teams.

Apparently, male rejection of women athletes has existed in a variety of sports, but most particularly in sports which have been traditionally "male oriented" as the following examples attest.

Patricia McCormick of Big Springs, Texas is a celebrated and courageous bullfighter. She has, during her illustrious career, fought larger bulls than any other woman and has killed over 300 of them. However, in the words of Carlos Arruza, great Mexican matador, "her defect is that she is a woman" (23:39). Officially she could never become a matador because no male matador would sponsor a woman in the ritual called the "alternativa" in which apprentices are advanced to senior rank.

Three women from England, hoping to "beat the men at their own game," announced their plans to enter long-distance auto races in Europe including the 24-hour Le Mans race. They elicited this comment from a sportswriter: "Stay home and maintain ladylike exteriors, sweeties" (50:8).

An Australian racing driver, apparently forced off the track by an auto driven by a lady driver from Holland reportedly had this to say: "Blast them birds, anyway. Why don't they stay in the kitchen where they belong?" (25:1D).

Officially, women have not been recognized as legal entrants in the Boston Marathon and the small group of women who do run each year must either join the runners after the official start of the race or disguise themselves and attempt to lose themselves somewhere in the large mass of contestants. When Mrs. Bingay ran the 26 mile course and crossed the finish line ahead of the 290 male runners, an official of the marathon, upon receiving news of her accomplishment, was quoted as making this announcement:

> Mrs. Bingay did not run in the Boston Marathon. She merely covered the same route as the official race while it was in progress. No girl has ever run in the Boston Marathon (1c:71).

As has already been mentioned, women jockeys have frequently met rejection from their male rivals. A veteran jockey commented that lady jockeys may be here to stay, but added the following:

> you know what will happen! They already have a separate dressing room. Soon they'll want lady valets to saddle up their horses and carry tack. Then they'll want a lady steward to look after their interests (8:43).

Still another male jockey demonstrated his feelings by cutting off Tuesdee Testa as they came out of the gate, a feat for which he promptly received a ten-day suspension (57:74).

Reportedly, a ranking United States tennis player viewed women tennis players as a destructive force in the major tennis tournaments. As he shared his ideas on how to "insure the survival and growth of tennis" he was quoted as saying:

> we've got to get rid of the girls in major tournaments. If they want to establish separate tournaments for the women as they do in golf, that's all right, but they don't belong in the same tournaments with men (53:19).

There may be several factors which have been instrumental in blocking the growth of sport for women in the United States, but, as the writer of one newspaper article stated, men's pride often blocks athletic equality.

> man's sore toe—his hairy-legged pride—has recently evolved as an ogre under the bridge . . . The ogre will not suffer the indignity of having a scented, flowery little woman compete against him (27:8A).

Referring specifically to male jockeys, for whom he expressed sympathy, the Reverend Thomas Boslooper expressed this opinion:

> here is one area in which women can compete on absolutely equal terms with men. Historically, women have been superb handlers and riders and physically we know that an athletic, medium-sized woman could certainly be the equal of a very small man. But here we run into an exaggeration of the classic male fear—the jockey's masculinity is being threatened by these women after he had escaped into a sport which was a kind of sanctuary from all the big men who had threatened him all his life (21).

Clayton Thomas, too, exclaimed that for many men there is still "a stigma attached to being beaten by a girl" (40:16). An interesting contradiction to that position, however, was offered by George Plimpton when he assayed some long-standing clichés about women and sport put to him by *Mademoiselle*. When asked if a woman should never attempt to win in sports competition against a man, Plimpton reportedly answered:

> No, that's nonsense. A man is always surprised, like being stabbed by a mugger, when it happens—but I suspect his feeling is ultimately one of admiraton. It's absurd to resent the fact that a girl is athletic. A good girl athlete is one of life's pleasures (37:197).

He went on to add:

> Obviously, if you play tennis or golf with a girl, it is much more fun if she's good at it. There is nothing more disconcerting than to play with somebody who constantly misses the ball completely—giggling sharply as she does so (37:197).

In professional sport the fight for equality of opportunity appears to be primarily a financial one. In 1968, when the tennis committee announced the prize-money list for the Wimbledon tournament, Mrs. Ann Haydon Jones, Britain's number one player, threatened to pull out of the competition unless the women's purses were raised. The winner of the men's singles was to receive $4,800 while the women's single winner would receive but $1,800. Mrs. Jones had some support for her move in Lady Churchill, who took up the women's cause and expressed her sentiments in a letter to *The Times*, and in Angela Mortimer Barrett, the last British player to win at Wimbledon, who reportedly described the tournament's offering as "an insult to our sex" (52:9).

The Ladies' Professional Golfers Association, the organizational magnitude of which reportedly exceeds that of any other professional group in women's sports, also fights the financial battle. Despite the fact that during the 1960's the women's pro tour had increased in number of tournaments, in size of galleries and, most importantly, in overall prize money available, the women still are waging an uphill struggle to secure increased television exposure and the sums of money that accompany television contracts. The differences between the earnings of the top women and top men pros have been substantial, to say the least, and the women pros seek ways of reducing the huge difference. A few examples may serve to illustrate the extent of that deficit. In 1967, Kathy Whitworth, for winning more tournaments than either Jack Nicklaus or Arnold Palmer, earned a sum of $32,937.50 for the year, which was approximately $17,000 less than Jack Nicklaus had earned in one tournament that year (28:62). From 1955 through 1968 Mickey Wright, a prominent woman in professional golf, for winning 75 tour events (including four Open championships and four LPGA titles) earned about $230,000, while Arnold Palmer over a similar period earned about $1 million for winning 51 tour events (15:37).

In 1968, just when it appeared that the Ladies' tour was going to win a most important battle, that of a signing a $115,000 television contract and join the men on Shell's "Wonderful World of Golf," the men's tournament committee found that the women were to be paid on the same scale as the men and insisted that Shell, the sponsor of the golf series, replace the women with men pros. The explanation of the PGA's rejection of the show was reported, as one put it, "I guess the men felt it wasn't going to enhance the game of golf" (52:9). The article mentioned at least two other things that wouldn't be enhanced, the men's wallets and their pride.

> There is always a possibility that women pros, playing from women's tees, will score better than the men (52:9).

When Gardner Dickinson stated it would hurt the men's professional image to play with the women and that the women should not get so much money, the ladies' response to the men's move, from Kathy Whitworth, president of the Ladies' Professional Golfers Association, was reported to have been:

> We were plenty mad at the time, but maybe we're better off this way. Now we know where we stand with the men. We know we're not going to get any help from them, and we'll have to do it on our own (18:22).

It appears that the male rejection has not been limited to women participants in sport. Elinor Kaine, a syndicated columnist, writes a column called "Football and the Single Girl," and recently wrote a book entitled *Pro Football Broadside* (15b). In New Haven, Connecticut where Miss Kaine had planned to cover a professional football exhibition game, she was told that no women were allowed in the press box at the Yale Bowl. One reason given for the denial of admission was that it was a tradition that only men be allowed in the press box. Miss Kaine obtained an order from a superior court judge ordering Yale and three other defendants to show why she should not be allowed her "equal opportunity" under federal and state civil rights acts (39:19). Apparently some women decided not to depend entirely on the available publications for recording the involvement of girls and women in the world of sport. Early in 1970 *Women's Sports Reporter* (published by the Score Publishing Company of Glendale, California) entered the sport scene as "Women's First Sports Magazine."

The role of women as participants, as spectators, and as reporters naturally will take its place as part of the continuing development in sport, and, will continue to be a factor to be reckoned with in the "wide world of sports." *Wisdom* magazine in an article entitled "Women In A Man's World" stated:

> Shortly after John Stuart Mill wrote his famous The Subjection of Women in 1869, the women's movement forsook its cloistered retreats and took to the market place. Feminism had become articulate enough to lift up its voice in public (63).

Now, 100 years later, women may say that feminism has become articulate enough to left up its voice—in sport.

The next chapter serves to illustrate that sport makes a contribution to the entertainment fabric of culture, a contribution which also appears to be neither trivial nor fragile.

REFERENCES

1. Bernauer, Edmund. "Physical Performance by the Female: An Apparent Superiority?" *In Focus and Perspective,* the 43rd Annual Conference Proceedings of the Western Society for Physical Education of College Women, Pacific Grove, California, 1967, pp. 41-45.
1b. Brody, Tom C. "At Last the Girls are Ours," *Sports Illustrated,* August 17 1964, pp. 68-69.
1c. Brown, Gwilym. "A Game Girl In A Man's Game," *Sports Illustrated,* May 2 1966, pp. 67-71.
2. Brown, Gwilym. "A Little Lace Goes A Long, Long Way," *Sports Illustrated* July 7, 1969, pp. 44-47.
3. Brown, Gwilym. "Carol is the Ladies' Mann," *Sports Illustrated,* July 12, 1965, pp. 22-29.

4. Chapin, Kim. "Goodbye Billie Jean, With Love From Nancy," *Sports Illustrated,* April 8, 1968, pp. 83-85.
5. Cohane, Tim. "She Has The Killer Instinct," *Sport,* July, 1969, p. 84.
6. Coleman, Janet. "Does A Woman Need Sports Appeal," *Mademoiselle,* April, 1968, pp. 196-197, 294-296, 298-299.
7. Gallico, Paul. *Farewell To Sport.* New York: Alfred A. Knopf, 1937.
8. Gianelli, Frank. "Girl Jockey Finds No Bad Feelings," *The Arizona Republic,* April 15, 1969, p. 43.
9. Gilbert, Bil. "Thank Heaven For ——," *Sports Illustrated,* November 27, 1967, pp. 72-82.
10. Glanville, Brian. "The Amazons," *Mademoiselle,* May 1965, pp. 166-167, 228-236.
11. *Golf Digest Annual,* "What's Ahead," February, 1969, pp. 11, 13.
11b. Gordon, Milton M. "The Concept of the Sub-Culture and Its Application," *Social Forces,* Vol. 26, October 1947-May 1948, pp. 40-42.
11c. Higdon, Rose, and Higdon, Hal. "What Sports for Girls?" *Today's Health* (published by the American Medical Association), 45:21-23, 74+, October, 1967.
12. Jares, Joe, "Off To Russia, Without Love," *Sports Illustrated,* July 12, 1965, pp. 20-21, 60.
13. Jenkins, Dan. "A Sudden Streak for Nancy," *Sports Illustrated,* January 30, 1967, pp. 8-13.
14. Jenkins, Dan. "Stop the World, the U.S. Is On," *Sports Illustrated,* May 2, 1966, pp. 26-29.
14b. Johnson, William. "Some New Babes in the Woods," *Sports Illustrated,* December 15, 1969, pp. 72, 75.
14c. Jokl, Ernst, et al. *Sport in the Cultural Pattern of the World.* (A study of the Olympic Games 1952 at Helsinki) Helsinki, Finland: Institute of Occupational Health, 1956, pp. 41-51.
15. Jupp, Nancy. "They Also Play the Game," *Golf,* March, 1968, pp. 36-38, 77-78.
15b. Kaine, Elinor. *Football: Broadside.* New York: Collier-Macmillan Company, 1969.
16. Kirkpatrick, Curry. "A Cool One Turned the Heat On," *Sports Illustrated,* July 7, 1969, p. 54.
17. Kirkpatrick, Curry. "In Stratford, Nobody Beats the Raybestos Brakettes," *Sports Illustrated,* September 11, 1967, pp. 92-93.
18. Kirkpatrick, Curry. "Relax, Girls, It's A Mann's World," *Sports Illustrated,* May 6, 1968, pp. 22-23.
19. Hartack, Bill. *Life,* "Lady Jockeys? Who Needs 'Em," December 13, 1968, p. 33.
20. *Life,* "Olympic Girls," photographs by Don Ornitz, July 31, 1964, pp. 38-47.
21. Lipsyte, Robert. "'It's Woman's Right to Play in Sports!'" *Milwaukee Journal,* (New York Times News Service), March 23, 1969.
22. Lovesey, John. "Quick Young Ladies of Quality," *Sports Illustrated,* April 19, 1965, pp. 108-110.
23. McCormick, Patricia. "A Brave Matadora Explains The Bullfight," *Sports Illustrated,* March 11, 1963, pp. 38-46.
24. Metchem, Rose Mary, "Les Girls in Des Moines," *Sports Illustrated,* February 17, 1969, pp. 34-39.
24b. Metheny, Eleanor. "Symbolic Forms of Movement: The Feminine Image in Sports," *Connotations of Movement in Sport and Dance.* Dubuque, Iowa: William C. Brown Company, 1965.
25. Mueller, Lee, and Gabriel, Joyce. "Women in Sports—I, 'Where To, Girls— the Kitchen or the Race Track,'" *The Arizona Daily Star,* (Newspaper Enterprise Association), April 6, 1969, p. 1D.
26. Mueller, Lee, and Gabriel, Joyce. "Women in Sports—II, There is Femininity Behind Their Prowess," *The Arizona Daily Star,* (Newspaper Enterprise Association), April 7, 1969, p. 8A.

27. Mueller, Lee, and Gabriel, Joyce. "Women in Sports—III, Men's Pride Often Blocks Lady Athletes," *The Arizona Daily Star*, (Newspaper Enterprise Association), April 8, 1969, p. 8A.

28. Mulvoy, Mark. "Miss Avis Against Miss Hertz," *Sports Illustrated*, November 27, 1967, pp. 62-63.

29. Myslenski, Skip. "This Coliseum Could Have Used Lions," *Sports Illustrated*, July 28, 1969, p. 38.

29b. Myslenski, Skip. "A P.T.A. Meeting is Tougher," *Sports Illustrated*, December 8, 1969, pp. 69-70.

30. *Newsweek*, "Measuring Up," February 22, 1965, p. 65.

31. *Newsweek*, "There Goes Barbara Jo," March 31, 1969, p. 87.

32. Orcutt, Maureen. "Are The Women Taking Over?" *The Book of Golf, 1968*, (produced for the PGA with the cooperation of *Golf Digest*) pp. 62-64.

33. Ottum, Bob. "Bully Buildup in Old Mexico," *Sports Illustrated*, October 30, 1967, pp. 20-23.

34. Ottum, Bob. "Dolls on the Move," *Sports Illustrated*, September 2, 1968, pp. 16-19.

35. *Parade*, "What Makes A Girl Beautiful," April 13, 1958, p. 6.

36. Parmenter, Cindy. "The Jockey is a Lady," *The Sunday Denver Post*, July 20, 1969, pp. 18-20.

37. Plimpton, George. "Does A Woman Need Sports Appeal," *Mademoiselle*, April, 1968, pp. 196-197, 294-296, 298-299.

38. Ryan, Pat. "Sprightly Boppers and a Cool Golden Swinger," *Sports Illustrated*, July 3, 1967, pp. 30-35.

39. *Salt Lake Tribune*, "Girl Reporter Hopes for Inside Look," (New Haven, Connecticut, AP), July 29, 1969, p. 19.

40. *Senior Scholastic*, "Girls in Sports—Are They on the Right Track?" March 21, 1969, p. 16.

41. *Sport Annual, 1969*, "A Flood of Gold Medals in Swimming," (produced by *Sport*) p. 49.

42. *Sports Illustrated*, "A Startling Invasion of Women," March 1, 1965, pp. 18-19.

43. *Sports Illustrated*, "Letters From the Publisher," November 27, 1967, p. 4.

44. *Sports Illustrated*, "Lithe Envoys To Our Latin Neighbors," May 6, 1963, pp. 28-32.

45. *Sports Illustrated*, "19th Hole," August 16, 1965, p. 67.

46. *Sports Illustrated*, "19th Hole," April 8, 1968, p. 114.

47. *Sports Illustrated*, "19th Hole," May 20, 1968, p. 100.

48. *Sports Illustrated*, "People," April 24, 1967, p. 60.

49. *Sports Illustrated*, "Scorecard," August 23, 1965, p. 10.

50. *Sports Illustrated*, "Scorecard," March 27, 1967, p. 8.

51. *Sports Illustrated*, "Scorecard," February 19, 1968, p. 10.

52. *Sports Illustrated*, "Scorecard," February 19, 1968, pp. 9-10.

53. *Sports Illustrated*, "Scorecard," June 16, 1969, p. 19.

53b. *Sports Illustrated*, "Scorecard," August 25, 1969, p. 12.

54. *Sports Illustrated*, "Why Can't We Beat This Girl?" September 30, 1963, pp. 54-57.

55. Steinhaus, Arthur H. "Exercise and the Female Reproductive Organs," in *Toward A Better Understanding of Health and Physical Education*. Dubuque, Iowa: William C. Brown Company, 1963, pp. 146-148.

56. Terrell, Roy. "A Dash of Style For Track and Field," *Sports Illustrated*, January 28, 1963, pp. 12-15.

57. *Time*, "Ladies in Silks," April 4, 1969, pp. 73-74.

58. Underwood, John. "The Winning Ways of Winnipeg," *Sports Illustrated*, August 7, 1967, pp. 20-25.

59. Underwood, John. "This Is The Way The Girls Go," *Sports Illustrated*, May 10, 1965, pp. 34-46.

60. Verschoth, Anita. "Some Dashing Dolls Debut in Dayton," *Sports Illustrated*, July 14, 1969, pp. 20-23.

31. Warner, Anne R. "Golden Harvest for the U.S.—and A Hero for Mexico," *Journal of Physical Education*. Yellowstone, Ohio: Physical Education Society of the YMCA's of North America, January-February, 1969, pp. 73-74.

32. Weiss, Paul. *Sport: A Philosophic Inquiry*. Carbondale, Illinois: Southern Illinois University Press, 1969.

33. *Wisdom Magazine*, "Woman In A Man's World," (The Wisdom Society For the Advancement of Knowledge, Learning and Research in Education), August, 1959, pp. 16-18.

33b. *The Woman Bowler* (official publication of the Women's International Bowling Congress), Columbus, Ohio, April 1969 and September 1969.

6

CHAPTER 8

Sport Entertainment — Big Pleasure, Big Business

From a theoretical standpoint, sport behavior, like all other forms of behavior, has been viewed by some sociologists as having a close connection with the entertainment industry and consumer consumption in equipment, facilities, and clothes. The statistics presented and conclusions drawn from studies cited by Lüschen (20:259) seem to suggest that sport today is a prominent leisure-time pursuit of people of all classes, not merely the upper classes. From an empirical standpoint statistics are not needed in order to conclude that sport is one of the indelible originals of the entertainment culture. The epoch of the "Super Spectator" as one writer called it appears to be undeniably upon us. Sport shows are produced in all sizes and in every setting from short informal gatherings to lengthy and elaborate productions held in festooned arenas around the world. Any spectator in America's over 200 million population can take his pick of a multitude of viewing pleasures. And apparently, most, if not all, Americans do so at a large expense. One survey revealed that money spent in spectator sports in 1953 approximated $230 million, while in 1967 the figure jumped to $433 million. Television's stake alone in sport in the thirty years since the first telecast has zoomed from zero to $150 million annually (13b:90). In fact, William Johnson, writing "Television and Sport," a five-part series of articles for *Sports Illustrated* proffered that sport has allied itself so irrevocably with television that it "has sold itself beyond the capacity to control its own destiny" (13b:86).

But, the spectator stampede to television, stadiums, and coliseums is not all of the entertainment picture. A startling boom in participation has characterized every sport, most especially since about 1954. Moreover, sport equipment has become a major product of American industry, insurance relating to sport is increasing each year, and gambling Americans annually bet millions of dollars on sport contests.

Money and leisure appear to have been major stimulants to, or perhaps the *sine qua non* of what was described by the *Wall Street Journal* as "the greatest sport binge in history." As stated in a special report on fun by Frank Trippett in *Look*, "At a paradoxical moment when the country seems obsessed with anger, the pursuit of fun is expanding in ever-quicker leaps." And, as the article continued, "To measure the phenomenon is to flirt with infinitude" (58:28).

Numerous technical periodicals and books, some of which are described in a preceding chapter under literature, present the vast and amorphous statistics of sport entertainment. These statistics, as well as those which follow, are not only difficult to interpret but become quickly obsolete. For that matter, to the social scientist, as Loy and Kenyon pointed out, "the facts themselves are largely trivial; it is discovering an explanation for them that excites the mind" (19:v).

Lack of explanations and encyclopedic thoroughness notwithstanding, this chapter will have served its purpose if it discloses a bird's-eye view of the meaningful figures in the sport dollar—players, participants, programs, and progress—and calls attention to the fact that in terms of entertainment, apparently culture "ain't seen nothin' yet!"

COUNTENANCE OF THE PROS—FRANKLY COMMERCIAL

Reuel Denney in 1957 asserted that by the business standard, which is "the most massive force" in culture, "the ultimate goal of any athletic ability is to provide sports entertainment for cash" (8:125). Some twelve years later, Bill Russell seemed to reaffirm this conviction by his statement: "I've been a professional entertainer, which is how a professional athlete probably should be classified" (32:19).

In 1969 there were 87 major league franchises in the sports of baseball, basketball, football and hockey, as contrasted to a total of 42 in 1959. In these sports, at least, money appears to be the name of the game; and, television seems to have become sport's electronic pleasure pill. As a crisp remark in *Variety* evaluated it: "Where video is concerned . . . sport is just another commodity."

Perhaps chief among the sport spectaculars is football. Long before John F. Kennedy rescued touch football from its proletarian sandlot obscurity, football was a popular viewing pastime. Today the remarkable surge in pro football—new teams, new leagues, franchise shifts—would befuddle even a certified public accountant.

To calculate the amount of money spent on stadiums to house this wunderkind certainly would require the services of a public accountant (for example, Houston built the Astrodome reportedly at a cost of $31.6 million and the proposed domed stadium in New Orleans was to cost somewhere in the neighborhood of $46.4 million). Pro stadium figures become quickly outdated and do not disclose the fact that football lives like a king in the ultimate of athletic facilities on most college campuses.

Although newspaper articles report variously contradictory figures on the football dollar, according to *Broadcasting*, a radio and television trade paper, the sums are nonetheless almost beyond comprehension. Apparently pro football received $34.7 million from the CBS and NBC broadcasting systems in 1969, a sum which is only part of the $53,198,650 total that networks, radio-television stations, and independents are paying for broadcast rights for 26 pro teams and 125 major college and university teams. The ABC system reportedly was expecting to pay $8.5 million to carry games of the merged football leagues on Monday nights in 1970 (33:B9).

As reported in a 1969 news item, something to look for in the near future appeared to be a television contract that could bring pro and college football as much as $200 million yearly and more firms willing to pay $60,000 a minute or more to advertise their products (1). An interesting comparative statistic is that reportedly in the 1968 Super Bowl Game a one-minute television commercial cost $135,000 (13b:88).

And what about football players' salaries? The NFL Players Association survey for 1966 and 1967 showed the mean salary figures for each team in the league and each of the eight playing positions. The Cardinals topped the list with a mean salary of $29,560 in 1967, while the Eagles were at the bottom of the list with mean salaries of $19,145. The quarterback position paid the highest mean salary—$32,658 (55). A partial 1968 statistic may complete the picture. Repeated winners, in this case the Green Bay Packers, earned an extra $60,000 to $70,000 per player in the three years between 1966-1968. That now-famous quarterback sneak executed by Bart Starr that led the Packers to victory over the Dallas Cowboys for the National Football League Championship in 1967 paid each player some $10,000 and put each in line for the $15,000 winner's share in the subsequent Super Bowl Game in January 1968, which, incidentally, they won (34:87-91). But, in the event one is led to believe that pro football doesn't hurt, medical expenses are reported to cost professional football teams more than $2 million a year (54:11).

A few published items perhaps of more interest than the impersonal football dollar, yet typical of its bigness, are these: It was reported that the citizens of Green Bay, Wisconsin quite literally own the Packers pro football team.

Packer stock has been sold to local people (at $25 a share, with a $5,000 limit), and it is understood that no dividends will be paid. Instead, the profits . . . said to bring $8,500,000 into the town each year are put back into the team (34:87-91).

Epitomizing the ultimate in the financial "fun and games" aspect of football is the fact that Danny Reeves bought himself a team named the Rams. Of this exclusive toy he was reported to have said: "Isn't it the dream of every American boy to own a football team?" (57:52).

In terms of fiscal structure the game of professional baseball, 100 years old in 1969, appears to have had strange combinations of good and bad times. Many journalists viewed it as being in deep trouble because attendance had sagged during the past decade or so. One sign of baseball's increasingly spectator-minded attitude, reportedly, was a recent promotion corporation formed solely to boost baseball on a nation-wide basis. It produced a major-league logotype for everything from bumper stickers to soup cans (26:47). The summer of 1969 saw other changes in the game of baseball: realignment of the structure of the two major leagues (an attempt to distribute and to increase "pennant fever"), attempts to combat the "pitching tyranny" (which had threatened to drive the fans from the ball parks) by lowering the pitching mound and decreasing the size of the strike zone, and the return of the "hitters" through the use of a "livelier" ball. These changes have been given as reasons for the revival of our national pastime. And, as noted by Mark Mulvoy, when baseball's new commissioner "exposed baseball's rebirth to the American public" at the annual All-Star Game he "converted the usually boring All-Star event into a three-ring circus." The affair was topped off by the centennial birthday dinner and the announcements of baseball's "greatests"—living team, player and manager and all-time team, player and manager. The game which followed seemed to prove "the bat was back"; the first half of the 1969 season seemed to prove that "the people were back" and many sportswriters seemed convinced that "baseball was back, too."

With expansion, attendance totals have increased more than 2,100,000 in the majors . . . Television ratings have stopped their abrupt plummet. Radio surveys, which are the best measure of outside-the-park fan interest, have astounded the advertising industry (24:15).

The fact that some clubs have sagging attendance while others report increasing numbers of admissions certainly has not been a recent phenomenon nor has it been peculiar to a specific sport. And, current reports revealed no general inclination of spectators to save money by staying away from ball games (football or baseball). In fact, a survey of athletic franchises showed no decline in spectator interest, but rather, that attendance was continuing to increase. Increasing attendance apparently has meant decreasing profits, however, for, as one report showed, runaway inflation has resulted in a profit decline for professional athletic teams. For example, when the Cardinals won the pennant and the World Series in 1967 and topped the National League in attendance (2,000,000 admissions), the team's net profit was the same as in 1966 when it finished sixth and drew fewer spectators (1,700,000).

It was reported that an NFL team that had not had an empty seat in its home stadium for several years was barely making $200,000 a year. Inflation seemed the obvious reason. From 1953 to 1968 the player salaries had increased 700 percent; administrative costs were up 745 percent while scouting costs shot up by 2,700 percent (13c:25). Reportedly the Kansas City Chiefs' (football team) operating expenses increased by nearly half a million dollars in one year, the Washington Redskins doubled their food and lodging costs in five years, the Minnesota Vikings, "noted for their parsimonious salaries," have doubled payroll costs in recent years, and the Cleveland Indians (baseball team) have lost money for the past few years. This report concluded with the remark that "even allowing for the normal amount of executive-suite pessimism, it looks as if the profit squeeze is on in sport" (51:8).

There are ways in which the players, too, eventually feel the profit squeeze. Contrasted with the picture that exceptional prospects in professional baseball receive bonuses reportedly as high as $200,000 and that a promising youngster may be guaranteed as much as $8,000 for a college education if he is signed by a professional baseball club was this picture: In 1967, an announcement of the World Series players' shares showed that the winning St. Louis Cardinals received less per man than the Philadelphia 76'ers got for winning the National Basketball Association championships; and, to take it a step further, the Cardinals got less for winning a seven-game World Series than the Kansas City Chiefs received for losing the Super Bowl. As the report pointed out, "There is a message in there someplace for baseball men" (50:14).

Nonetheless, the evidence has been rather conclusive that in terms of exorbitant spending in baseball, no less than football, the sky is the limit. Although stadiums almost always lose money, the public shells out millions of dollars to meet debts falling due on ball parks. One report noted that the Louisiana legislature was asked to guarantee a $95 million bond issue to pay for a stadium in New Orleans that had been estimated originally to cost $35 million; voters in Kansas City were asked to approve a $43 million bond issue to finance the building of twin football and baseball stadiums, which, although it passed, was not enough to meet rising costs; as of this writing, Washington Stadium had lost $6 million in seven years forcing the District of Columbia to appeal annually for advances from the federal government. The report concluded:

None of which is doing sport any good. New venues, new stadiums, new leagues are all wonderful things—but not when they leave the citizens of a community feeling gulled (52:13).

Basketball, which now encompasses the United States, with its franchises extending from coast to coast, "has further enhanced its reputation by distinguishing itself in that all important field, money" (44). In 1967, Wilt Chamberlain and Oscar Robertson, two of basketball's super stars, ended their annual holdouts and signed to play for one year, reportedly for a combined total of $365,000. In 1968, Wilt Chamberlain signed a long-term contract with the Los Angeles Lakers, reportedly for an amount in excess of $1 million, with some estimates running as high as $3 million for five years. The battle between the National and American Basketball Associations over the services of UCLA's Lew Alcindor was concluded when the 7-foot center signed a contract with the Milwaukee Bucks, reportedly for a figure and "fringe benefits" in excess of $1 million, although the offer from the younger American Basketball Association was supposedly much larger. Following the 1969-1970 basketball season, talented collegiate players benefited from the bidding war of the two professional basketball leagues. Several of them reportedly signed million-dollar contracts.

Money talks in hockey too, which has been called the fastest growing "in" sport. The National Hockey League in 1967 expanded from six to twelve teams and the prediction was that it would change the entire character of big-league hockey, which formerly was called "a tight little business controlled by a few men." The six clubs spent an estimated $65 million on franchise fees, stadiums, and players who already were reportedly "perhaps paid more now in relation to their accomplishments than any other team athlete" (4:35-36). By 1969, the sprawling twelve-team network gamble seemed to be "paying off in five of the six new cities, as imaginative owners with local experience lure more and more fans into shiny modern arenas" (27:64).

The rise in salaries of hockey players accompanied the game's expansion. Bobby Orr and Bobby Hull perhaps have been the best financial symbols of the current hockey boom. When negotiations broke down in his $100,000 salary request, Hull said he would retire. His stand did not go unnoticed.

His retirement lasted one game. Petitioned by their fans before the season opener against St. Louis ("Give Bobby 100 Grand—Don't be Cheap," said one sign), the Hawks relented and signed their 29-year-old star for $100,000 (39:68).

Orr's three-year contract was at a reported $250,000 and the trend seems to be that more players will be asking for more and will get it.

If soccer lacks the financial pizazz generated by other team sports in the United States, it has made up for it in the rest of the world. In Italy, financiers, shipowners, auto manufacturers, oil executives, and others annually try to outbid each other for top soccer players. In 1967, by the end of such a bartering session, an estimated $8 million dollars had been invested, the biggest buyer spending $650,000 for one player and an estimated $1.7 million in all (48:8). A top ranking player like Luis Suarez made an estimated $42,000, in 1967, plus additional side benefits. As far back as 1963, the transfer fee (required from the purchasing team) paid for Angelo Sormoni was $680,400 (15:28). Recently it has been reported that one of the world's highest paid athletes was a soccer player from Brazil whose salary was estimated at $400,000.

Among the individual sports, the saga of money has reigned supreme in the golf world for many years. Arnold Palmer's total winnings for golf tournaments in 1966 were reported to be $154,692.24 (47:40). In 1967 he was labeled by his manager and biographer, Mark H. McCormack, as "the first athlete to become a walking, breathing million-dollar corporation in his prime" (23). In January 1969, Palmer's overall tour earnings to that point were $1,165,565, a figure which amounted to $800 for every round he had played, or $50 for every hole, or $11.65½ for each stroke he had taken in tournament play (53:8). The first winner of the United States Open Championship in 1894 won $150. The winner in 1969, Orville Moody, won $30,000 for the tournament alone plus all the benefits from endorsements that accompany being an Open champion. Victory in the 1968 Open for Lee Trevino brought him $1 million in commercial endorsements.

Television exposure accorded golf tournaments is a year-round big business venture. Twenty-four cameras were used for ABC's "Wide World of Sports" television coverage of the Open Championship in Houston in June 1969. And, since women also play the game of golf, an interesting historic sidelight is that starting in 1966 the USGA and ABC televised the last day of the Women's Open Golf Tournament. Six players vied for $32,000 with a first prize of $10,000, the highest in LPGA history to that date (14:77).

The Professional Bowlers' Tour, as Melvin Durslag reported, had experienced eight years (as of 1969) of success on national television, and, as the PBA pointed out, because bowling has four times as many participants as golf, "almost every time it goes head-and-head against the prestigious game of golf, bowling knocks it into the creek" (9:28). In 1958, the Professional Bowlers' Association was formed and in bowling championships the "pots" are growing larger each year. The professional tour expanded from three tournaments in 1959 worth $47,000 to 35 tournaments in 1968 worth $1.8 million. Wayne Zahn, winner of the 1966 Firestone Bowling Tournament, went on to become the leading money winner in the pro circuit, with almost $55,000 in earnings, while Jim Stefanich won $25,000 for winning the 1967 Firestone tournament alone (31:86-88).

A one-time king in sports' money world is boxing. Fighters in the WBA Championship elimination tournament held in the Houston Astrodome in 1967 to pick a successor to Muhammad Ali (Cassius Clay) all received purses of $50,000, with the exception of one who received $22,560. A crowd of 13,946 people paid $92,560 to see the fights (17:12). This elimination tournament was said to represent "the final takeover by TV of a major sports field" (22:20).

Tennis has become more of a business and is gaining in television exposure. Typical of the modern approach to tennis is the statement that "even the amateurs are getting their money over the table." After all, as noted in this report, Australia's tennis player Roy Emerson as an amateur received about $27,000 a year ($10,000 as a public relations consultant for a cigarette company, $6,000 as a racket consultant, and about $11,000 in tax-free expenses paid by tournament promoters). And, according to this writer "there is the hypocrisy of a sport in which amateurs refuse to turn pro, because that could mean taking a cut in salary" (56:57). The writer, however, pointed out that in this country, "little that surrounds the game of tennis is likely to appeal to him [youngsters] much," although increasing the financial incentives could change the situation. As the structure of tennis competition changes (open tournaments) and as the money available in professional tennis continues to increase, the situation may be resolved and financial incentives could lead to the United States players being the best in the world. As an example of increased professional incentives, in 1966 the International Professional Tennis Association, descendant of Jack Kramer's professional group, paid Dennis Ralston, top-ranked U.S. amateur tennis player, $70,000 for a two-year contract. And, according to Frank Deford, the professional tennis players' tour "is becoming bigger, better organized and, most important of all, more lucrative . . . ready to rake in the big money the way golf has" (7:58).

Skier Jean-Claude Killy, winner of everything in sight (in 1967 he won 16 of 20 races, three gold medals at Grenoble and two straight World Cups), reportedly "has been schussing through a hail of new-minted gold . . . about $2 million worth of contracts for three years" (45:4).

Dr. Fager, a one-in-a-lifetime racer, was "the kind of mystical horse" whom the experts voted the best grass, handicap and sprint horse of 1968, along with the coveted "Horse of the Year" honors. All in all, he earned $1,000,642 and his owners syndicated him for an almost unbelievable $3,200,000 (41:34).

Jai alai, whose origins are said to be "as mysterious as those of the Basques, who play it best," required a court that cost $200,000 to build when it was brought to Miami, Florida, and some $12 million in bets were reported as being handled that year (43:22-27).

BIG BUSINESS—FINAL TAKEOVER

James Reston of the *New York Times News Service* observed that "'Bigness' is both the dominant trend and curse of our time. Megalopolis and the conglomerates, the giant nations, giant corporations, giant universities are all in control" (3). This general theme of the time may be viewed as being equally decisive in the takeover in the sport world.

Strictly Professional Business

The year 1969 may have marked the beginning of pro sport becoming strictly business, complete with profit motives and union demands. An expert on labor-management was hired to represent the Major League Baseball Players Association, and, after almost four months of negotiations between baseball players and owners, baseball's first strike since 1889 was resolved. Negotiations included a $1,350,000 player pension hike, a reduction from five to four years in pension eligibility requirements, and various improvements in medical benefits. In the future, maybe the negotiations will go in the direction of the reserve clause by which owners control players' contracts from year to year. As one editorial facetiously put it, "perhaps demands in the future will center around the elimination of double headers, a five or six-day week . . . a salary scale for infielders, outfielders, utility players" (59:28).

An earlier claim had been staked in 1967 by the then newly organized Hockey Players Association. Several concessions were won from management at that time: minimum salary limit $10,000 (up from $7,500), more meal money on the road, pay for playing in exhibition games, a major medical plan, and a modernized pension plan (25:40–41).

In 1968, the National Football League Players Association threatened to strike unless their demands were met by the club owners. Although training camps were opened on schedule they were attended only by rookies and free agents pending the settlement of the player dispute. Negotiations were finally completed, with players being granted a pension of $1600 a month at age 65 for ten-year men, $3,000,000 for their pension fund to be paid over two years, a minimum wage of $12,000 for two-year men and $13,000 for three-year men, $280 exhibition-game pay for a five-year man and $70 for a two-year man. One player, after the first workout in 90° weather, thought the timing of the settlement could have been better and facetiously remarked, "I think we settled too quickly. How about another vote?" (40:23).

It has been reported that professional football players, like baseball players, are interested in taking a closer look at the clauses in their contracts which tie them so closely to the team that drafted and/or signed them.

The rift between golf's touring pros and club pros came to a head in 1968 over the matter of money, among other things. While the club pros had a regular income without the pressure of competition, the touring pros on the other hand had little such security. Most of the big names of the game broke from the PGA (Professional Golfers' Association) and rallied under the banner of a splinter group, American Professional Golfers Inc. The break away from PGA's control appeared to be confirmed when several contracts were signed with tournament sponsors, and, as the report concluded:

> Only a firm voice in its own matters would bring the touring pros back into the PGA fold. Otherwise, it was obvious that the PGA was now out of the major tournament business (42:46).

When the settlement between the two factions was finally reached early in 1969, both sides had backed down from previously held positions; but the agreement did, in effect, give control of the tour to the players.

Amateur Business

As if to match step with the pro sport world, and some persons consider it more professional than amateur, the Olympic competitions have become vast economic enterprises, too intricate and elaborate to detail in any brief accounting book. A few selected observations are presented to give the reader a thumb-nail grasp of the immensity of the economics of this, the greatest sport investment in the world.

Tokyo was said to have changed its face for Asia's first Olympics in 1964. As John Kieran in his book, *The Story of the Olympic Games, 776 B.C.–1964,* described:

> A new city was being born just to accommodate the Olympic Games . . . There was the same convulsive rebuilding, remodeling and restoration as had followed the 1923 earthquake and the horrendous fire bombings of World War II. And this third occasion unquestionably was the most expensive, because the costs reached the astronomical figure of 700 billion yen—or $2 billion by American financial measurement (16:363, 365).*

Some specific figures of Japan's preparation included these: The organizing committee had over 500 persons on its payroll. The national

*From the book *The Story of the Olympic Games* by John Kieran and Arthur Daley. Revised Edition Copyright, ©, 1969 by J. B. Lippincott Company. Reprinted by permission of the publishers.

stadium was enlarged at a cost of $2.8 million. In all, Japan was reported to have spent better than $56 million for sports facilities, $16.8 million for operating expenses, and $280 million on new roads (6:38-41).

Bank officials reported that Japan, as sponsor of the 1964 Olympiad, spent 18 times as much money for installations as did Mexico. The Mexican government, on the other hand, by sponsoring the 1968 Olympics, was expected in time to show a $40 million dollar profit, which would represent probably the first time in the history of the modern Olympics that the Games have been in the black. At any rate, The Banco Nacional de Mexico reported revenues amounting to $192 million, with $153.2 million being spent on installation, organization, and administration of the Games. Other economic by-products reported were impressive additions to Mexico's communications facilities (3,200 new private telephone lines; 2,290 direct telephone lines; 1,300 private telephone switchboards; and 91 new international circuits), and a new wave of tourism to Mexico (2:ID).

As of this writing, Denver, Colorado had already spent 20 to 22 million dollars just for its effort to get the Winter Olympics in February 1976 and in preparing the structures to host the Games. UNIMARK, International Corporation for Design and Marketing, estimated that $1½ million would be spent in communications media alone if Denver would be successful (which it was) in its bid for the Games.

Brutal Business

Commercial affiliations in sport and an athlete's own desire to improve his performance seemingly have produced something of a drug culture in the world of sport. The trend of the pill, capsule, vial and needle to become fixtures of the athletic locker room and the problems created in this turned-on world have been explored in numerous articles. *Sports Illustrated* presented a comprehensive and authoritative study of this vastly complicated problem in a series of three articles (11). These articles cannot be effectively compressed in short abstracts here. They merit complete reading. Perhaps a brief note from another article will serve to highlight the commercial aspect of drugs, if not to summarize the overall problem facing sport. It is concerned with British cyclist Tommy Simpson who collapsed and died while competing in the Tour de France. Apparently, the report revealed that "among those interested in high-quality performances are the companies who hire leading cyclists to advertise their wares . . . the tour was their premier showcase" (49:7). The telling headline to the whole sport drug business may be that which appeared in *The Economist*, reportedly on Simpson's death. The headline read, "Death of a Salesman."

Profitable Business?

The question of how much longer television networks can continue to broadcast sport events in the face of the skyrocketing prices demanded by sport organizations is being asked with increased frequency. The production of sport events has become a losing business for the networks and they are faced with the fact that the sponsors have simply refused to pay the prices asked for advertising time. CBS has experienced difficulty in obtaining sponsors for its coverage of professional football. NBC is reported to be anticipating a loss of $2 million on the "Game of the Week" (baseball) and has been unable to find sufficient sponsors for the World Series, traditionally the "number one attraction." It has been estimated that ABC must accept a loss of $4 million for the rights to televise the 1972 Summer Olympic Games. And on the "biggest attraction in sports," the Super Bowl Game, NBC reportedly lost $1.55 million in 1969. Obviously the networks are concerned. Vice President of CBS Sports, Bill Mac Phail, was quoted as saying:

> In any other business we'd be arrested for throwing money away. We're carrying sports purely as a public service, like news, but we can't take a financial beating indefinitely (10:7).

Stanley Frank went on to explore the possible repercussions of continued resistance on the part of the sponsors and the continued insistence by the sports organizations.

> For years, people in sports have been exploiting television as though it were the fabled golden goose, an inexhaustible source of riches. TV revenue assures profits to owners of major-league baseball and football franchises before they sell a ticket, and pro athletes, of course, are the new plutocrats of American society . . . It is obvious that fantastically inflated salaries are coming from teams' TV income—and that's only half the story. TV also is underwriting players' pension funds that were boosted to giddy levels by recent threats of strikes in baseball and football (10:8).

And, of course, if television coverage of sporting events must be curtailed or in any way reduced by inferior telecasting there will be another large group of "losers"—the viewing public. More recently William Johnson, writing for *Sports Illustrated*, took an in-depth look at the intricate relationship between sport and television and concluded that sport has come to a "life and death dependence on the dollars of commerce" (13d:36).

What bothers some sports promoters and writers is the belief that the professional athlete may be pricing himself out of business with super star contracts, minimum salary rules, and "fantastic" pension plans. Art Rooney, president of the Pittsburgh Steelers football club, was reported to have said that the requested $18,000,000 pension commitment over a period of four years would give a ten-year veteran $40,000 a year at the age of 65.

SPORT ANYONE?

Reuel Denney in 1957 documented the specialization in sports in two ways, by observing the business methods necessary to a university's department of athletics, and, "by observing the decline of interest in sport activities among younger Americans" (8:123). Whether this was, or now is, a legitimate documentation, it tends to be obscured by recent writings that suggest there are millions of Americans who at least pay for participation in one sport or another. Frank Trippett, in "The Ordeal of Fun," in *Look* pointed out the dismal failures in the pursuit of fun (not limited to sport, of course), but also presented "a statistical banquet" of funscape facts. In one vastly surveyed recent year, for example, Americans went swimming 970 million times, played outdoor sports 929 million times (26 million softball players alone); and bicycled 467 million times. Three and a half million skiers are reported to spend $1.1 billion annually; there were 100,000 practitioners of *Mu Duk Kwan Tang Soo Do* (Korean karate). In 1967, 41 million Americans used about 8.3 million boats and spent some $3 billion in doing so; there were 10 million golfers on 9,615 courses; 94,000 tennis courts; 10 million horseshoe pitchers; 150,000 mountain climbers; and about 2000 sporting goods manufacturers (58:32, 34).

As one might suspect, the sporting aspect of the fun quest is not limited to suburban America. A special section of the *Saturday Review* revealed the holiday habits of world leaders. Although it was pointed out that the vacation pastimes of leaders differ as widely as their ideologies, it was interesting to note that the accompanying pictures showed former Presidents Franklin D. Roosevelt in a swimming pool, Woodrow Wilson shooting a daily round of golf, Warren G. Harding "letting go" with a game of golf and one with the caption, "Who can forget Ike with his shiny putter." Even among such leaders of the Kremlin as Khrushchev and Gromyko, swimming, shooting and cross-country skiing were depicted as vacation pastimes (35:40). For that matter, Teddy Roosevelt's cabinet was often called the "tennis cabinet."

Trippett suggested that while "the fun seeker is universally applauded," it is not because the fun quest is now moral where it was once immoral. Rather, he declared,

> This is because it is now profitable where it was once unprofitable . . . Fun has become a consumer product (58:34).

A brief overview of sport-participant fun as a consumer product is the concern of the following section.

In defiance of H. L. Mencken's statement, "If I had my way any man guilty of golf would be ineligible for any public office . . . and the females of the breed would be shipped off to the white-slave corrals," golf appears to be the fastest growing participant sport. As one writer stated, it is "a fantastic mixture of pleasure and business that seems to turn everyone who touches it to gold" (36:17). In 1931, four fifths of the 5,691 courses in the United States were private country clubs. In 1967, of the 9,333 courses, less than half were of this type (36:19). Whatever the reasons for the golf explosion (from the democratization of the game to the golf cart), apparently course construction is far behind the lures of the game and the crush of new players. In 1967 there was only about one course for every 1300 golfers, although in 1969 an estimated 400 courses were expected to be added to the 9,615 now listed in the United States (12). Golf club maintenance in 1968 was estimated to cost $360 million. A good golf course costs from $5,000 to $10,000 a hole to build and approximately $4,000 per hole per year to maintain. Some public courses are bombarded with 70,000 rounds of play a year. Some golf course superintendents (called agronomists) command salaries of more than $20,000 (13:62). Spending by golfers in the United States alone for golf products topped $1 billion in 1969, more than is spent on any other sport. More and more electric and gas golf cars (over 147,000 at present counting) will replace caddies, and more women will enter the golf scene. It was estimated that at least one million residents occupied golf-oriented residential communities in 1970 (12).

Other writers suggest that bowling best epitomizes the change that has overtaken sporting America. Current enthusiasm may not differ from that of Sir Francis Drake who, when the Spanish Armada was advancing on England in 1588, insisted upon finishing his game of bowls before repairing to his ship, but there is a fresh face on this sport. As Ray Cave described it,

> Born of the automatic pin-setter, reared lavishly with vast capital and full-grown in chrome, fluorescent lights and razzle-dazzle, bowling managed . . . to get America out of the alleys and into the lanes. The modern bowling establishment is as respectable as a split level and as encompassing as a supermarket (5:15).

In 1969, it was reported that some 40,000,000 persons were bowling in North America and that in the United States alone $2.5 million a year is spent on this sport. While there were only 48 contestants in the Firestone Tournament of Champions in 1967, it was reported that the forty million everyday type of bowlers are "brashly stepping onto the next lane, and, in many cases, matching the established pro strike for strike" (31:86-88).

The fifty-ninth American Bowling Congress Tournament in Des Moines, a 69-day tournament with 27,000 contestants and total prize money of $500,000 doubtlessly proved that bowling is rolling up the ratings. However, some observers, as Melvin Durslag pointed out, are stumped for an explanation of its popularity.

the noise is deafening. The environs often are smoky and the suspense is reduced to this: either the ball knocks down the pins or it doesn't (9:28).

The nation's surge to the waters has been one of the most startling phenomena within recent years. Although some may not call boating a sport in the traditional sense of that word, its mystique certainly belongs to the sporting world. For all the varied pleasures of life afloat, *Newsweek* reported that "more than 13 million Americans spent at least one night on boats" in 1969. There were "8.4 million boats, ranging from sunfish to sloops, from prams to power yachts," and "700 U.S. manufacturers turned out crafts as fast as they can mold fiber glass and stitch sails." Most people, *Newsweek* noted, "have only a fleeting yen to battle the sea." Much of the pleasure for some sailors comes in showing the boat off "even while looking forward to buying an even bigger status symbol next year." Some of the boats are not only lavish and garish, costing as much as $150,000, but, as one dockmaster observed, they may never even leave the dock (28:58).

In order to get a picture of the popularity of the more unusual water sports, perhaps one might turn to the surfing boom. Although at one time surfers may have been described as a "pretty scruffy lot," more recently they have been accorded the virtue of having "fought their way out of the sociological swamps," as reported by Bob Ottum, to become "cool, nervy, graceful, clear-eyed, four-square, uniformly lovely, thrifty, brave, reverent, kind and only slightly crazy" (29). Ottum in 1966 highlighted surfing's unique excitement with such statistics as: there are more than 50,000 eastern surfers by rough estimate; at Virginia Beach (Va.) there are more than 2,000 boards in town on weekdays, and weekends bring more; in Florida four years ago there weren't four surfboards and now there are maybe 7,000 surfers and 2,500 have their own boards; in Miami, a disc jockey ran a test by calling all surfers to rally—more than 17,000 showed up; more than 4,000 surfers hit Gilgo Beach each day during the weekend (29:30-37). A more recent article presented these statistics: *International Surfing*, one of the two national magazines devoted to the sport, recorded 350,000 surfers, almost all of them teen-agers; a large manufacturer of custom boards said there were 400,000 surfers; an executive secretary of the United States Surfing Association said there were more than half a million surfers in California and another half a million in the East and that the rate of growth is 20 percent a year; the *New York Times* gave the count as several million surfers in the United States and stated that the number almost doubles annually (30:97). This is convincing evidence that business is also riding in on the surfer's wave of enthusiasm.

Perhaps for lack of diligent sportswriters, many sports with startling numbers of participants go unreported. The "little sports," as Jim Murray called them, may one day capture the attention, money, and literary talents of the sport entertainment world. Meanwhile, a few interesting comments about one so-called "little sport," lacrosse, may serve to place it in a deserved larger perspective even if the economic picture is missing. Lacrosse has been called America's fastest growing sport. One article reported that in Minnesota some 115 years ago, long before the Twins and the Vikings came to town, the Indians were playing lacrosse. They called it ball, and it was more like intertribal warfare, but it seemed "much like contemporary lacrosse without the rule book" (21:W3). Another writer, placing it in contemporary perspective, reported that 112 colleges fielded teams in 1969, twice the number fielded a decade ago and declared:

> at some prep and high schools lacrosse has become so popular that athletic directors refuse to grant it varsity status out of the fear that their top baseball, track and tennis players will defect to it (18:49).

One further note regarding a "little sport," little league baseball, seems worthy of attention in this listing. Founded by Carl E. Stotz in 1939, little league baseball had attracted some two million boys in 6,158 leagues in 28 countries by 1965. Yet, as Lloyd Shearer reported, Stotz, who would no longer have anything to do with the "Frankenstein" it has become, declared:

> I became utterly disgusted with its philosophy . . . Originally I had envisioned baseball for youngsters strictly on the local level . . . keeping the game as simple as possible (37:6-7).

Little league may be many things, but simple, it is not.

Today's unprecedented popularity of most sports has been described by some writers as being due, for the most part, to the equipment of the "plastics age"—fiber glass-reinforced plastics, acrylics, cellulosics, nylon, phenolics, vinyls, amino plastics, and "those famous poly sisters"—ethylene, styrene, vinyl-chloride. Reportedly, when Gary Player swung his fiber glass clubs well enough to win the U.S. Open at St. Louis, it opened "the $210-million-a-year golf-equipment industry to a mad controversy over the merits and demerits of glass vs. steel shafts" (38:37). The changes and economics of sport equipment which are too numerous to mention here are chronicled in various sources. The reader is referred to the article quoted above as exemplary, not only of the colorful revolution in sport equipment but of its influence on American sport and its related industry.

Lest the sport transformation and influence be pictured solely as impersonal monetary phenomena, a few isolated observations are noted in concluding this section. The American Medical Association formed a tennis association in 1967 and it boasts some of the best tennis players in the country. Tournaments are held each year in various spots throughout the United States; the 1969 tourney held in Tucson, Arizona brought over 200 players. Some states such as Kentucky have public libraries that lend sports equipment as well as sport books. About Kentucky this was reported:

> The thought is that if a boy borrows a baseball he might want to read about Mickey Mantle—and then one day he might just want to read . . . In the program's first three weeks there was but one loss—a broken bat (46:9).

In 1969, the New York Mets "turned away 8,000 paying baseball spectators one night because 8,000 nonpaying fans happened to appear at the game in response to a free-ticket promotion" (24:15). And in San Francisco it was reported that "as many as 8,000 youngsters, rich kids and poor kids . . . file into Candlestick Park each day to see the Giants play—free" (24:13). And major league teams not only opened their gates to four million nonpaying spectators in 1969, but let another three million in at reduced rates (24:17).

The Illinois Sports Council was formed to organize the Illinois Panathlon, "the first major organized effort of any state to back sports." Its purpose was stated quite simply:

> To promote a sports-educational program for the total population of Illinois, thus instructing each individual in how to enjoy his leisure hours in a more wholesome program of activity within his means (46:9).

And, the idea of sport in education relates this section to its next one, the educational aspect of sport.

REFERENCES

1. *Arizona Daily Star* (New York, AP), "Jets' Super Bowl Triumph Brings Changes for Future," January 19, 1969, p. 3B.
2. *Arizona Republic (The)*, "Olympians Reassemble," January 31, 1969, p. ID.
3. *Arizona Republic (The)*, "Sometimes Great Strength Is A Marked Disadvantage," April 20, 1969, p. 7.
4. Axthelm, Pete. "Crashing Into A New Ice Age," *Sports Illustrated*, November 5, 1967, pp. 34-37.
5. Cave, Ray. "The Fresh Face of Sport," *Sports Illustrated*, August 21, 1961, pp. 10-15.
6. Connery, Donald S. "Tokyo Changes Face for Asia's First Olympics," *Sports Illustrated*, May 8, 1961, pp. 38-41.
7. Deford, Frank. "A Man To Lead the Pros Out of the Darkness," *Sports Illustrated*, June 20, 1966, pp. 58-62.
8. Denney, Reuel. Chapter 6, *The Astonished Muse*. Chicago: University of Chicago Press, 1957, pp. 121-137.
9. Durslag, Melvin. "Still Rolling Up the Ratings," *TV Guide*, April 19, 1969, p. 28.
10. Frank, Stanley. "Greed is the Name of the Game," *TV Guide*, August 9-15, 1969, pp. 6-10.
11. Gilbert, Bil. "Drugs In Sport," Part I (June 23, 1969), Part II (June 30, 1969), and Part III (July 7, 1969), *Sports Illustrated*, pp. 30-35, pp. 64-72, pp. 30-42.
12. *Golf Digest Annual*, "What's Ahead," February, 1969, p. 11, 13.

13. *Golf Magazine*, "Guardians of the Green," March, 1968, pp. 57, 62.
13b. Johnson, William. "Television and Sport," (Part 1), *Sports Illustrated*, December 22, 1969, pp. 86-102.
13c. Johnson, William. "Television and Sport," (Part 2), *Sports Illustrated*, January 5, 1970, pp. 23-29.
13d. Johnson William. "Television and Sport," (Part 5), *Sports Illustrated*, January 26, 1970, pp. 30-36.
14. Jupp, Nancy. "They Also Play the Game," *Golf* (Incorporating *Golfing*), March, 1968, pp. 36-38, 77-78.
15. Kane, Martin. "The True Football Gets Its Big Chance," *Sports Illustrated*, March 27, 1967, p. 28.
16. Kieran, John, and Daley, Arthur. *The Story of the Olympic Games 776 B.C.–1964.* Philadelphia: J. B. Lippincott Company, 1965.
17. Kram, Mark. "Then There Were Six," *Sports Illustrated*, August 14, 1967, pp. 12-15.
18. *Life*, "The Little Brother of War," photographs by Arthur Rickerby, April 18, 1969, pp. 49-56.
19. Loy, John W., Jr. and Kenyon, Gerald S. (editors). *Sport, Culture, and Society.* Toronto: The Macmillan Company, 1969.
20. Lüschen, Günther. "Social Stratification and Social Mobility Among Young Sportsmen," in John W. Loy, Jr. and Gerald S. Kenyon (editors), *Sport, Culture, and Society.* Toronto: The Macmillan Company, 1969, pp. 258-276.
21. Mackay, Bill. "When The Indians Tied The Redskins Three All," *Sports Illustrated*, December 11, 1967, pp. W3-W4.
22. Maule, Tex. "The Once and Future King," *Sports Illustrated*, July 10, 1967, pp. 19-21.
23. McCormack, Mark H. *Arnie.* New York: Simon and Schuster, 1967.
24. Mulvoy, Mark. "Baseball Booms Again," *Sports Illustrated*, August 4, 1969, pp. 12-17.
25. Mulvoy, Mark. "Bobby Stakes An Orr Claim for Everybody," *Sports Illustrated*, September 2, 1968, pp. 40-41.
26. *Newsweek*, "A New Ball Game," December 30, 1968, p. 47.
27. *Newsweek*, "Boston's Orr: Fire on Ice," March 24, 1969, p. 64.
28. *Newsweek*, "The Joys of Life Afloat," August 4, 1969, pp. 58-63.
29. Ottum, Bob. "Riding the Wave of the East Coast's Surfing Boom," *Sports Illustrated*, July 18, 1966, pp. 30-37.
30. Rogin, Gilbert. "An Odd Sport—And An Unusual Champion," *Sports Illustrated*, October 18, 1965, pp. 96-110.
31. Ronberg, Gary. "Over 30 Is Over The Hill," *Sports Illustrated*, April 10, 1967, pp. 86-88.
32. Russell, William F. "I'm Not Involved Anymore," *Sports Illustrated*, August 4, 1969, pp. 18-19.
33. *Salt Lake Tribune* (Washington, AP), July 27, 1969, p. B9.
34. Sanders, Jacquin. "Bart Starr: Nice Guy Finishes First," *The Reader's Digest*, (condensed from *Chicago's American*, August 18, 1968), September, 1968, pp. 87-91.
35. *Saturday Review*, "The First Resorts, A Roundup of Vacationlands Preferred by World Leaders," March 8, 1969, pp. 39-111.
36. Seitz, Nick. "Golf: Big Business, Big Pleasure," *The Book of Golf*, (produced for PGA with the cooperation of *Golf Digest*), 1968, pp. 17-19.
37. Shearer, Lloyd. "Little League Baseball," *Parade*, May 28, 1961, pp. 6-7.
38. Smith, Liz. "Sport Moves Into the Age of Plastics," and Richard Meek, photographer of "Only the Game Remains the Same," *Sports Illustrated*, September 27, 1965, pp. 32-37.
39. *Sport Annual*, 1969, "Money Talks In the NHL," (produced by *Sport*), p. 68.
40. *Sport Annual*, 1969, "Pro Football Player Strike," (produced by *Sport*), p. 23.
41. *Sport Annual*, 1969, "The Name Is Dr. Fager," (produced by *Sport*), p. 34.
42. *Sport Annual*, 1969, "The Touring Golfers Revolt," (produced by *Sport*), p. 46.

164 *Sport is Cultural*

43. *Sports Illustrated,* "High Speed Jai Alai," photographs by Jerry Cooke, February 19, 1962, pp. 22-27.
44. *Sports Illustrated,* "Letter From The Publisher," October 23, 1967.
45. *Sports Illustrated,* "Letter From The Publisher," November 18, 1968, p. 4.
46. *Sports Illustrated,* "Scorecard," August 23, 1965, p. 9.
47. *Sports Illustrated,* "Scorecard," December 19, 1966, p. 40.
48. *Sports Illustrated,* "Scorecard," July 31, 1967, p. 8.
49. *Sports Illustrated,* "Scorecard," August 14, 1967, p. 7.
50. *Sports Illustrated,* "Scorecard," November 20, 1967, p. 14.
51. *Sports Illustrated,* "Scorecard," February 19, 1968, p. 8.
52. *Sports Illustrated,* "Scorecard," May 20, 1968, p. 13.
53. *Sports Illustrated,* "Scorecard," January 20, 1969, p. 8.
54. *Sports Illustrated,* "Scorecard," February 24, 1969, p. 11.
55. *Sports Illustrated,* "Scorecard," April 21, 1969.
56. *Time,* "Anyone For Sense," September 15, 1967, p. 57.
57. *Time,* "Pros In The Playground," January 7, 1969, p. 52.
58. Trippett, Frank. "A Special Report On The Way You Play The Ordeal of Fun," *Look,* July 29, 1969, pp. 24-34.
59. *Tucson Daily Citizen,* "Best Yet to Come: Yaz Signs Contract For Top AL Dough," February 27, 1969, p. 28.

PART IV

Sport is Educational

"an education of the whole person in which the physical takes its proper place in the unfolding of the intellectual, social, emotional and aesthetic powers of the individual."

————JESSE FEIRING WILLIAMS

The concept that sport is educational may seem to be somewhat redundant in the sense that throughout this book sport has been shown to educate the personal, social, and cultural dimensions of man, and, in a sense, without benefit of a cent of the taxpayers' education dollar. The two chapters which follow, however, are meant to show some aspects of the genesis and growth of sport in the school system and its relationship to educational goals.

That sport is a part of the mosaic of the school system is an obvious fact. As Ernest Dimnet put it, "Sports are still, and often avowedly so, the essential part of the school life . . . School news in America is Sport news. Notre Dame is a Catholic college, certainly, but it is that much less than it is a stronghold of football" (9:63-64). And, although football may not be the king it once was, in the words of one writer "it lives like one" (52). Great efforts are being made to preserve intercollegiate football even in the face of rising costs that picture it to be a losing business.

But, football is not the only aspect of sport in education. Sports of all kinds, from archery to wrestling, are organized and integrated within the school system in three ways: 1. the physical education program, 2. the recreation and/or intramural program, and 3. the intercollegiate athletic program. Beyond this, there is a professional program designed to prepare teachers and leaders in these areas. Despite the many hashed-over questions of values, the sport program in the schools, whether it be as part of physical education or athletics, may be said to be based upon the assumption Joseph Lee may have had in mind when he declared that "if one wishes to know what a child will be, then he should direct his form of play" (24).

The direction sport has taken in education and the impact of certain influences upon it, both from within and outside the schools, is the concern of the next two chapters.

CHAPTER 9

Physical Education

ITS PROPER PURPOSE

If the proper study of mankind is man, the proper study of physical education is sport. Physical educators have a special responsibility to educate, and thus have used and studied sport, as well as dance, games, and designed exercise, in order to accomplish the objectives of education. In the vernacular of physical education, these objectives have been variously classified, but generally they are acknowledged to include the development of the following: neuromuscular skills; organic fitness; socioethical behaviors such as sportsmanship, fair play, and so forth; and intellectual, or mentimotor or cognitive skills. Influential scholars and leaders have variously expressed these objectives in meaningful and perhaps more colorful language by such expressions as: "play enables Jack to become more Jack"; "play is nature's hand on the back of the child pushing him to educate himself"; "how about some muscle?" "The skill-learning years are the great golden decade"; "to move is to learn and to learn is to move"; and so forth.

Although such descriptions of the objectives of physical education might seem to be merely a game of semantics, they have been necessarily prompted, in some instances, in order to defend the proposition that physical education is a way to learning, and because periodically in the history of education, physical educators have been confronted by the query: "Why physical education?" Equally persistent have been the rise and decline in prestige of physical education in the schools. Some critics have at times insisted that physical education, as one of the so-called "fads and frills," should be eliminated from the schools in favor of purely intellectual endeavors and the development of the school's basic educational program—that of providing a liberal education. Such critics have discovered intermittently that the mind is not sent to the classroom and the body to the gym—that more is involved in the educative act than the dichotomous separation of mind and body.

Other critics, while holding physical education in high esteem at times when there is a need for physical action—war, safety, health, fitness—have denied that it has any value beyond the physical. A sampling of articles published in the popular magazines in almost any given decade reveals abundant literature expressive of recurrent public concern for physical fitness, and, a lack of literature concerned with physical education. One such typical cross section from the 1960's includes such titles as: "Physical Fitness Factory" (*Popular Mechanics,* 1960), "Let's Close the Muscle Gap" (*Reader's Digest,* 1961), "Toughening Our Soft Generation" (*Saturday Evening Post,* 1962), "Our Flabby Youngsters: Myth or Reality" (*Good Housekeeping,* 1962), "Exercise Programs Help Youngsters' School Work" (*Scientific National Life,* 1963), "School Where Fitness Counts" (*Reader's Digest,* 1964), "Physical Activity Aids the 3 R's" (*Senior School,* 1965), "Putting Muscle into Mark" (*New York Times Magazine,* 1965), "In My Opinion Our Muscle Mania Has Gone Too Far" (*Seventeen,* 1966), and "Physical Fitness: A School Community Responsibility" (*Parent's Magazine,* 1969).

Noting the "everlasting tension between ethical ideal and everyday reality," Jan Brockhoff wrote:

> A look at modern programs of physical education would only confirm the absence of a societal ideal or set of ideals. Seldom do these programs carry significant values beyond narrowly defined hygienic and physical fitness objectives. The scientific method . . . has yet to contribute to the formation of ideas that would elevate physical education above prophylaxis and recreation (3:30).

Brockhoff observed further that many may share the lament of the medical scientist Carrel that "our modern society is no longer capable of producing an elite that combines intelligence with imagination and courage" (3:30).

Be that as it may, physical educators, in defense of their programs and sometimes at the promptings of their academic associates or the urgings of national leaders have continued to argue in favor of one or all of the objectives they purport to serve. The repeated ventures of introspection prompted by the what and why of physical education have culminated within recent years in the question: Is physical education a discipline, or, more specifically, is it an academic discipline? The literature concerned with this question is too vast to chronicle in the present volume nor is it the purpose herein to explore the justifiable cause of physical education in the schools. Some literature which seemed to mark a turning point in the general treatment of ideas about physical education has been presented under the topic heading "Sport as an Art Form," appearing in Part III. From the writings of Eleanor Metheny (28) and others (32) may be traced the triumph of the principle that human movement experiences, as they occur in sport, dance, and other forms of physical activity taught in the physical education program, are among the expressive-communicative nonverbal arts. Like any other perceptual experience (seeing, hearing, speaking), movement experiences are "too much like thought to be less than thinking." In fact, the term "human movement" has been proposed by many persons as being a more appropriate one than physical education, which is poorly understood by the layman. As Harold Vanderzwaag pointed out, however, "human movement 'as an umbrella' . . . is also extremely ambiguous and nondescriptive . . . it entreats analysis" (59b:36). And, as Thomas Sheehan put it, "Individual interpretations of the proper study of physical education generally have not met with universal acceptance" (36:59). More importantly, within the context of this book, whether or not physical education has had a substantial impact on the sport and commercialized recreation that plays such a distinct role in American life is a debatable point.

Whatever may be the failure of physical education within the sport world at large, it is most readily acknowledged by physical educators themselves, many of whom declare that the various "publics" simply do not know what comprises the field of physical education. Although physical education and athletics are considered to be members of the same species, they are different creatures in many ways. Yet, surveys of opinions frequently reveal that physical education is described or defined as something related to the football or basketball program at the varsity level (55:141). Guy M. Lewis, in a well-documented article appearing in *Quest*, pointed out that accommodation to varsity athletics was the key factor in the transformation of the physical education profession. According to Lewis, "from this point formulation of a philosophy was merely a practice in justifying the existence of programs already sanctioned by higher authorities" (24b:42). The report of the athletic program at the varsity level is revealed in the next chapter. That description leads one to conclude that athletics, at least, has captured the eye, energy, and pen of various publics.

The account that ensues, on the other hand, may lead one to conclude that while writers of the day may extol sport and/or athletics, few extol physical education. If the account is brief, therefore, it is because the popular literature gives scanty treatment to physical education. If it is one-sided, the cause may be the already noted confusion about the why of physical education and its relationship with athletics. At the same time, it should be noted that, just as is the case with physical education, the literature gives fuller treatment to art and music, for example, than it does to art education or music education.

A LIBERAL EDUCATION?

The concepts that the objective of physical education in the school is *exercise,* that it is a *requirement,* and that it seems to lack relevance to a *liberal education* were pinpointed, albeit tongue-in-cheek, in a recent article by John Ciardi. Ciardi gave the following impression of the profession of physical education and "gym" classes: Granting that "a given gym teacher might be a decent, though misguided, person," gym is "a fraud imposed upon the hapless young."

> any healthy boy can get all the exercise he needs . . . chasing girls . . . there is no need for that . . . (swimming) requirement to have a point: the point is to have a requirement . . . I damned gym . . . and the stupidity of college administrators so confused they . . . could imagine such . . . to be any part of a liberal arts education (5:21).

Lest one conclude, however, that accusations about physical education as purely "body-centered" and bearing no relation to the more serious educational purposes for which school exists come merely from adults or from humorous intent, the following rather typical news item appears to dispel that notion. A 17-year old student wrote a scathing letter which appeared in the *Manchester Evening Herald* protesting her grade of "C" received in an archery class. *Time* magazine reported her complaint, which was that "in the jet age, the space age, the atomic age and the age of pushbutton warfare Manchester High makes no distinction between brains and brawn" (56:46). *Time* noted further that her charge to change the honor roll system and " 'get back on our planet' " brought praising editorials from other newspapers, congratulatory phone calls and messages, one of which came from a school board member who " 'estimated that 200 other bright youngsters missed the honor roll for . . . low physical education grades.' " This board member concluded that rewarding well-rounded sampling rather than academic achievement was symptomatic of what's wrong with the schools.

In 1969 an editorial which appeared in *The Charleston Gazette* (West Virginia) made a similar appeal. Titled "How Many Pushups for 'A' in Latin?" the editorial concluded:

> It is difficult to understand why school administrators didn't long ago abandon a system that permits physical education grades to lower (or raise) academic averages (59c:155).

Edmund Burke, who cited this editorial, pointed out the import of the fact that the *Gazette* had a circulation of 63,860, the largest in West Virginia, and that the state legislature was in session at the time the editorial appeared.

IS IT PHYSICAL?

As mentioned previously, many supporters of physical educators who give them praise and mandatory laws requiring school time and facilities for physical education do so on the basis of its "physical" reasons for being. Publicly, physical education often has been judged by evaluating its contributions to the fitness of men (particularly as revealed in the draft statistics). A doctor who writes a regular newspaper column stated:

as long as the fun-and-play concept dominates the program of physical education . . ., it won't prove adequate . . . I propose that physical training at school be considered chiefly as work . . . simple sitting-up exercises which any teacher may supervise . . . if one watches a company of recruits in the army . . . he will see what I have in mind (29b).

Another columnist, in protesting the board of education's attempt to change the state law requiring one period of physical education daily, wrote:

how about the over-all picture of a good body in a sane mind? Man is composed of two parts, and his enjoyment of muscle-flexing is not the least (35).

This writer, perhaps hoping to add stature to his proposal, added that the President's Committee for Youth Fitness was not made up of coaches and "P.E." men but of "laymen in the academic glades and some dedicated gents of Cabinet level."

As if to add frosting to the mind-body dualistic reasons for physical education, a member of the National Education Association executive board stated that "physical education should be compulsory because increased physical activity parallels increased mental activity."

OR ANTI-PHYSICAL?

Apparently many people, however, had not been sold on physical fitness—those who go in for anti-exertion and anti-sweat devices and tables to exercise on without getting tired—until, of course, along came the joggers of America and the fitness craze was on once again as it has been intermittently throughout man's history. Along with the fitness craze came the question of "fitness for what?" The matter of fitness, however legitimate and for whatever reason, has led to much enterprise without direction and to a hodge-podge of reasoning. Janet Coleman declared that "keeping in shape is a sexual preoccupation, although hardly anyone admits it." She asserted that the strategy of gym teachers "is to treat physical fitness as some kind of obligation or biological duty, about as pleasant as cod liver oil or spinach soup."

Think of the force-fed exercise of horrid mandatory gym classes, a discipline as necessary to children as joining the Marines (6:295).

In fact, according to Miss Coleman, from the time one begins to play, sports are institutionalized in such a way that "it is very rare to hear a sport described in terms of a private moment, or a personal 'happening,' a 'listening to the body'."

On the other hand, some persons have decried the fact that physical education class is precisely the place where they don't get much exercise of any kind. One such story is told by a teen-ager whose unconventional observations about why she hated high school appeared in the magazine *Seventeen*. For this student, physical education—with its huge classes, sitting around, checking gym socks and calling roll—was among the reasons that high school was a painful way station on the road to college. On what was described as a fairly typical situation,

> we all suited up, did exactly one forward roll apiece, and then spent the rest of the time sitting on the gym floor in silence (39:273).

THE IMAGE

Without a doubt many physical education classes are too large and many may be taught by teachers who themselves are confused about the purposes of physical education. But if there is one thing that tends to compound the problems of an already inadequate supply of good teachers, it may be the image of the woman physical education teacher commonly portrayed in the popular media. Exemplary of this image was one humorous, yet typical connotation, which came by way of a cigarette advertisement. It seems that Thorwald Dockstader—sophomore, epicure, and sportsman—had a date with a physical education major named Peaches Glendower. She was:

> a broth of a girl with a ready smile and a size 18 neck. She took Thorwald down to the cinder track where they did 100 laps to open the pores . . . after playing four games of squash, six sets of tennis, 36 holes of golf, nine innings of one o'cat, six chukkers of lacrosse, and a mile and a quarter of leapfrog . . . they went ten rounds with eight ounce gloves—exchanged a firm handshake and went home to their respective whirlpool baths (37).

The plight of women in sport, and the image therein, has been detailed in Chapter 7. The evidence from the literature leaves little doubt that the sport "muscle moll" is a thing of yesteryear, or perhaps a figment of some writer's imagination. But, the seeming present preoccupation of writers to portray the woman in sport as a "thing of beauty" also may lead one to conclude that it does not matter so much whether or not sport is educational—it matters only that it is beautifying.

Needless to say, the foregoing illustrations, which represent all the present authors could uncover in the popular literature, leave the question which Delbert Oberteuffer once asked still unanswered:

> Does physical education still mean to many . . . an enigma, an educational ambiguity, either a jolly good clown to have around for morale purposes or a walking incarnation of Veblen's concept of barbaric ferocity (30:46-56).

Whether or not the growth of sport has anything to do with physical education, and whether or not the growth of professional sport has marked a decline in the growth of amateur participation may be factors quite outside the influence of physical education. Part of this picture is presented in the next chapter. Nonetheless, of concern to physical educators is the plight of the average sport participant whose story may be in one sense poignantly summed up in this want ad which appeared in the *Los Angeles Times*: "Mediocre tennis player wants better player to rally twice a week, $2.50/hour" (41:9).

CHAPTER 10

Athletics

Although the idea of physical education in its broad sense has not captured the imagination of writers in popular literature, writers of the day seem to see the presence of competitive sport in schools and colleges as considerably more than of token interest. For all concerned, athletics seems to offer, above all, an educational paradox. The various "publics" are divided, vague, and ambivalent about its place, value, and conduct. Institutional guardians of education are not sure themselves of what is most valuable in that particular treasure called athletics. On at least one point, however, there appears to be general agreement—athletics is a form of entertainment. Directed toward entertainment, athletics needs, besides players, a battalion of coaches, stadiums, equipment, officials, news media, and downtown boosters clubs. The costs amount to millions of dollars. The players' talents seem to come alive only in partnership with a large corporation of investors whose interests may be in contradiction to his education. Since there is no shortage of athletic talent, shortcutting educational goals may be, or may seem to be, an economic necessity for the athlete who wants to be endorsed and who, therefore, must show promise of a certain profit to the institution. In short, today's athletes seem to be, as stated in *Life*, "the finished product of a system in which . . . fathers prefer quarterbacks to valedictorians, and football is synonymous with patriotism" (25:34B). Some of the strands which run through this account of athletics, and therefore, of sport, are unfolded in the ensuing pages.

IT BEGAN

Sport, in one form or another, has always been a part of the school system. Those who have chronicled the history of sport and education have made distinctions between the meanings of the words sport and athletics. Such distinctions may do little more than document a shift

174

n attitude and in interest brought on by increased spectator involve-ment. "Historians have not recorded," wrote Myles Jackson, "the name >f the incipient athletic director who first turned away from watching :he players on the field and counted spectators" (15:176). Suffice it to ;ay that after 1870, about the time college football was born, inter-collegiate athletics grew rapidly. In the years between 1906 to 1916, as old by Guy M. Lewis, athletics stepped from the status of being con-;idered amusement to being considered as serving educational purposes (24b). In 1929, a report entitled *American College Athletics* presented a serious indictment of practices in intercollegiate athletics. As stated by Earle F. Zeigler, "There was no question but that semiprofessionalism had arrived in college sport" (61:110). Since that time sport in education, nore specifically, intercollegiate athletics, has had a troubled history. Part of its rocky road has concerned strong conflicts in values.

J. W. Keating suggested that because the terms sport and athletics have been used interchangeably, confusion had resulted in "the futile attempt to outline a single code of behavior equally applicable to adically diverse activities." Sport, as Keating explained it, is "a kind of diversion . . . for fun, pleasure, and delight . . . dominated by a spirit >f moderation and generosity." Athletics, on the other hand, is "a com->etitive activity . . . for victory . . . characterized by a spirit of dedica-ion, sacrifice, and intensity" (21:25). Keating notwithstanding, people n America have tended to equate sport in the schools with athletics and o attribute to athletics, therefore, those virtues commonly held for sport.

ACKNOWLEDGED VALUES

From the various segments of society and various types of literature, >ne finds these viewpoints expressed by the many persons who have xtolled the value of athletics.

The *New York Times* survey of the basketball scandals in 1951 re-ealed these arguments against athletic reforms:

Football (or basketball) brings in the money that pays for . . . all the minor sports that we could not otherwise afford . . . There's nothing wrong in free rides for players who might not otherwise get a college education (13).

An editorial in *Teacher's College Record,* addressed to the point that America can manage with few champions but needs more athletes, ontended the following:

Our production of the specialized champion matters little . . . Few enterprises provide as direct an opportunity for such learnings as self-reliance and . . . the happy sturdiness of body and character . . . as does athletics practiced in the proper perspective and born of widespread participation (54:483).

A *coach and player,* Willis M. Tate, made these observations:

to understand and be at home with physical strain; to think under pressure; to cope with competition; to learn how to snap back from defeat; responsibility, self-discipline, sacrifice, respect for others (53:8).

A *physical educator,* Robert Singer, testified to these values:

provides athletically gifted with a means of further skill development; personal relationships; brings out the spirit, pride, enthusiasm of people; physical fitness of participants; and such values as fair play, ethics, leadership, ability to win and lose graciously (38:147).

A *president* of the University of Michigan stated of their football team that "their appearance in the Rose Bowl did more for the school's image than anything the regents or president had done all year" (34).

A Big Ten *Commissioner,* Bill Reed, said he saw no evil when 60,000 persons pay

to watch a teenage quarterback direct his team to the Rose Bowl . . . Seeing a qualified student perform athletically under pressure with 80,000 or 100,000 sitting in judgment makes me imagine the same man, years later, making vital executive decisions . . . if . . . football symbolizes . . . values like pride and discipline and respect for orderliness . . . we ought to be proud of it (29).

A *sports writer,* arguing that when education minimizes competition or equates progress to the pace of dullards, athletics justify their cost stated:

the force of athletics is one of the last outposts giving this land its heroes . . . we villify our political heroes . . . ignore our business heroes . . . But, as a competitive nation, we worship our sports heroes . . . And—let's face it . . . schools are in the public entertainment business (11).

A noted *scientist and educator,* Joseph Kaplan, while writing to the point that football coaches should clean house or else, described what he called the "salutary lessons of football," wherein a faculty member can see coaches and players work as in a laboratory under a strict plan

the mental demands . . . range of plays and assignments, the necessity for the player to learn, not only his job, but those of other players . . . a complex course that includes some mathematics, . . . physics, and, considering the demands on the body, not a little chemistry . . . a succession of great moments of individual selflessness and courage (20:38).

When the Cincinnati Board of Education ordered elimination of inter school athletics, among other programs, in order to curtail spiraling school budgets, a *chief of police* and school officials expressed concern about a possible rise in juvenile delinquency because of a lack of sport to provide an outlet and keep school morale high.

Associate Director of the Institute for Psychosomatic and Psychiatric Research in Chicago, Daniel Offer, wondering whether the theories concerning adolescents derived from work with disturbed patients would also be applicable to a normal, well-adjusted group, examined teenage boys in two high schools in suburban Chicago. Among the study's high lights was this fact:

Teachers that teach intellectual courses (literature, art, science) are rarely mentioned as meaningful figures. The most respected teacher is the athletic coach who, the students feel, is the only one who treats them as individuals (31:78).

James Simon Kunen, of SDS (Students for Democratic Society) fame, who may be classified as one of the more "visible" members of the younger society, reminisced about his "rowboating" days at Columbia University in an article appearing in *Sports Illustrated.* Although declaring that there was "no real social value in sports," Kunen explained with caustic candor his belief in giving all of oneself for something:

That's a gutty game, football . . . tied up with those ego-masculinity things. You have to be sufficiently angry to play it well . . . The key to crew is to kill yourself. Then, even if you lose, it's O.K., you've really won. If you kill yourself rowing and win, that's even better (40:6).

And whether or not "it's all part of the Protestant ethic, all shot through with capitalist values," as Kunen put it, he acknowledged that, "I'm a prisoner of the ethic myself. I have to win. I can't stand to read reviews of books by other kids." And, whatever the values of sport may be, apparently these values are tinged with danger.

VALUES: TINGED WITH DANGER

Starting with the 1920's, perusal of the popular literature outside the fields of physical education and athletics reveals a persistent theme. The title of an article, "The Great God Football," written by John R. Tunis for *Harper's* in 1928 appears to tell a story very much like that told in articles written since that day. The following listing is exemplary: "Prometheus or Frankenstein" (S. Fogler, *Journal of Educational Sociology,* 1950); "The Revolution in Sports" (E. S. Blanchard, *Harper's,* May 1956); "American Sports: Play and Display" (Gregory Stone, *Chicago Review,* 1955); "Money, Muscles—and Myths" (Roger Kahn, *Nation,* July 6, 1957); "Athletics: The Poison Drug in Our Schools" (James B. Conant, *Look,* January 17, 1961); "College Football Has Become a Losing Business" (Myles Jackson, *Fortune,* December 1962); "Apartheid in Sports" (Robert Conley, *New York Times,* October 15, 1963); and "The Big Business of Sports is Odds-On to Get Bigger" (James Tuite, *New York Times,* January 6, 1964).

Similarly, the titles of articles, all of which appeared in just one periodical (*School Activities*) during the years 1961 to 1965, reveal the concern about athletics: "School Athletics on Trial," "Public Pressures and Their Effect on Athletics," "Athletics—Unquestionably the Same," "Twelve Killers of High School Athletics," "Who Lets the Game Get Out of Hand," "Who Says We Gotta Win?" "Athletics are a Menace to Education," "Inter-School Rivalry: Curse or Cure?" and "The Education-

7

Athletics Nonsense." As these titles suggest, the primary concern may not be so much about the values to be derived from athletics as the question of whether it is educational.

IS IT EDUCATIONAL?

The intrusion of athletics into the spirit of the academic life of the schools has been angrily deplored from the very beginning. A story that is told about the glorious Gothic spires of King's College, Cambridge very early placed the issue of athletics versus academics in its perennially "hot" perspective. "The King's eight-oared shell won four times on the four successive flights of the May Races, the most important event of the Cambridge spring." The response from all over Britain was voluminous and critical: "The King's crew was obviously spending too much time in its boat and too little time in studies" (54:483).

Since that time, caustic distinctions have been drawn between the proper business of education and the business of athletics. In 1951, correspondents of *The New York Times* conducted a study of forty colleges and universities in twenty states. The study disclosed a wide difference in treatment of athletes, but among the bad features which showed up in large and small institutions was that of the lowering of academic standards. Charles Grutzner, who wrote a series of six articles on the college basketball scandals of that era, quoted A. Whitney Griswold, then President of Yale University, as saying:

> The confusion of values represented by semi-professional "big time" athletics in our colleges and universities is a reflection on the intelligence of the American people and a betrayal of the tradition of higher learning (13).

Those that decry football call it, in the words of one observer, "a pain in the academics." Others cast doubt on whether schools are academic or athletic institutions. Ernest Dimnet, in describing education paradoxically as one of the obstacles to thinking, asserted that:

> the predominance of sport in schools . . . not only crowds out what is or should be more important but it creates an atmosphere in which important things are made to appear superfluous, or are even described in extremely disrespectful slang (9:64-65).

James B. Conant probably needs no further identification here because he focused the attention of a large portion of the nation on the "vicious overemphasis" on sports in the schools. Along with the harm to the physical and psychological development of youngsters, Conant made the dour observation that sport in the schools harmed academic life (7).

Numerous stories do give potent testimony to the truth of the assertion that athletes get an unbalanced program of 75 percent athletics and 25 percent study. For example, before the Big Ten passed the anti red-shirt rule in 1957, those students seemed to have five or six years in which to get a "doctorate in football," as one editor put it.

When a promising player began to do well in his studies and was in danger of normal graduation, the coach often would persuade him to "adjust" his courses and thus spread his credits over five instead of four years (51:20).

While nobody knows how much red-shirt clinging to players goes on in colleges today, there appear to be other escape clauses to four balanced years of study. One such escape hatch from educational aims is that of "double standards." How much favoring of athletes has affected educational standards is difficult to measure because of many overlapping factors. It is generally recognized, however, that such double standards as the following do exist: matriculation by waiver of some entrance requirements; a greater leniency in absence from classes, upgrading of academic performance of athletes in order to keep them eligible. One question that arises in reference to physical education as well as other subjects is whether varsity athletes should be excused from physical education. This question does not lend itself to a categorized yes or no answer because various physical educators themselves hold differing views (many coaches are also physical educators). Some suggest that an athlete should not be required to take "double courses." Probably the great majority, however, respond with the belief that the athlete should be expected to attend physical education classes as he would any other class given for credit. As for other classes, almost daily state directors are asked by local school administrators to rule on, or express opinions about, excusing varsity athletes. (18:6).

The repudiation of educational tasks by coaches has been considered to be one of the paradoxes of education. Some suggest that the profession of physical education frequently is used as a place to "hide" athletes. A typical commentary on this state of affairs was one in *Sports Illustrated* under the title, "Lower Learning." The article described a master's degree in sports administration in which students study business, law, journalism, and education, and work in the ticket office, booking department, maintenance and payroll departments among others. In view of the thesis of this book, it would be churlish if not downright ignorant to raise the question of whether there is a need to prepare students in such a profession as sports administration. Obviously sport, like any other facet of society, can support many professional ramifications not now available yet needed. Nonetheless, the commentary raised valid doubts about the kinds of "work" studies provided and concluded with this somewhat tongue-in-cheek description of a degree in sports administration: "scheming to sell a 15¢ hot dog for 35¢, Doc., or scheduling split double-headers, so the fan has the privilege of paying two admissions" (46:16).

Another large area of concern regarding the repudiation of educational tasks is that of the inept athlete, or as Edward Rutkowski put it, "the 'dumb ox' . . . who is passed under alumni pressure, by the teacher, or the inept, boisterous coach tolerated by the academic world as a concession to the alumni" (33:30).

Whether or not athletes are dumb has been the subject of numerous investigations. The copious data from such studies show: Athletes are dumber, smarter, and finally, no different from other students. The theory of compensation, however, does not seem to hold. Brain and brawn, as noted in Chapter 1, are not mutually exclusive qualities. The larger question in this dialogue, however, is concerned with whether athletes are students or entertainers first.

EDUCATION VERSUS ENTERTAINMENT

A few thousand years ago, Juvenal concluded: "Two things only the people anxiously desire: bread and circuses." The troubled history of athletics suggests that perhaps schools have been arduously attempting to satisfy one of those desires. An experienced coach, football player, and one-time member of the Ethics Committee of the American Football Coaches Association, asserted that "intercollegiate athletics is, frankly, entertainment for the public and student body, personal glory for players and coaches, and profit when possible" (12:32).

When diverted to commercial ends, athletic contests appear to become entertainment circuses and gladiatorial type of events which encourage winning at all costs and such well-known avenues to winning as subsidizing, circumventing rules, arguing with officials, and recruiting players who do not qualify as bona fide students. The question of the need to win has its pros and cons, but, as John Bridgers, ex-Baylor coach and coach of the Dallas Cowboys, was reported to have said:

> In pro football, it's obvious you must win. In college football there's sometimes talk of other goals, but when you get right down to it, that's what really matters there too.

Some concerned individuals identify many "half-truths" which breed malpractice:

> admission of athletes who fail to meet regular requirements; irregular methods of dispensing financial assistance . . . needless jobs conceived and created for sports competitors; lightened academic loads . . . extending an ordinary four year college term to five or six; clandestine out-of-season workouts (12:31).

Others assert that what is at issue is the "college-perpetuated myth that athletes are students first; that their sport is an avocation." Among the most caustic critics of athletics in education has been, and still is, Robert Maynard Hutchins, former chancellor of the University of Chicago, who ousted intercollegiate football on the University of Chicago campus in the 1930's. At the age of 69, in a news interview, he expressed his continued disdain:

> The industrialization of athletics . . . is almost identical with the industrialization of any other process that goes on in the commercial world. Not interested in educating these young people, not interested in what happens to them after graduation, all you want to do is make as much money, get as much publicity, as possible (29).

In answer to the question of what the result of the abolition of professional sports from universities would be, he replied:

> The abolition of intercollegiate football at the University of Chicago was the greatest single thing the University of Chicago ever did. The best students from all over the world flocked into the university as a result (29).

Be that as it may, as students revolt against the so-called "irrelevance" of much college teaching (whether or not "their idea of relevance is that of a nursery" as Harvard's Paul Freund put it), the possibility of irrelevance appeared to be expanded in the university's preoccupation with athletics. Today, amid the strife of student revolts against intercollegiate athletics and concern over the plight of the black athlete, the question of what to do about collegiate athletes who are paid to play games and who frequently end up without an education has been brought into sharp focus. Writing about what he called the "Underground Railroad" ("a mysterious but highly efficient network operating for Negro athletes who want to play college-level sports but simply do not have the grades, or the intelligence, or the disposition to meet the academic requirements"), William Johnson pointed out that Bob Presley, Negro center for the University of California basketball team at Berkeley, was a perfect example of calculated recruiting resulting in the admission of a boy to the school purely because he was an athlete.

> the combination of the Underground Railroad and the easy-entrance path to Berkeley raises a broad—and by no means new—question of academic ethics vs cold opportunism in college recruiting (17:53).

If one is tempted to conclude that it is only the Negro athlete who ends up without an education, there is ample evidence that white players as well have come to sad endings academically. One report cited such examples as Texas quarterback James Street, who dropped out of school after the Cotton Bowl because he was too far behind in school; LSU's Pete Maravich, who was suspended for cutting classes; Purdue's Rick Mount, who dropped out of school after the basketball season ended. The writer of the report made the "modest proposal" that "for every player who fails to graduate within nine semesters . . . subtract one athletic scholarship that the coach can offer in the next academic year" (51c:10).

The National Collegiate Athletic Association's 1.6 rule, which required that a student do academic work equal to a minimum of C minus before getting a scholarship, was believed by some to be a step toward ensuring that athletes be bona fide students, although as one writer stated, "1.6 does not bar a college from admitting a dubious student and feeding him courses in dancing and knitting for four years while he plays football" (47:11). In 1968 NCAA colleges voted to eliminate that part of the rule which specified that the athlete had to maintain 1.6 academic work. The rule was said to be "crimping recruiting . . . but its true effectiveness is most obvious where athletic excellence, not scholastic aptitude, was once a prime concern" (48:6).

The fact that the athlete himself sometimes considers that he is not a student is exemplified in statements made in an acceptance speech by Allen Brenner, captain of Michigan State's football team, at the time he was honored for his prowess as an athlete and scholar (a 3.7 average in pre-law). According to the report, Brenner stunned the audience with these comments:

> Playing college football is becoming a delusion. It takes too much . . . time . . . The plight of the player-student is almost impossible . . . players cannot finish their education in four years. The athlete needs responsible help—not under-the-table help, but something like a five-year academic program. I implore your consideration (50).

And, while some complain that the athlete is an exploited, paid employee rather than a student, there are those who bemoan the financial burden of intercollegiate athletics.

A COSTLY VENTURE

Although one may not share the conviction of one college dean that the intercollegiate athletic program is designed "to lure to our campuses muscular giants . . . to increase the collection of trophies . . . to afford the alumni the chance to wave a pennant and indulge in maudlin and nostalgic reminiscing, and to keep up with the next campus," no one is unaware of the millions of dollars spent on such programs (22). That college sports represent a big business seems to be an acknowledged fact. And, that some sports have become a losing business is a story receiving increased attention and publicity. In 1962, Myles Jackson documented the argument that college football had become a losing business. As of 1961, he noted, "the cost of fielding a three-platoon football team was as high as $760,000 (*Fortune's* estimate) for schools that operated at big-time levels of competition" (15:119).

Since that time "inflated football" has become to some a frightening spectre. In 1968, a report of a survey compiled of the Pacific Eight schools revealed that three universities were operating "in the red" while the other five were not expected to remain "in the black" more than three to five years. Five of the eight schools were reported as operating an athletic budget in the range of $1-1.5 million; two in the range of $1.5-2 million; and one had a budget of more than $2 million. The football budget at the average school in the conference increased 97.3 percent in 10 years, from $221,410 to $436,948. Financial aid to athletes increased an average of 148.7 percent; cost of athletic equipment rose 87 percent, athletic travel, 75 percent and recruiting expenses, a staggering 151.7 percent (1). The story appeared to be similar nation-wide. In the Big Ten Conference, for example, despite massive crowds for football, six schools lost money in 1968. At Michigan, a report showed that the intercollegiate athletic budget had risen from $1.5 million to $2.2 million in just two years (49:18).

Football plants at such places as Alabama and Tennessee are among the most luxurious in the country, and, only recently, Bear Bryant was reported to have said it should be easier to win a national championship at Alabama, "where a man can have the whole state going for him, all those doctors and lawyers helpin' out with recruiting" (16:31). Yet, in the 1968 season the Southeastern Conference had a most embarrassing experience when its top three powers lost to outsiders. After "the most disastrous major bowl setbacks in its history," Southeastern Conference coaches clamored for more athletic scholarships, and, as this reporter wrote:

> In a period when universities as a whole are pleading poverty over escalating athletic department costs, it is strange to find anyone asking for the privilege of increasing the number of scholarship grants (58).

Thus, the cycle appears to be a never-ending one and the question becomes: "Who's to blame?" It is to this question that many writers have addressed themselves.

WHO'S TO BLAME?

A veteran sports writer, John Lardner, in an outspoken article which appeared in the 1950's diagnosed the "creeping sickness which turns fine young athletes into bums and cheaters whose only goal is easy money." He was referring to the celebrated cribbing case in which 90 cadets were forced out of West Point, but which he stated was not the fault of the players, the coaches, or the fixers. "Overemphasis," he stated was the main symptom, "the chronic aspect" of the disease (23).

Still others blamed the presidents (or chancellors) of the seven schools involved in the 1951 basketball scandals and the executive director of the National Collegiate Athletic Association of being "ultimately respon-sible for the recruiting tactics which corrupt young athletes while they are still in school" (42:11).

Others at the time of the 1951 scandals placed the responsibility not only on university executives, but, more particularly, on athletic directors and coaches who

> place final approval on grossly commercialized sports programs which employ athletes to produce gate receipt revenues, increase institutional prestige, hike enrollment quotas, and appease alumni . . . and have permitted relaxed academic standards (14:65).

Some get more specific, arguing that coaches themselves are at fault.

> Coaches who use athletes for self-aggrandizement and personal prestige, remain in coaching and continue, consciously and/or unconsciously, to contribute to the moral degeneration of these students and a skepticism incongruous with youth (12:33).

Joseph Kaplan, a brilliant scientist and educator and recognized authority on the problems of intercollegiate football, challenged the coaches to improve the ethical and academic climate of the sport. Coaches, he declared, should not receive "grandiose, spectacular bonuses," should not "route an athlete, not truly qualified for college work into some snap course," must stop "breaking contracts," must stop offering "inducements to a player beyond what national or conference codes on aid permit," and need "not be a martyr permanently" because of the job's unique pressures. Furthermore, "unless the football specialist can justify himself academically, at a level something above amateurism . . . there can be no room for him in the classroom" (20:33).

While coaches may make money, many of them apparently agree that man does not live by bread alone. There are the overzealous alumni. Darrell Royal, football coach at the University of Texas, declared that coaching was a wonderful profession and only disturbing because

> people give you too much credit when you win and too much hell when you lose. I'll be the same person and do the same thing when we lose, but people won't believe me. I won't change, but the people will (44:14).

Finally, there are those who place the blame for the pressures exerted on intercollegiate sport at the doorstep of the American legacy—an individualistic social order which "exalts profit making" and "extols competition." This writer, Paul Governali, also a coach himself, wrote further that

> because most businessmen do not understand education, its ideals and principles . . . they can only understand and judge intercollegiate sports by applying business criteria to determine what success is . . . equate winning with profit, and losing with loss (12:31).

A countervailing view comes from George Young, a well-known long distance runner and teacher, who expressed a conviction that the percentage of unethical people in college sports is far lower than it is in society in general. Referring to the NCAA as the "Sin Committee,"

Young declared that "no segment of American society is making a more determined effort to police itself or to publicize its own misdeeds than is college sports" (60:101).

The naked point of all this may be that, as Reuel Denney declared of college football in 1957 when he wrote "The Decline of Lyric Sport," "the sport generates so much distrust within collegiate circles themselves that those really unhappy with it are its producers" (8:119-120). At any rate, the confusion and malpractices surrounding sport in education, an area of educational experience that seems to have value in and of itself, call attention to the absence of simple moral courage on the part of the faculties, and persistently underline the need for reforms. Almost everybody is offering some solutions.

SOME PROFFERED SOLUTIONS

The literature reveals numerous suggestions for correcting abuses in college as well as high school and junior high school athletics. Some persons would abolish completely interscholastic programs (and marching bands) in favor of devoting a period a day to physical education class instruction and intramural programs. Among such persons is James B. Conant, former president of Harvard University (7). Stanley Elam, editor of *Phi Delta Kappan*, the professional educators' journal, reported that the response of the majority of nearly 200 schoolmen was in agreement, in a general way, with Conant's views (57).

Another writer, pointing out that since higher education and competitive athletics have different goals, the connection should be severed. Proposals for severing the connection included getting the financial facts into the open and getting on record such problems as

> student time spent in promotions, stunts, scholastic concessions made to athletes, special tutoring, amount of administrative and faculty time spent on problems; if the decision is made to eliminate athletic programs (as distinct from physical education) offer to turn over the program to any group interested in maintaining it (19).

Thus, a community or an alumni group could sponsor athletics and also education without fooling itself into "thinking that if a school has a first-rate competitive team, it follows that the school has a good educational program, even a good physical education program" (19).

Those who favor retaining intercollegiate athletics, particularly football, give consideration to the slashing of costs. The "most likely candidates for surgery" advanced have been recruiting, financial aid grants, and two-platoon football (one athletic director stated that two-platoon football costs in excess of $100,000 annually above the cost of a single platoon). A vote, however, to request that the NCAA return to one-platoon football met with stern opposition by several coaches, who reasoned that "the caliber of football and the quality of the 'show' would go down inviting fans to take their patronage to the pros" (1).

Others have explored such suggestions as raising ticket prices; requesting money from other university funds; cutting coaching staffs; decreasing the number of scholarships (except the Southeastern Conference as noted previously); "taking the plush out of the athletic dorms and the steaks off the training tables"; or "play an 11-game schedule," said Fritz Crisler, Michigan's athletic director, but "this would be out of step with the general educational philosophy . . . for it would require games when students are not yet at school" (49:18). It was to become apparent, however, that the NCAA rules committee didn't share Fritz Crisler's belief because it gave a seal of approval to the scheduling of an eleven-game football schedule beginning with the 1970 gridiron season.

A different idea in athletic assistance came from Ames, Iowa, where farmers were asked to donate beef for Iowa State University's training table. The plan gave priority on reserved seats, preferred parking benefits, and a banquet to any Iowa farmer who donated a beef to help reduce the annual training table expenditure. The author of this news item offered the comment that Iowa State

> ought to close down its 20,000 capacity stadium, shuck off some of its seven football coaches, and let the girls in home economics classes make peanut butter sandwiches (43:11).

Some persons have even considered the possibility of making pure amateurism work. In 1952, coach Clair Bee pointed out that Johns Hopkins had made "pure amateurism" work since 1937, and "with conspicuous success in eleven sports, including football, without collecting a dime" (2:80).

Within recent years, such a solution may not seem like heresy. It is apparent that many persons envision a new or alternative concept of sport in education which may include many of the aforementioned solutions. In fact, stiffer academic standards, increases in college enrollments, and student concentration on studies as well as other avenues of interest, some persons view as meaning the demise of big-time intercollegiate athletics. In *Sports Illustrated,* a picture of Ohio State's Coach Woody Hayes looking downcast while an archer practiced in Hayes' beloved football stadium appeared to symbolize "widening student interests and the stern demands of modern academics . . . the passing of a frenzied football era" (4:98).

Serious questioning by students of athletic priorities, which began on some campuses in 1969, seemed to lend credence to the predictions that big-time athletics was on its way out. In a student referendum at the University of Buffalo, for example, approval was given to reinstate a $12.50 athletic fee per student per semester with the provision that the plans and priorities of the athletic department would be reviewed by a committee of students and faculty members. The referendum was clearly no mandate for big-time athletics; it gave priority to intramural and recreational activities over varsity sports. As reported in the *New York Times News Service,* the sport editor of the student newspaper said:

> The big myth is that you need a big intercollegiate program to have a big intramural program . . . facilities are rarely available for nonvarsity recreational sports (27:2B).

At San Francisco State College it was reported that the Associated Students organization allocated the activity fees to the Third World Liberation Front and the Black Students Union and cut the athletic department allocation from $48,000 to zero; the amount of $12,000 was later granted in order to meet certain contractual obligations (59:66).

As for the contention that athletic scholarships are not readily available to those who need them and would not otherwise get an education, some persons imply that scholarships are too easy to come by. One athletic director was reported as saying:

> When I played, a kid would have cut off an ear to get an athletic scholarship . . . Now just about anybody who is warm and has a pulse rate can get a scholarship in some sport somewhere (59:74).

Some educators are shying away from the term "scholarship," claiming that the word "grant" is more accurate. The reason, they conclude, is that "outright gifts to students are based more and more on need, rather than exceptional academic ability." Furthermore, figures are cited to show that almost anyone today can borrow money for college expenses—colleges have loan programs; commercial banks promote educational plans; the federal government lends about $200 million under its National Defense Education Act and guarantees another $250 million of loans by private lenders; church, civic, and professional groups and many states offer sources for college loan plans (26).

A remarkably candid and a disturbing self-portrait of the university community is presented by John Underwood in a well-researched series on the coaches' dilemma appearing in *Sports Illustrated* (59:66-76). The coaches—"bewildered, angry and disillusioned, no longer certain of their mission or, in some cases, of their relevancy"—may take some solace in the ample evidence that their concerns are shared by many persons, some of whose thoughts are recorded in this well-written series. Underwood examined the plight of "the desperate coach" confronted by student activists who regard him as a neofascist racist; insidiously threatened by hostile faculty factions that resent his preeminence or that empathize with student rebels in order to establish themselves as good guys; and caught in the vice of current "disdain for traditional verities." As Underwood noted, the behavior that a coach fears most and that challenges his reason for being is the willingness of the athlete to quit.

> When athletic rivalries don't mean as much, when loyalty to race or a social cause is more demanding than loyalty to a school . . . team, when . . . discipline and hard work are made to appear suspect (and a little foolish) . . . the coach is faced with the ultimate threat: that the game he teaches may not be relevant (59:75).

Yet, for all the avowed evils and malpractices laid at the doorstep of intercollegiate athletics, and for all the proffered solutions and predictions, some persons still think in terms of bigger and better offense and defense. In a commentary called "Eye In The Sky," it was reported that the increasing use of videotape instant playbacks was anticipated. Although cost had been a prohibitive factor, a videotape representative was reported to say that "the gear that now sells for $25,000 may be available next season for as little as $10,000 to $12,000 because broadcast quality reproduction is not necessary" (45:19).

Another report cited the instance of Ohio State's Woody Hayes suggesting adding one dollar to the price of football tickets in order to pay for a synthetic field. Apparently, "What Woody Wants Woody Gets," because the fans started sending in their money without even waiting for the price boost. Reportedly, "other OSU departments were beginning to get their noses out of joint because checks were arriving for the field and not for the usual university needs" (51b:14).

Recently, and for the first time in its history, the Big Ten voted to make its stadiums available to professional football teams. The move was prompted in part by the fact that athletic departments could use the additional rent money.

This is all part of the current picture of sport in education, even though it may remind some teachers to refer to that letter which appeared in the *Houston Post*:

> Dear Coach:
> Remembering our discussion of your football men who were having troubles in English, I have decided to ask you, in turn, for help. We feel that Paul S., one of our promising scholars, has a chance for a Rhodes Scholarship, which would be a great thing for him and for our college. Paul has the academic record for this award, but a Rhodes Scholar is also required to have other excellences, and ideally should have a good record in athletics. Paul is weak. He tries hard, but he has troubles in athletics. But he does try hard.
> We propose that you give some special consideration to Paul as a varsity player, putting him in the backfield of the football team. In this way we can show a better college record to the committee deciding on the Rhodes Scholarships. We realize that Paul will be a problem on the field, but—as you have often said—cooperation between our department and yours is highly desirable.
> During intervals of study we shall coach him as much as we can. His work in the English Club and on the debate team will force him to miss

many practices, but we intend to see that he carries an old football around to bounce, or whatever one does with a football, during intervals in his work.
Sincerely, (10).

Despite the complex problems just mentioned, educators as well as any other segment of society may well be asking if there are not some profound educational reasons why many students are devoted to athletics. And, as John Erskine suggested: "The teacher of any subject, even though he is a sworn enemy of what he calls the athletic craze, may well hope that craze will continue in full vigor until all other subjects are taught from the same system" (9b).

REFERENCES

1. *Arizona Republic (The) (Los Angeles Times Service),* "Platoon Football Costly Venture," December 1, 1968, p. E9.
2. Bee, Clair (as told to Stanley Frank). "I Know Why They Sold Out To the Gamblers," *The Saturday Evening Post,* February 2, 1952, pp. 26-27, 76-80.
3. Brockhoff, Jan. "Chivalric Education In the Middle Ages," *Quest,* Monograph XI, Our Heritage, December, 1968, pp. 24-31.
4. Cantwell, Robert. "Say It Isn't So, Woody," *Sports Illustrated,* September 11, 1967, pp. 98-118.
5. Ciardi, John. "Confessions and Vengeances," *Saturday Review,* March 8, 1969, p. 21.
6. Coleman, Janet. "Does A Woman Need Sports Appeal?" *Mademoiselle,* April, 1968, pp. 196, 294-296, 298-299.
7. Conant, James B. "Athletics: The Poison Ivy In Our Schools," *Look,* January 17, 1961, pp. 56-60.
8. Denney, Reuel. "The Decline of Lyric Sport," Chapter Five, *The Astonished Muse.* Chicago: The University of Chicago Press, 1957, pp. 97-120.
9. Dimnet, Ernest. *The Art of Thinking.* New York: Fawcett World Library, 1966.
9b. Erskine, John. "Education: The Greeks Had a Technique For It," *New York Times Magazine,* January 29, 1939.
10. Fuermann, George. *The Houston Post,* June 6, 1967.
11. Gianelli, Frank. "Athletics Do Justify Cost," *The Arizona Republic,* September 29, 1963, p. 1C.
12. Governali, Paul. "The Physical Educator as Coach," *Quest,* Monograph VII, December, 1966, pp. 30-33.
13. Grutzner, Charles. "College Emphasis on Sports Found to Victimize Students," Report of *New York Times* Survey, March 18, 1951.
14. Hobson, Howard. "How to Stop Those Basketball Scandals," *Collier's,* December 29, 1951, pp. 26-27, 65ff.
15. Jackson, Myles. "College Football Has Become A Losing Business," *Fortune,* December, 1962, pp. 119-121, 174-184.
16. Jenkins, Dan. "This Year the Fight Will Be In The Open," *Sports Illustrated,* September 11, 1967, pp. 28-34.
17. Johnson, William. "Collision on the New Underground Railroad," *Sports Illustrated,* February 12, 1968, pp. 52-53.
18. *Journal of Health, Physical Education and Recreation,* "Should Varsity Athletes Be Excused From Physical Education?" 32:6-8, 1961.
19. *Journal of Higher Education,* "The Education-Athletics Nonsense," Volume 34, no. 9, December, 1963, pp. 487-490.
20. Kaplan, Joseph, and Cohane, Tim. "To Football Coaches—Clean House or Else," *Look,* December 9, 1958, pp. 33-34, 37-38.
21. Keating, J. W. "Sportsmanship, As A Moral Category," *Ethics,* Volume LXXV, No. 1, October, 1964, pp. 25, 35.

22. Kirkpatrick, Harold L. Talk delivered at a Joint Conference of Western College Physical Education Association for Men and Western Society of Physical Education for College Women, October 29, 1964, Reno, Nevada.
23. Lardner, John. "My Case Against Sport," *American*, October, 1951, pp. 24-25, 111ff.
24. Lee, Joseph. *Play in Education*. New York: The Macmillan Company, 1929.
24b. Lewis, Guy M. "Adoption of the Sports Program, 1906-39: The Role of Accommodation in the Transformation of Physical Education," *Quest*, Monograph XII, May, 1969, pp. 34-46.
25. *Life* (editorial), November 29, 1968, p. 34B.
26. Lindberg, Peter. "The College Cost Picture: Is It So Grim?" *Better Homes and Gardens*, March, 1969, pp. 8-16.
27. Lipsyte, Robert. "Director Bothered By Campus Life," *The Arizona Daily Star* (New York Times News Service) March 11, 1969, p. 2B.
28. Metheny, Eleanor. *Connotations of Movement In Sport and Dance*. Dubuque, Iowa: William C. Brown Company, 1965.
29. *Minneapolis Star (The)* (*Chicago Daily News* Service), Interview with Robert Maynard Hutchins and Bill Reed, August, 1968, p. 2D.
29b. Myers, Garry. "Regard It As Work," *The Denver Post*, September, 1964.
30. Oberteuffer, Delbert. "Sanity and Satire," *Professional Contributions*, No. 4, The American Academy of Physical Education, 1955, pp. 46-56.
31. Offer, Daniel. *The Psychological World of the Teen-Ager*. New York: Basic Books, 1969 (also reviewed in *Newsweek*, June 30, 1969, p. 78).
32. *Quest*, Monograph IX (The Nature of a Discipline), December, 1967.
33. Rutkowski, Edward. "What Is Football?" *Journal of Health, Physical Education and Recreation*, September 1967, pp. 30-31.
34. Ryman, Marsh. "An Athletic Director Looks At Physical Education," National College Physical Education Association for Men, *68th Annual Proceedings*, January, 1965.
35. *San Francisco Chronicle*, January 25, 1959.
36. Sheehan, Thomas J. "Sport: The Focal Point of Physical Education," *Quest* Monograph X, May, 1968, pp. 59-67.
37. Shulman, Max. "On Campus," advertisement for Marlboro Cigarette Company, 1962.
38. Singer, Robert. "Status of Sports In Contemporary American Society," *The Physical Educator*, December, 1966, p. 147.
39. Sorenson, Holly. "I Hated High School," *Seventeen*, August, 1968, pp. 272-273, 334.
40. *Sports Illustrated*, "Letter From The Publisher," June 16, 1969, p. 6.
41. *Sports Illustrated*, "Scorecard," August 15, 1960, p. 9.
42. *Sports Illustrated*, "Scorecard," May 8, 1961, p. 11.
43. *Sports Illustrated*, "Scorecard," June 12, 1961, p. 11.
44. *Sports Illustrated*, "Scorecard," December 25, 1961, p. 14.
45. *Sports Illustrated*, "Scorecard," December 11, 1965, p. 19.
46. *Sports Illustrated*, "Scorecard," February 13, 1967, p. 16.
47. *Sports Illustrated*, "Scorecard," January 22, 1968, p. 11.
48. *Sports Illustrated*, "Scorecard," April 1, 1968, p. 6.
49. *Sports Illustrated*, "Scorecard," May 13, 1968, p. 18.
50. *Sports Illustrated*, "Scorecard," March 24, 1969, p. 17.
51. *Sports Illustrated*, "Take Off Those Red Shirts," October 17, 1960, p. 20.
51b. *Sports Illustrated*, "Scorecard," December 15, 1969, p. 14.
51c. *Sports Illustrated*, "Scorecard," April 20, 1970, p. 10.
52. *Sports Illustrated*, "The Bear Bryant Hilton," October 11, 1965, p. 42.
53. Tate, Willis M. "Light Observations of a Rank Amateur," National College Physical Education Association for Men, *67th Annual Proceedings*, January, 1964, pp. 8-11.
54. *Teacher's College Record*, "More Athletes, Not Fewer," March, 1961, pp. 483-484.

55. Thomas, Charles. "Physical Education's Failure," *The Physical Educator*, December, 1960, pp. 141-142.
56. *Time*, "The Connecticut Yankee," August 1, 1960, p. 46.
57. *Tucson Daily Citizen*, "Do We Overemphasize Competitive Athletics," May 11, 1961, p. 37.
58. *Tucson Daily Citizen*, " 'Bear' Howls For Aid After Bowl Disaster," (Los Angeles—AP), January 8, 1969, p. 27.
59. Underwood, John. "The Desperate Coach," (Part I), *Sports Illustrated*, August 25, 1969, pp. 66-76.
59b. Vanderzwagg, Harold. "Sports Concepts," *Journal of Health, Physical Education, and Recreation*, March, 1970, pp. 35-36.
59c. Welch, J. Edmund. "A Challenge Answered," *The Physical Educator*, December, 1969, p. 155.
60. Young, George H., and Paxton, Harry T. "I Serve on the Sin Committee," *Saturday Evening Post*, April 30, 1960, p. 101.
61. Zeigler, Earle F. *Problems In The History and Philosophy of Physical Education and Sport*. Englewood Cliffs, New Jersey: Prentice-Hall, 1968.

Epilogue: Just Around the Corner

By what yardstick does one measure the comparative significance of contemporary sport with that of any other period in history? Or, for that matter, how does one weigh the permanent significance of sport against its present seeming importance? The history of sport indelibly records each new era as one in which sport emerged as supreme, and almost every decade or two in the present century has been labeled by some writer or another as the golden age of sport. Early American sport, perhaps only a "thug on the outskirts of town," is nonetheless remembered by some nostalgic fans as a glorious, untamed spectacular of roughhouse and riot. The 1920's and 1930's were seen and reported by Paul Gallico as "the wildest, maddest, and most glamourous period in all the history of sport." Yet, Robert Boyle in 1963 declared that "the so-called Golden Age of Sport was not the Twenties; it is now." The *Wall Street Journal* called the period that followed, "the greatest sport binge in history." Yet, in the 1970's sport seemingly will burst into an explosion unparalleled in previous times. Its salutary appeal and ubiquitous presence is a fact of contemporary history one can hardly deny.

Although many hazards await the writer who ventures to reveal sport in all of its aspects, no matter. Work on this book has come to mean the equivalent of the excitement and challenge awaiting the participant in the arena. Perhaps this, after all, is what really makes sport so captivating. Anyone can call the shots, make speculations, proffer solutions, find his own meanings, and weave his own story without even having to leave his living room arm chair.

Practically any minute now, it seems, some other persons and another set of circumstances will supply a new batch of material from which writers everywhere will mine their new exciting tales. As Paul Gallico said, "the past is not an honest guide to the future, the records of these valiants are not carved in rock but writ on sand." And, since the teller of stories will always be in demand, perhaps the reader will venture across the threshold of his own time and speculate about tomorrow's sport stories. Some questions may serve to spark the imagination:

Will the 1980 Olympics be the first of the "open" Olympics and will the terms "amateur" and "professional" be abolished in principle as they are in practice?

Will the World Series of baseball be, as Jim Murray put it, "played any year now between two squads of adding machines?"

Will the 400 hitter return to baseball?

Will the coach run college athletics or will the students?

Are we facing the greatest crisis in sport history, as Hank Iba declared?

Will professional sport creep down into the elementary school?

Will coaches and college presidents continue to quit at a record rate?

Will the hippie replace the athlete as the idol of kids, as Mel Cratsley warned?

Will sport stand as the last bastion of the male prerogative or will it offer to women a new frontier for equality?

Will international sport be distorted for pragmatic purpose or be shelved because it fails to accomplish that which it may not have been designed to achieve?

Will the prestigious position of sport be altered in the next decade?

This sampling of questions is perhaps enough to invite the reader to ponder at least one further question. Recall the passage in Plutarch where Themistocles, when asked whether he would rather be Achilles or Homer, replied: "Which would you rather be, a conqueror in the Olympic Games or the crier who proclaims who are the conquerors?"

Index